GEORGE M. COHAN: THE MAN WHO OWNED BROADWAY

By the author

GEORGE M. COHAN: THE MAN WHO OWNED BROADWAY

MR. LAUREL AND MR. HARDY

George M. Cohan: The Man Who Owned Broadway

John McCabe

1973
Doubleday & Company, Inc., Garden City, New York

ISBN: 0-385-01578-x
Library of Congress Catalog Card Number 72–89328

Printed in the United States of America

For
Mary Cohan Ronkin
who is as grand as her name

CONTENTS

INTRODUCTION

George M. Cohan's world was the theatre, his family, and a few friends. Of these, the theatre, *his* theatre, came first. It could not have been otherwise, given his heritage and life pattern, a pattern well established by his seventh year.

His theatre, the one in which he was born and reared, is perhaps too amorphous to define. Variously called "pure entertainment," or "just entertainment" or "entertainment for its own sake," this is theatre of the commodity market. It is Broadway.

Artistically, Broadway has never been well regarded because the high visibility of its commercialism make this aspect seem its prime essential. Actually, the commercial theatre in America has a rich history of the innovative and significant, as Brooks Atkinson has shown so memorably in his *Broadway* (1970). At the same time, no one has much praised that part of Broadway which *is* elementally commercial—entertainment *sui generis*—that lighter entertainment which seems to satisfy one of mankind's basic and perhaps indefinable needs. It may well be that pure entertainment needs no apologist or advocate. Certainly its intrinsic values have been little discussed and just as certainly many critics infer that pure entertainment rarely reaches the dignity of art. Such critics tend to think that the best drama is necessarily probing or corrective in its ends. Playwrights themselves have accepted this view on occasion. Terence Rattigan, in categorizing his kind, says that "every playwright who's born into the world is either an Ibsenite or a Chekhovian"—presumably, that is, either a creator of "well-made" plays more or less sociologically oriented or of "formless" plays psychologically oriented. In America, either an Arthur Miller or Tennessee Williams.

But surely there is a third category of top rank playwrights, a category of which Rattigan himself is no mean examplar. These are the Entertainers.

Rattigan, Noël Coward, Howard Lindsay and Russel Crouse, George S. Kaufman and Moss Hart, Garson Kanin, Oscar Hammerstein II, Marc Connelly, S. N. Behrman, and Neil Simon are only a few among good playwrights who represent and who in varying degrees advocate the primacy of entertainment in the theatre. Noël Coward puts it without apology, indeed with a touch of asperity: "The primary and dominant function of the theatre is to amuse people, not to reform or edify them." The best Entertainers demonstrate that although "pure entertainment" is not profound in essence, it is something more than a form of relaxation or respite from stress. They recognize what entertainment is for most of us: a need—a need of a kind perhaps best illustrated by a comparison of two words commonly used for seasonal work leave. In the United States we define "vacation" generally as a getting *away* from something, as a release. In Britain, the brighter, happier word "holiday" is used, a word which connotes going *to* something, going indeed in celebration.

What the Entertainers at their best are going to, what they celebrate, is life itself in mostly its positive, holiday aspects. The best of the Entertainers, in Sean O'Casey's words, are those who realize that life is inevitably a dialectic of joy and despair—but who, when they go out at night, always look up at the stars.

George M. Cohan was Broadway's sovereign Entertainer in the early years of this century.

Little of Cohan remains in the American theatre. He is something of an unforgettable forgotten man. Outside of perhaps ten songs, there is not much evidence of him today. In recent years his best play, *The Tavern,* has been revived by knowledgeable theatre people who recognize it for what it is, one of the great American farces. This recognition at least seems not likely to diminish. The dramatizations of Cohan's life in film (*Yankee Doodle Dandy,* 1943) and musical theatre (*George M!,* 1969) were loosely structured entertainments which emphasized the man's musical work but barely examined his life and thought. Ward Morehouse's 1943 biography, *George M. Cohan, Prince of the American Theater,* outlines Cohan's life in interesting detail but with little psychological depth, and with scant evaluation of Cohan's artistry.

Cohan, then, remains unknown except as a derbied vaudevillian who waved an aggressive American flag, wrote "Over There" and a few other stirring songs, and who stands as archetype for the glories of turn-of-the-century show business. He has never been the critics' darling except as a performer and even that rather late in life. In 1968 Brooks Atkinson who had reviewed appreciatively a number of Cohan's productions over the years said on reflection, "What he had does not really enrapture me."

Many major critics of the American theatre, with the prominent exception of George Jean Nathan, said or implied the same at one time or another. But Cohan was not much interested in critics. As perhaps the most popular audience figure in the American theatre of his day, he could afford to disregard the critics. At his zenith Cohan was "all the candy" in multiple aspects adding up to a form of genius. As his friend and fellow performer, William Collier, put it: "George is not the best actor or author or composer or dancer or playwright. But he can dance better than any author, write better than any actor, compose better than any manager, and manage better than any playwright. That makes him a very great man."

It is the purpose of these pages to create not so much the biography of a man as the biography of his work and creative spirit—to sound Cohan the Entertainer from his lowest note to the top of his compass. This is not a wide range but it is deep in its intense theatricalism and its unique coloration. In the early years of this century, George M. Cohan struck a note in the American heart which has not yet stopped sounding. It is important to know why. It is more important to understand the style and substance of the man who, whatever the artistic legacy he left, was for many years the most successful individual in the American theatre, the Man Who Owned Broadway.

From the first it has been the theatre's business to entertain people, as it also has of all the other arts. It is this business which always gives it its particular dignity; it needs no other passport than fun, but this it has got to have.

—Bertolt Brecht

Whatever you do, kid—always serve it with a little dressing.

—George M. Cohan to Spencer Tracy

GEORGE M. COHAN: THE MAN WHO OWNED BROADWAY

1. THE ROAD

George Michael Cohan was almost certainly born on July 4, 1878, at 536 Wickenden Street, on Corkie Hill, in Providence, Rhode Island. Until Ward Morehouse discovered the Cohan baptismal certificate which carries a July 3 birthdate, there had never been any doubt that the real live nephew of his Uncle Sam had been born on any day other than the Fourth. The baptismal certificate hardly settles the matter. As was not unusual at the time, the birth was not recorded in the civic registry of Providence. There is, however, circumstantial evidence writ large that the July 3 on the baptismal certificate is a clerical error. Cohan's birthday was always celebrated on the Fourth of July by his parents, Jeremiah ("Jere" or "Jerry") and Helen ("Nellie") Cohan, and this many years before that date began to have profitable connotations for the Yankee Doodle Dandy. The utter probity of these two remarkable people who early taught their son that a man's word was his impregnable bond is the strongest proof that Cohan was indeed born on the Fourth.

It is a rare mother who is not sure of her own child's birthday and on this point Cohan's mother is explicit enough. In *Theatre Magazine*, May 1922, she wrote an article which begins: "Of course I think the babe born to me on Independence Day, 1878, is a fine boy. He seems to me the best son in the world. That is a delusion which most mothers share." And virtual confirmation of the July 4th birthdate comes from Cohan's father. Jerry Cohan, known for his vigorous rectitude, was hardly the man to lie to his diary. On July 3, 1882, he records: "Got a little present for Georgie's birthday tomorrow." The very casualness of the entry in a book intended for his eyes alone bespeaks its integrity. George M. Cohan, despite Ward Morehouse's guess that "he came to believe it himself," never doubted—his widow attests—that he was born on Independence Day.

The matter is not unimportant. There was a mystique, a self-created mystique, in which he identified himself indelibly with everything elemental to American life. This he could not have done in quite the way he did had he known he was born on the 3rd of July. From his earliest days he was, he said, profoundly "impressed with the fact that I had been born under the Stars and Stripes, and that has had a great deal to do with everything I have written. If it had not been for the glorious symbol of Independence, I might have fallen into the habit of writing problem plays, or romantic drama, or questionable farce. Yes, the American flag is in my heart, and it has done everything for me."

Jerry and Nellie Cohan would not have countenanced a fraud, even one so minor as pretending to a false birthdate. Both reared in the exuberant pietism of nineteenth-century Irish-American Catholicism, they subscribed to an honesty which permeated every aspect of their personal and professional lives. "Georgie," Jerry told the boy many times, "two things I want you to remember. Be honest, and—if you can't boost, don't knock."

Jerry Cohan lived both these aphorisms. Born on Blackstone Street in Boston on January 31, 1848, he was the son of Michael Keohane and Jane Scott, both immigrants to this country from County Cork, Ireland. Michael's ancestors spelled their surname "O'Caomhan" but he simplified this to "Keohane" which in turn became "Cohan" at the time of their entry to the United States. The pronunciation of the name by those who bear it, with one interesting exception, is Co-HAN. The exception was George M. Cohan who always said CO-en, as in "Cohen." He was the only one in his family to do so, and this is possibly derivative from his intimate friendships with many Jews in the theatre, particularly his much-loved only partner and sometime brother-in-law, Sam H. Harris.

Jerry Cohan, after brief schooling, was for a time surgeon's orderly in the Civil War and served for a few years as a saddle and harness maker in Providence. The tedium of this work he relieved by creating variations on Irish dance steps he had learned as a youth. He was particularly fond of the clog, a sprightly step whose lively rhythms were ultimately to be impregnated in much of his son's music. Jerry developed an act of his own for which he wrote the music, playing both harp and violin. After attaining rough proficiency in both these instruments, he left harness-making for bookings with various minstrel companies, billing himself as an "Ethiopian Comedian." He became a staple act in New England vaudeville of the 1870s. Never a star turn, his ambitions were amply realized in the joy of being a professional. Jerry Cohan never had a star complex. He loved the showman's life and this was transferred directly, effortlessly, to his son. As Jerry saw it, the only thing bad about "the show business" (the definite article was dropped by the profession only in recent years) was loneliness. For such a naturally convivial man, family life was as necessary as breath. A strong sense of "family" was another gift from Jerry to his son.

In 1874 Jerry had just concluded a tour with Sharpley's Minstrels in Elgin, Illinois, when a letter came from his sister in Providence to tell him of a lovely young Irish girl she knew, Helen Frances Costigan, with a spirit and outlook very likely to interest him. Helen Costigan—Nellie—daughter of Ellen Breen and John Costigan, a skilled carpenter in Providence, was a girl of remarkable personality.

A born mimic and raconteur in an age when girls did not do those things, she impressed Jerry as having the two essentials to be the wife of a strolling player—amiability and patience. Their courtship was brief. They were married in June 1874 despite the opposition of Dennis Costigan, the uncle for whom Nellie was housekeeper. Costigan said vehemently, "I don't trust a man who changes his collar every day." Without a honeymoon, the Cohans began a life of trouping that would end only when they were on the outskirts of old age.

Jerry's first job as a newlywed was to organize a Hibernicon, a form of Irish vaudeville featuring songs, dances, and rapid-fire sketches. He proudly led his bride to a front seat before the initial performance and after the show anxiously asked her opinion. She thought it was mildly silly. But as the troupe went its determined way through New England and occasional box-office disasters, Nellie began to see why the theatre was in Jerry's blood. She noticed that entertainment, even as basic as this, cheered the spirit of both performers and audience. This was something she could warm to. She helped by working both as ticket-seller and ticket-taker, an act of consummate dexterity. She enjoyed watching the company at every performance and liked them all except a haughty actress who persistently needled the new Mrs. Cohan with unsubtle comments about her intrinsic lack of value to the group. The catty lady had designs on Jerry and when her hopes were crushed she walked out an hour before a matinee. "And now here's a real chance to help your husband," she said smilingly to Nellie before departure. An appalled Nellie realized what faced her. Never before on a stage, she went on. She knew the lines from her many nights of watching, and despite nerves and a tendency to speak too softly, did the entire show with gusto. She loved it all.

It was all very exhilarating for a few months but pregnancy brought her up short. She then seriously wondered what she was doing on a series of one-night stands junketing around in drafty and frequently near-empty theatres. She returned to her relatives in Providence and gave birth to a girl, Maude, who lived only nine months. To forget her loss, Nellie entered more vigorously into Jerry's work. He now billed them as "Mr. and Mrs. Jerry Cohan" and wrote a number of vaudeville sketches incorporating rich, rapid-fire patter (JERRY: Does Chicago? NELLIE: No, but Niagara Falls!), a song or two and a few clog dances. Jerry was fascinated with words, and, although not gifted as a playwright, wrote poems unendingly. Most of his verse was slight, of the jingly variety, and humorous. On occasion he could rise to a purpose. One of his poems had a stanza his son always remembered as basic guide to the creation of Cohan lyrics:

My son, there's lots can rhyme and write
In different ways and measure;
And sprinkle "nearlys" left and right
With speed, at ease and pleasure.
But high-flown metaphoric stuff,
With literary glisten,
Creates no jewel, smooth or rough,
Unless it's got the "listen."

It was a lesson George learned well. He came from a remarkable father. In Jerry's later years when he became well-known, Broadway was continually amazed by his gentleness, his instinctual honesty, and the modesty which he wore always and well. His son inherited the honesty. Frank Ward O'Malley recalling Jerry across the years said, "He was a man sweet of soul, and infinitely gentle. He had an instinctive courtliness which was old-fashioned even in his day. Broadway is not a gentle place—no one gives anyone anything willingly—but even its hardest inhabitants always gave Jerry the respect and love he so bountifully deserved. He was the definition of 'gentleman.'"

After the death of their first child, Jerry and Nellie went

back on the road with an Irish variety show, *The Molly Maguires*, a production Jerry eventually took under his own management. They had not been with it very long before Helen became pregnant, and, in 1876, Josephine was born. From the first, grace was Josie Cohan's hallmark, and in one sense she was the most talented of that imperishable act, the Four Cohans. Her technique as a dancer was exquisite, and her gracefulness was mirrored in her personality.

Nellie always returned to Providence to have her babies, and just as regularly she went out on the road when they were able to travel. "People used to ask me why I took on the trouble of carrying Josie and George as infants around with us," Nellie said in later years. "Why, they weren't any bother at all. They could be parked in a trunk or even a dressing table drawer, and fortunately they were both very good little babies. I can remember carrying George onstage in an act Jerry wrote called *The Two Dans*, and that tiny little baby loved it. I could tell. He was four months old—his birth kept me in Providence for three months, the longest period Jerry and I ever had to be apart—and when my little boy was brought out on that stage, I just knew he felt good to be there. A stage, after all, is a place of love."

The Cohans in their barnstorming days were held together principally by love. "It was a joke, our pennilessness," said Nellie. "I don't think anyone could blame me for wanting a home I could call my own, away from some of those overly theatrical types, and where I could raise my children without having to run eternally for a train or rehearse in some dirty barn of a theatre. But my husband was always an optimist and he kept us happy. I could sew adequately and thus the children were always well dressed. But lack of money always bothered us. Mr. Cohan would never take a salary from anyone for my work. He was just too proud. He always said that if he couldn't earn our living, he might as well give up the show business. And he just couldn't give it up. He couldn't and I knew that. It was a very hard life. Sometimes we didn't have streetcar fare and we carried the children for miles in our arms to the theatre. Still, somehow, when we got to the theatre, and we put the children to sleep in a drawer or a trunk, it was worth it because my husband made it worth it. He loved what he was doing so much that we all caught fire from him."

Nellie remembered George as "an odd boy in many respects." He loved to take baths, many every day if he could. Always two a day at least. He never fought other boys, always avoided childhood battle. He was what was called in those days an "old child," always preferring the company of his elders. He did not dislike candy but he asked for apples, and liked to give them away, especially to the elderly. He wept at the sight of beggars or the infirm. Nellie said, "He had a prim little habit of dividing the money we gave him into two parts. One half he would put in a pocket on one side of his coat. The rest he placed in a pocket on the other side. I often asked him why he did this and he answered that he 'liked to feel that his pockets were full of money.' He would start up the street for a walk . . . thoughtfully but observant. 'What are you looking for, Georgie?' we would ask him. 'Poor old people,' he would answer. If he saw any, he divided all his money among them. If returning from his walk, he met any children, he always emptied his pockets for them." This was a habit Cohan was to resume in the years of his fame when down-on-the-luck actors learned how to approach him with the correct story.

Young George was a mimic early. In boardinghouses, actors would give him toys or chat with him, and he would frequently imitate his benefactors for his parents and compound the imitation by assuming the names of those he imitated for days at a time, answering only to the new name. Nellie was always struck by his habit of watching crowds. Somehow, it did not seem to her a boyish pursuit, looking at people as they walked down the street. It was as if he was aware early that he was apart from the crowd, always to one side of life's mainstream. "We four," said Nellie, "were sufficient unto each other."

It was in his fourth year that George began to evolve the jingles which would one day mature into his songs. His first complete composition was brief, and he asked Jerry if he would like to hear it. Jerry was enthralled until he heard George's piping voice lilt out:

"Damn it to hell!
DAMN it to hell!
Damn it to hell!
DAMN it to hell!"

Jerry terminated the audition, suggesting that the lyrics were unsuitable, but he told Nellie that what little there was of the tune seemed first rate.

Jerry was sufficiently stimulated by George's apparent taste for music to make him take violin lessons. "How I hated it!" George recalled fifty years after the event. "For one thing, my instructors weren't terribly good. Every time Dad hired someone to lead the small orchestra which always toured with us, he would give the leader an extra five dollars to teach me the violin. For some reason, the leader of every orchestra we ever had played the clarinet only and could pick out a few things on the piano. That was bad enough, my having awful teaching, but the thing that really got me down was the incessant practice. Sometimes I'd be sawing away, looking out of the window at the kids playing baseball, and the tears would roll down my nose and never stop. Many years later when the Four Cohans had done very well and we were headliners in vaudeville, we were in San Francisco, and I was lunching with Dad at the beautiful Palace Hotel there. I remember that an orchestra was playing in a little balcony overlooking the dining room, and the first violin stepped out between the numbers and did a very accomplished solo. We enjoyed it very much. I turned to Dad and said, 'You see, if you hadn't finally called off those music lessons, I might be a fine violinist like that fellow.' Dad reached over and patted me on the arm. 'That's right,' he said, 'but you'd probably be working here instead of eating here.'"

When George was five, B. F. Keith entered the life of the Cohans for better and for worse. Keith became the most powerful figure in American vaudeville and his tyranny over performers was notorious. Under the twin pressures of greed and a puritanical wife, Keith overworked his employees and overscrutinized their personal habits. In 1883, he opened a small theatre in Boston at which he developed the pattern for all his later vaudeville operations. He had an unerring eye for talent. He hired Jerry after seeing him on the informal variety circuit which then swung erratically through a number of New England towns. Jerry at the time was playing with Nellie in a "two-act," the children having been sent for a visit to friends in New Jersey. Keith wired Jerry: CAN YOU OPEN FOR FIVE SHOWS A DAY? Jerry replied: I TRIED TO LEARN A TRADE BUT I CANT CARRY A DINNER PAIL TO YOUR MACHINE SHOP. But Jerry's friends in vaudeville convinced him that Keith, hard taskmaster though he was, constituted an open door to better things. Keith through subtle flattery and the promise to pay for the children's train fare prevailed on Jerry to become a Keith regular. It was never to be a fully satisfactory relationship but as Keith told him often, "It may be hard work, Jerry, but it's always there."

It was during the early days of the Keith association that George and Josie, seven and eight-and-a-half years respectively, became working members of the Cohan act. Josie had been practicing high kicks and hand-springs which she slowly worked into a contortion number. George continued under peripatetic musical tutoring and was pressed into service as second violinist in the house band of every theatre they played. On one occasion George was actually taught violin by a violinist. "In two weeks," George said, "I knew all there was to be known about the violin. The teacher himself said so. He sent me back to my father with a note which read 'Impossible to teach this boy any more. *He knows it all.*'"

Outside of six weeks in 1884 at the E Street School in Providence, George M. Cohan had no formal schooling. Unlike many men of extensive accomplishment who lacked and later much regretted the lack of education, Cohan rarely thought about school. He learned all he needed to know in order to do splendidly the one thing he loved best, and anything not grist for that mill did not exist. Jerry was never conscious that his son was being deprived. To an old stager, making a livelihood in the field of one's choice had prior claim over formal training of any kind, a viewpoint not many will challenge.

Jerry made one experiment with his son. Wondering briefly if George might not have an affinity for home life, Jerry sent him for a trial run with some family friends, the Higginsons of Orange, New Jersey, who had often sighed the lack of children. The experience was debilitating for everyone. In putting George on the train to his folks a few weeks later, Mr. Higginson with jolly but utter sincerity said, "Georgie, tell your father, mother, and sister that we think just as much of them as ever." Jerry, Nellie, and Josie had just been engaged for the tour of a Western melodrama, *Daniel Boone on the Trail,* starring Captain Jack Crawford, the poet scout. Since everyone in the cast was expected to do at least two jobs, there existed some hope for George's employment if only as second violin. "I was second violin," George said, "because I carried a violin and sat right next to the first violin. My most vivid memory of the Daniel Boone show is that of its three acts, I never saw the second or third. During that time, I was always asleep. It was without doubt the worst show I ever looked at."

He looked for six months in the multiple capacities of semi-musician, song-book vendor, and pseudo-cowboy. The members of the troupe were expected to dress Western even offstage, and George delighted in it. But the greatest thrill came when he led the street parade, the preliminary ballyhoo for the show. George was astride a donkey, followed by Jerry beating a large bass drum with Josie and Nellie close behind atop an old stagecoach from which they threw show-bills. The Cohans left the troupe when George got into a fight with a young actor playing an Indian. But there had been progress. "While with this show," George admitted, "I developed very fast. The day we left the show . . . every member of the company admitted that I had developed. Even the manager told my father that in his opinion Georgie had developed into the freshest song-book boy in America."

Jerry had been yearning for his own company, and after a tour with his old Hibernicon, teamed up with a comedian friend, John Barker, to form the Bijou Comedy Company which set out on a rigorous six-month tour, frequently playing six times a day, six times a week with mandatory all-day Sunday rehearsals. The shows presented were fast-paced farces and afterpieces, and from this formidable indoctrination, Cohan developed a sense of what made people laugh, and not infrequently on the tour, he had practical experience in what did not make people laugh. "Those were frantic days," he said, "but it was there that I learned that farce must be swiftly done, and that the only way to know if something is funny is to try it out before an audience. The audience really writes comedies, they are the ones who decide what one should do."

During this period, George made his solo debut. Despite his antipathy to the violin, he was aware that if he could do some bizarre bowing and tricky runs he might merit feature billing. Jerry gave him his chance to do a single during an engagement at Waldron's Opera House in Haverstraw, New York. After a graceful dance by Josie, George came out, bowed briskly, and went into "The Beautiful Blue Danube" with flourishes, or what he thought were flourishes. The audience did not seem to mind, which relieved George a great deal. He began to rehearse of his own volition and when, as was inevitable with the Cohans, they returned to Boston and the Keith circuit, George approached Keith's new general manager, E. F. Albee, and announced his availability as a great new trick violin act. Albee asked him his price and George casually said that he would leave it to Albee to pay him what he thought the act was worth. At the end of the week George opened his pay envelope and found six dollars. He turned indignantly to the tenor sharing his dressing room and said, "Can you beat that? Albee said he'd give me what the act was worth and he hands me six dollars." "What's the extra dollar for?" asked the tenor.

Incensed, George took down his card, *Master Georgie—Violin Tricks and Tinkling Tunes* from the proscenium billing and put it and his violin in the prop trunk, never to be used again. His enthusiasm leaped to baton twirling. He had often envied the pontifical drum majors who strutted at the head of show parades and he was sure that if he could create some unusual effects with the baton he might do considerably better with Albee. He mastered a complicated set of twirls, consolidated them into a juggling routine of sorts and sang as climax a rousing coda:

"I'm Major McPlugg
With the comical mug;
I'm as happy and free
As a bug in a rug."

To surprise his family, George displayed the act during an engagement at Austin and Stone's Museum in Boston. All went well until the end when the baton flew out of his hands accidentally, hit the orchestra leader across the head and broke his violin. To square things he gave his violin to the leader; the baton went into the prop trunk.

In the spring of 1889, Jerry felt that there was enough mature Cohan talent to make up a complete family vehicle. He formed a unit billed as "The Cohan Mirth Makers—The Celebrated Family of Singers, Dancers and Comedians with their Silver Plated Band and Symphony Orchestra." The family never varied in number, but the rest of the company, depending on box office intake, swelled or ebbed like the tide. When business was good, the "Symphony Orchestra" had eight members; in bad times it diminished to a single piano player. The Cohan Mirth Makers' program was catholic:

1. Grand Overture, "Bridal Rose"—Cohan's Symphony Orchestra.

2. "Retiring from the Stage"—the clever one-act comedy sketch—Mr. and Mrs. Jerry Cohan

3. Miss Josephine Cohan—Queen of Terpsichore.

4. Master George Cohan as "The Lively Bootblack"—Master Cohan's Own Conception of Buck and Wing Dancing.

5. Jerry Cohan as "The Dancing Philosopher."

---

10 MINUTES INTERMISSION
During which Master Cohan will offer for sale
Autographed Photographs of this fun-creating family.

---

6. Grand March Selection—"Gladiator"—Sousa.

7. THE FOUR COHANS in Jerry J. Cohan's Original Comedy with Songs and Dances:

"GOGGLES DOLL HOUSE"
concluding with the famous "Dancing Dolls"

The Dancing Dolls were George and Josie who leaped to rhythmic life at the end of the sketch. Almost incredibly, the Cohan Mirth Makers took this act on six hundred one-night stands throughout the country in the next two years. Cohan remembered that ". . . during that time, we hired and discharged at least half a dozen bands. Toward the end of the second season, during one of our bandless periods, the piano went on a spree, so we had to close up all together and go back to Keith's."

Before they did, they played a benefit near Boston that was to remain in Jerry's memory for decades. The show was for the Pilgrim Fathers Society at Revere Beach. "It was a well-behaved, sedate crowd of Puritans that confronted us," said Jerry. "They were very attentive. Our best efforts were greeted with frosty smiles and sometimes gentle applause. We were angry, oh so angry. But we didn't let up. No, we banged away at 'em till they thawed out. Well, by the time George and Josie had done their famous doll dance, exhausted all their encores, and taken bows and bows, I had to make a speech. I told them that my family was proud of applause and praise coming with such sincerity from the hands and hearts of those whose ancestors made it possible for the present generation to dwell in peace in this free land. And, I added, 'We, too, have some claim upon your regard, which you will acknowledge when I tell you with pardonable pride that Boston is my native city. My great grandfather was a soldier, a regimental surgeon, and served on many a bloody battlefield in the war of the great rebellion.' Tremendous applause and emotion. I went on: 'We might be enrolled as sons and daughters of the Revolution'—cheers and cries of 'Yes, yes!'—'and we should, we would, but for the fact that my ancestor fought on the wrong side. He surrendered with Cornwallis to the Continental Army.'" The audience, Jerry reported, had the flexibility to laugh moderately.

Return to Keith's was the other end of the pendulum swing for the Cohans. No matter how far they toured, or how long they played in the rest of the country, they always came back to Keith's, Boston. That, and North Brookfield, Massachusetts, were their only stopping points of any duration. At Keith's they were under the pressures of five shows a day, occasionally more, and restrictive rules of conduct more suitable for convent girls than working actors. The opposite flavor prevailed at North Brookfield. A pleasant country town in the center of the state, fifty-five miles from Boston and in George's words, "looking as though a scenic artist had painted it on the side of a hill," North Brookfield was the home of Jerry's mother. This town was the Mirth Makers' only chance to receive mirth instead of giving it. One might expect the children of this peaceful town to be in awe of this much-traveled, cocky stranger from the outside world, but George quickly became the leader of the town youngsters. He was made captain of the pre-teen baseball team and doubled as their coach. One of his teammates was the man who became his lawyer in the years ahead, Dennis F. "Cap" O'Brien.

Cap had reason to be grappled to George's soul with hoops of steel. He was his first and for many years only confidant, and it was Cap who gave George the idea for his first great song hit. One summer, after George had begun to write songs, the boys flopped down on a bench to rest after a spirited baseball game. It was early evening and George looking up in the dimming sky said, "Cap, what is that star that always comes out first and shines so brightly?" "Why, that's Venus, George." "Venus. Beautiful. Just beautiful." George never forgot the star, and not long after wrote what he was always to call his best song, "Venus, My Shining Love."

Most ev'ry one has a sweetheart,
With beautiful eyes that shine;
I'm not acquainted with your love,
But you're well acquainted with mine.
Excelling all other ladies,
Fairer than any, by far;
You must admit that the brightest of all
Is Venus, my shining star.

Venus, beautiful Venus, how bright you shine;
None shall e'er come between us, sweet Venus mine.
None, as bright as my darling, so far up above.
Venus, my beautiful Venus, my shining love.

Cap O'Brien in their boyhood days also served as George's mentor for spelling and grammar on occasion. George was to reciprocate this aid practically at a later date by lending his friend the money he needed to go to law school, and in time Cap became the most astute theatrical lawyer in New York.

Following a North Brookfield summer in 1891, Jerry wrote a slight and strenuously paced farce, *Widow McCann's Trip,* for the family and they began an extensive western tour when a wire came asking if the Four Cohans could come to New York at once. The Atkinson Comedy Company, a producing organization, wanted the Cohans to appear in a dramatization of George W. Peck's hilarious novel, *Peck's Bad Boy and His Pa.* George was to star as Hennery, the title character who makes life a roaring hell for his parents and neighbors. Jerry was the boy's father, Nellie the mother, and Josie the bad boy's girl friend. Hennery Peck is something just this side of a monster in the novel which in late nineteenth-century America sold millions of copies. Hennery is a happy, free wheeling rogue who revels in his father falling downstairs or into a scummy horse trough. The book's great success, its most recent editor, E. F. Bleiler, believes, was due to its serving as the focus of rebellion against the goody-goody sentimentalism of the times. It is, Mr. Bleiler points out, "a cruel book, for there is a strong element of pain in its situations . . . not cruel because G. W. Peck was a cruel man, but because he lived in an era when practical jokes were almost a cult. It was written for a generation that liked its humor strong, imaginative, and painful—for the other person."

The stage adaptation of the book was called *Peck's Bad Boy* and many of the harsh practical jokes of the novel were preserved. The only significant difference between the book and the play is that in the latter Hennery is more pleasant, is in fact, as the play's program stated carefully, "that incorrigible lad with the heart of gold." There is in this definition something very close to the boy George M. Cohan was and the man he became. At the age of thirteen when he assumed the role of Hennery he already had six very active years of show business to his credit. By the time he starred in *Peck's Bad Boy,* he had grown beyond his years, and yet had still not experienced some of the natural growth processes of boyhood. Bleiler says of Hennery, "The Bad Boy is often coarse, but he is also vigorous, ingenious and imaginative." For "coarse" read "deceptively mature" and one has an essential description of George M. Cohan at thirteen. In many ways, he was Peck's Bad Boy, the stage Hennery, all his life—the person Leslie Fiedler calls the quintessential good bad boy. "The Good Bad Boy is, of course, America's vision of itself," says Fiedler, "is authentic America, crude and unruly in his beginnings but endowed by his creator with an instinctive sense of what is right."

In the stage version, Peck's Bad Boy faces his natural enemy, the mature world, with cocky enthusiasm. So, too, with young George. He described himself as the happiest kid in the world when the play opened at a Monday matinee to a peanut-eating audience that yelled with laughter at every move he made. The play abounds in physical indignities for the adult characters. The climax occurs in act three. Hennery, in swiftly ascending action, frightens his mother into hysterics, heaves a scuttle of coal into his father's face, belabors the grocery store keeper with a slapstick, pushes an irate policeman into a washtub of foaming suds and tumbles the screaming hired girl out of the window. This was heady stuff for young audiences and particularly for an ebullient young leading man already well disposed toward himself. Cohan recalled: "When the matinee performance came to an end, I wended my way to the dressing room with the frenzied shouts of approval still ringing in my ears. I was firmly convinced that that guy Booth had nothing on me."

George's self-regard was mountainous by the time he attained the alley in back of the theatre at the end of the performance. Waiting for him was a large portion of his afternoon audience. Cohan describes how ". . . a great shout went up from the band of urchins who not only clogged up the alley, but were also hanging on window sashes and fire escapes in their frantic efforts to get a look at the famous bad boy in the flesh . . . 'Hurray! Hurray! Hurray!' It was the first big thrill I'd ever known. I was surrounded in a second."

The boys in the alley sent up another round of cheers, applauding wildly. George smiled, shook hands with many and walked among them regally. He had gone only a few feet when his world was upended. A fist caught him squarely, followed by another blow. Squashy potatoes were hurled at him as he ran a gauntlet of flailing attackers. Thus, at an early age, did Cohan become the victim of the "let's-see-if-this-guy-is-really-tough" syndrome which some portrayers of villainy have experienced at firsthand from their public. Considerably battered, George reached the hotel and was not ashamed to find comfort in his Nellie's arms.

The company manager did not find the experience unusual. He said that it was the ambition of every kid in America to take a punch at Peck's Bad Boy, and if George wanted to keep the role he would have to get used to it. The Cohans had a family meeting to discuss the very real possibility of leaving the play if, as seemed likely, the harassment was to continue. Jerry assured George that no one would blame him for giving up the role under the circumstances. But George was determined to keep his stardom despite the cost. "The result was," he said, "that for the following thirty-five weeks I fought my way out of every popular-priced alley on the ten, twenty and thirty cent circuit."

George M. Cohan was not born a fighter; he became one. His life-long penchant for belligerency was now imbedded.

2. THE ROAD TO NEW YORK

From the time he realized that the heart of the American theatre was New York, George made it his destination. Jerry and Nellie had played there briefly various times but they always considered themselves "road" actors and were not unhappy at the designation. Throughout long, hard years on the road, George wanted desperately to succeed in New York. In his years of maturity, by a typical turn of fate, it was the long hegira leading to New York that he principally remembered. The disheartening encounters with greedy managers, the drafty theatres and foul-smelling dressing rooms, the dirty railroad coaches, long hours of travel and those dreadful times when the audiences would not come—were remembered with affection. It was, for all its terrible impositions on the spirit, the only time when he had somewhere yet to go, and Cohan was always a man who needed somewhere yet to go.

George's self-esteem was growing despite the management of *Peck's Bad Boy* giving the Cohans their notice on the grounds that George was making life a quiet little hell for the stagehands with aggressive demands for better lighting. The Cohans went out into the hinterland to the place where the gold was (and in large measure still is) for variety performers—state and county fairs. During the summer of 1892, they earned $2000, for them at the time an astronomical sum. Jerry, unaccustomed to an ample bank account, needed to lighten that burden, and he succumbed to the authorship of a three-act farce, *Four of a Kind*, which despite its title needed ten actors in addition to the Cohans. The scenery was expensive, $450 in those days of cheap labor and inexpensive materials, and Jerry was always generous with actor salaries. To break even, the company would have to bring in $150 a performance which they did for only two weeks. Savings depleted, it was back to the variety act and great discouragement.

But not all was loss. In the summer of 1892, George learned his first big lesson in dramaturgy by watching *A Gilded Fool* by Henry Guy Carleton, a comedy written for the genial light comedian, Nat Goodwin. This was a great opportunity for George to see how a play of general appeal could be tailored into a vehicle for a specific talent. In his career Carleton was first a writer of verse tragedy but his failure there turned him almost savagely to the writing of farce. He constructed *A Gilded Fool* to make money, and in focusing the play on Nat Goodwin he was in a position to make a great deal of money. In the nineties Goodwin was America's most polished actor of light comedy. His playing was affable and slightly bemused as if the world was too much to contemplate with any degree of seriousness. He became Cohan's first favorite actor, and the Goodwin acting style was subsumed by the younger man.

Only fourteen, Cohan had the thrilling opportunity to see *A Gilded Fool* come to life. "We happened to be laying off that week," he said, "and so I hopped on to my old home town, Providence, to see my favorite comedian, Nat Goodwin, in the first night of a new play, and incidentally it was my first night of any play. Was I excited! Well, if you had been sitting beside me in the first row of the gallery, you would have thought that I was a kid on the verge of a nervous breakdown waiting for that curtain to rise on the first act. I witnessed the entire first four performances of *A*

Gilded Fool, Thursday and Friday nights and the matinee and night performances Saturday. After the first performance I said to myself, 'Now, there's a pretty good play, but the trouble is that it's too long drawn out. I wonder how they'll remedy that fault and bring it down to cases?' And so I began making mental notes and fixing up the play in my own way. At the second performance much to my surprise and delight I discovered that several of my ideas had actually been adopted, such as the dovetailing of a couple of scenes and the elimination of a long stretch of dialogue. At the third performance at least another ten minutes had been deleted and again I patted myself on the back and said to myself, 'Well, they've done everything I've thought of so far. Now we'll see how my ideas jibe with theirs at the two performances tomorrow.' When the final curtain fell on the fourth performance Saturday night, they were right down to normal playing time and now had what to my mind was a perfect comedy. It was the first time I had ever got a slant on how plays were doctored and pulled together, and although mine had been all what you might call absent treatment, I took full credit in my own mind for having done the whole job myself."

In this fashion did a very young professional set the groundwork for his later ability, miraculous it seemed to some of his peers, of taking a play in great trouble and shaping it into a success. Cohan learned to be miraculous through concentration and hard work at an early age. Years later when Goodwin became a close friend, Cohan told him the story of his experience with *A Gilded Fool,* and added with a straight face that he had doubtless projected the improvements the play needed via mental telepathy. Goodwin smiled appreciatively, paused and took a closer look at his young friend. "By God, knowing *you,* maybe you did!"

Thanksgiving week of 1892 found the Four Cohans at Robinson's Theatre in Buffalo where they intended to stay for two, possibly three weeks. They remained a year. The Four Cohans caught on because they made a commitment to as wide a range of entertainment as their considerable talents could offer. They did things they never knew they could, and these they discovered simply by the doing. The public liked the Four Cohans in their basic act, and the management wanting to keep them on, asked for variations of their songs, dances, and sketches. The Cohans responded by ". . . putting on sketches, specialities, dancing acts, farces, pantomimes, melodramas and any other forms of entertainment the management asked for," said George. "One week I played my own mother's father, mother being cast for the old general's daughter, and I for the general."

It was during this period that George began to think seriously of writing. Heretofore, little sketches he wrote had been exercises to pass away the time, but in Buffalo he encountered the works of the first playwright to put a lasting impress on him, the man whose general theatrical philosophy George M. Cohan was to practice all his life.

Dion Boucicault, a nineteenth-century Irish playwright little remembered today (save for a brilliant revival of his *The Shaughraun* at the Abbey Theatre in Dublin in 1967) was an Entertainer. He wrote a wide range of potboilers but his theatricalism was so rich that Bernard Shaw put Boucicault in the company of Molière, Goethe, and Ibsen for his skill in stimulating audience emotion. Boucicault offered his audiences a well-integrated blend of sentiment and laughter sauced with lively song and set against colorful scenic effects. This was to become the operative formula for many Cohan plays. During his Buffalo stay, George appeared in two plays of Boucicault and remembered them as the kind of theatre that gave him the deepest satisfaction. "Boucicault," Cohan said, "is the model for me of what a good playwright should be. He tells the story quickly, he gives you some basic, exciting emotion, good plot twists, with a *lot* of laughter and some charming songs. And, above all, thank God above all, Boucicault is fun."

Boucicault's plays inspired George to write beyond the sketch form. He completed a one-act play and took it to

Jerry who helped him greatly by pointing out dialogue which was extraneous. It was Jerry who first encouraged his son in the use of colloquial dialogue, pointing out that most audiences enjoy hearing characters speak the way the audience speaks. Next, George turned to song-writing and Jerry gave him even greater encouragement. George felt so encouraged that he sent a brace of songs to a prominent New York publisher whose reaction was swift:

> Dear Sir:
> Your songs are not publishable. Please do not send any more.

Cohan's first encounter with a critic infuriated him and he wrote all the more. The determination to go to New York flared anew and in one remarkably sustained performance in front of Jerry, displaying a mix of sincere egoism, lofty rage, and flaming determination, George vowed that once he got to New York he would, in succession, own his own music publishing house, build his own theatre, and write and star in his own plays. As it turned out, he was quite wrong about these events' order of succession.

George's heart was now unalterably in New York. More and more the family's provincial tours frustrated him because these engagements seemed circular experiences, without goal. Moreover, he suspected (correctly) that Jerry was happy where he was. Jerry was not without ambition, and going to New York would be pleasant enough but with due process and all in good time. George bluntly urged a concentrated job hunt in New York. Jerry's reciprocal bluntness in telling George that it was none of his business what the bookings were was uncharacteristic, but he felt he had to put a foot down. George decided to run away; his unrequited passion for New York could bide no delay. In the best tradition of the melodramas he was then playing in, he packed a bag and wrote a note to his mother:

> Goodbye, mother. Don't worry about me. I'm on my way to New York to sell my songs and plays and get a job in a Broadway show. Dad doesn't seem to think that I amount to anything, but keep a-praying for me and everything will come out all right. Please don't let anybody try to bring me back, because my mind is made up to fight it out alone.
>
> Your loving son,
>
> GEORGE

For all its obligatory theatrics, the note was sincere. George had finished a very full apprenticeship in show business, and New York was his inevitable destination. Only fifteen, he had already developed an appearance of agelessness that was to stay with him all his life. A small man, he never gave the impression many small men do of trying to walk tall. He was remarkably lithe and self-contained, resembling in essence if not in detail the man who was to portray him years later on film, James Cagney.

The particular afternoon in June 1893 when George wrote his farewell note to his mother, he was never more sure of himself and his destiny. He packed his bag and was putting the note under his mother's door when Jerry walked in, grinning. Jerry had a gracious and warming smile, and wore it often, but when he grinned it was a clear sign of nervousness. "Listen, son," he said, "I've been thinking about that matter you spoke of today—you know, about New York—and your mother and I have decided to take your tip and go there." At this moment in the lives of the Four Cohans, a subtle ascendancy, a loving ascendancy, occurred.

George began to direct the artistic destinies of the family. He never again challenged his father on matters of discipline, and Jerry from that time on never disputed George professionally. The Four Cohans were either ready for New York or it would be necessary to have the contrary proved and Jerry came up with one sure way they could get an engagement there. Their faithful if exasperating old standby, B. F. Keith, had taken over the Union Square Theatre and was going to open it as a vaudeville house on Labor Day next. One more thing, Jerry told George. "Listen, son, the next time you want to run away, you come and tell me about it, and we'll all run away together, the four of us. What do you say, boy, eh?" George was still boy enough to weep in relief and gratitude. Jerry, it turned out, had discovered George's plans from the ticket agent at the depot who had been struck by the fact that only a single Cohan was leaving town.

The summer before their booking in New York, the family went to Rocky Point, Rhode Island, for a summer casino engagement. In his autobiography, Cohan writes, "The only incident of any importance that happened to me during the two months we lingered there was that one Monday they ran short of a sister team, so I had to put on skirts and do a sister song and dance with Josie." Perhaps that was the only incident of importance from a middle-aged coign of vantage, but when George was fifteen that pleasant summer he fell in love with Julia Mackay, an attractive young lady his own age, then storming the portals of show business as a baritone. She wanted to go only where Georgie went, and they planned to elope in Boston prior to a descent on New York with the family. The happy couple boarded a Narragansett Bay paddle-wheeler and sang cheery songs to each other all the way to their first stop in Providence. The singing ceased after they had boarded a train for Boston and were politely detained by a detective friend Jerry had called in to waylay the youngsters. Julia was crushed but George was understandably resilient. He had a greater love.

3. NEW YORK

The Four Cohans spent the last three days of August in a boardinghouse just off Union Square polishing and reworking *Goggles Doll House,* the act Jerry had worked out for them over the years. The act, a skillful blending of all their specialties, was tightened into a fast-paced twenty-minute production with Nellie and Jerry's quick comic patter intersticed with Josie's dancing and George's singing-dancing-talk piece, *The Lively Bootblack.* George's was the least entertaining of the segments but it had a boyish vitality which was reasonably diverting.

When the family arrived at Keith's Union Square Theatre for their first music rehearsal, the stage manager, a man who knew and respected Jerry, handed him a wire. "Sorry, Jerry, but the boss wants it this way." The telegram said that the Four Cohans were to be fragmented during the one-week engagement. E. F. Albee, the tyrannical general manager for a tyrannical owner, had decreed that the Cohans were to split into three separate acts. It was a particularly hard blow for George because he realized that he was especially vulnerable without the support of the family and it was all the more frightening because this was Union Square. The Union Square of 1893 was not the worn, sooty demesne it is today. It was then the heart of a splendid theatre district, the glittering focus of top professionalism in acting, playwriting, and producing. And for George now to be presented on his own was a challenge he did not want to meet.

He complained loudly to Jerry and was prepared to elaborate on his anger when Josie's warning look checked him. Josie had the quality of being able to hold George back when he was obstreperous, a not unusual state for him. Jerry agreed that doing the act as a unit was ideal but Albee's word on such matters was law. Better to open in segments than not open; better to get a foothold and then return to the four-act. George agreed, grudgingly, but he was determined to give his segment, the bootblack number, every benefit that extended rehearsal could offer. He was told by management that extended rehearsal was impossible, each act being allotted five minutes with the overworked rehearsal pianist. George took fifteen minutes to the intense irritation of the other acts, the stage manager, and the pianist. The climax was an argument with the stage manager, and George's lofty rejoinder that he was an artist, too intelligent to go around the country having fights with piano players and stagehands. He added that there was little doubt that everyone present backstage would, one necessary day, be working for him. At this moment Jerry arrived and, eyes glittering with anger, took George to the dressing room. George had never seen his father in full rage ever, and he had sense to forestall what was likely to be the worst moment of his life. He said, "Dad, I'm so dead crazy to make good here in New York that I can hardly think straight. I'll apologize to the piano player, to the stagehands, and everybody else in the theatre if you want me to. I was wrong and I'll admit it. A fellow can't be any more reasonable than that. Nothing of the kind will ever happen again, Dad, I give you my word."

The assistant stage manager bustled in with the time sheet giving the performers their place on the bill. To be comparatively late on the bill, like next to closing, was not merely status but security, too. Booking agents only looked at the late acts on the bill. The stage manager ticked off the Cohan slottings: Josie was fourth, not bad; Jerry and Nellie were sixth, quite good; George was to open the show. Disaster. Number one slot was the nadir of billing. Trying to entertain while the audience was straggling in, talking among themselves until the substantial acts appeared—this was impossible and all vaudeville performers knew it. Opening was for animal acts, for acts with noisy alarums and excursions; it was not the place for a bright young lad with convictions of grandeur.

George exploded in bitter complaint and this time Jerry did not have the heart to stay him. New York engagement or no, to open the bill was demeaning. Even Josie, the quiet Cohan, spoke up. To split up the four-act was bad enough; to place George on the level with animal acts was not fair. She suggested they give up the engagement and Jerry agreed only if Nellie said yes. She did, unhesitatingly. They were about to inform the management when the stage manager came by, calling out, "Ten minutes to curtain, ten minutes to curtain." George knew instantly that he would go on, and before he did, he gave his family a largely self-exhortatory pep talk in which he assured them that by next week he would be in the middle of the bill. He included a line from a play he had just written to the effect that he would turn victory into defeat and added that God was the only possible source of help for the other acts. "I'll get even with Keith and Albee, see if I don't!" he shouted to Jerry as he took his place in the wings.

George heard the introductory vamp to his number and for the first time in his life walked out into the spotlight of a New York theatre and sang Cohan lyrics—Jerry's:

"I'm called the Lively Bootblack
For my style and occupation,
When work is done I like to play
By way of recreation.

My cousin is an actor boy;
He's often been before you;
I know you're fond of dancing,
So a specimen I'll show you."

Then he threw himself into a vigorous, board-pounding Irish reel concluding with a double heel slap, an unabashed signal for applause. Silence. Trying to appear unruffled he went into the second verse of the bootblack song:

"I sneaked into a fancy ball
With whiskers made of false hair.
The dancers couldn't dance at all;
I taught them how to waltz there."

Whereupon into a spirited waltz clog, with another applause-begging finish. Silence. Sweat appeared on his forehead—in the slang of a later era, flop sweat. Ignoring it, he walked to downstage center and recited "The Bootblack's Dream," a pathos-soaked poem with a Horatio Alger ending. On the last words, he raised his voice in fervent climax, paused and then bowed impressively. Silence. Now close to the audience he looked over the glaze of the footlights and what he saw did not reassure him. There were about thirty-five people out front, a dozen of whom were reading newspapers.

Gritting his teeth through a forced smile, George said, "Ladies and gentlemen, I will now offer for your approval my own conception of the most difficult terpsichorean art, commonly known as buck and wing dancing. I wish to call your particular attention to the fact that the steps are of my own invention and that no other living dancer has ever been able to master the same routine." The buck and wing was dexterously done, topped by a finish which became a Cohan trademark. This was a spirited run up the side of the proscenium arch, back down across stage for a run up the other side, and back to center stage for a breathless bow.

Silence this time was broken only by one gentleman turning the pages of his newspaper with unnecessary vigor. George ran to the first entrance, turned, gasping as he bowed. By now the silence was assertive.

He ran to his dressing room, fulminating against Keith and Albee, and hurled his bootblack box against a pitcher of water which broke, spattering a bewildered Jerry. Nellie and Josie ran out of their room as the house manager came in to tell Jerry not to worry about the pitcher. The family watched as the manager hustled George out in the hall where the boy was tongue-lashed for his petulance and above all for his ill-treatment of Jerry. George admitted to dereliction of duty, agreed that his actions had been immature, but after all, he told the manager with deathly seriousness, he had been treated rottenly. Everybody in the organization, and George was specifically including Keith and Albee, was against him. "If you ask me, I think I've been treated pretty rottenly by the whole outfit." To this point the manager had been grave but George's passionate solemnity was not to be borne. The manager began to laugh, and other performers who had stuck their heads out of dressing rooms to witness the incident joined the laughter. Josie, Nellie, and Jerry heard it, came out into the hall and fell into the fun. The laughter grew, cleansingly, but for George it was the final indignation, the bitter coda to his New York debut. He walked to his dressing room and slammed the door, glowering into his mirror as he creamed off the make-up. The laughter persisted until he was forced to laugh at his own dour reflection. He dressed quickly, ran into the alley and around to the box office where he bought a ticket for standing room. He was in time to see Josie do her skirt dance to great approval. He grew dour again.

He walked sulkily through Union Square and leaned against a lamp post. Thinking of Josie, he said to himself, "And *that's* what a good spot on the bill will do!"

4. THE ROAD AROUND NEW YORK

For the remaining seventeen performances of their contract (three a day, 12:05, 5:20, and 7:25), George learned the precise meaning of a trouper's phrase already old in the nineties—to die standing up. His audiences continued to read newspapers. His continuing failure he attributed to the sparseness of audience so early in the show; there were a dozen or so out front each time he did his act and George could never understand why they didn't read their newspapers out in the lobby. The light was certainly better out there. At the final performance for the Cohans, however, the augury was positive. The house was packed, and George knew that a packed house is almost always eager to be entertained. Backstage the buzz went that the audience had started laughing at the box office. George was received enthusiastically throughout his act, even winning an encore for his waltz clog. Excited, he added two one-line jokes which brought appreciative roars. This uplifted him almost to loss of control but he held on, saying over and over, "Keith and Albee, I'll show them!"

At the beginning of "The Bootblack's Dream" recitation, he knew he was holding his audience. They were listening to every word, seriously, intently. George paced it well and had reached the most potent dramatic section which tells of the patchwork bootblack falling asleep on a doorstep to dream he was a rich man's son. Suddenly a loud noise from the gallery obtruded. "Fight! Fight!" And it was, a crawling, eye-gouging affair engrossing everyone in the house. George continued but the brawl howled on. He asked the piano player to rush into his side-run-up dance but even this failed. George ran off in the hopes that his return for a bow would settle things a bit but when he came back for the bow even the piano player was watching the fight. Everybody in the theatre, to a man, was facing the wrong way.

As he stamped off indignantly to his dressing room, the property man stopped him to share his anger. George was told that the fight was faked, a plant, a plot specifically set to ruin his act. The property man said he had proof of this perfidy: "I heard the whole thing cooked up. I know the two guys that started the thing and I also know they were planted there purposely to kill your act." "Who were they?" George asked. "Keith and Albee," the property man whispered. "They went up there disguised as a couple of Spaniards, and pulled the whole thing off just to get even with you for taking money for that act you did here this week." The property man strolled away, whistling.

George was seething when he reached the dressing room and to top his evening, Jerry handed him a wire from their booking agent:

> CAN BOOK JOSEPHINE COHAN FOR SINGLE DANCING SPECIALTY AT KOSTER AND BIALS OPENING MONDAY NIGHT. SALARY SAME AS FOUR COHANS ARE RECEIVING JOINTLY FROM KEITH.

George's anger ignited. He was not going to let a woman earn his living for him, he announced, even if the money was fine. Jerry said nothing but in putting on his make-up, he hummed to himself. Jerry always hummed when he was controlling his temper.

It was a discordant ending for their first New York engagement. For George, the Union Square Theatre episode did several things. As a result of it, he developed a phobia on matters of billing which transcended vanity although that flavoring was unquestionably there. He knew that being seen by an audience at their most receptive moment could make or break an act, and that sometimes a single engagement could determine one's future in the theatre. He learned that to get proper billing one frequently had to fight for it. Jerry was a gentleman in all senses, and could not be expected to stand up strongly to gristle-headed managers and bookers. George decided that he must adopt an anticipatory belligerence for the health of the act. In the years just before Broadway he was frequently called a fresh guy, a know-it-all, and a smart kid. He was, and he had to be.

Josie's progress was not to be marveled at. As the most talented member of the Four Cohans at this juncture in their lives, the invitation to play at Koster and Bial's, the leading vaudeville theatre in the United States, was almost inevitable. A taste of Josie's quality can be found in a review of her work by a *New York Dramatic Mirror* critic:

> When she capers about the stage executing her intricate steps, her dainty feet seem to scarcely touch the floor. She is all alive . . . she goes through her graceful evolutions with such an apparent lack of effort that it is a positive pleasure to watch her. She is a living proof that dancers are born, not made . . . Though she shines principally as a dancer, Miss Cohan is talented in other ways. She is a gifted comedienne, and can sing a song as smartly as any soubrette on the stage, and with those wonderful eyes of hers she can give meaning to even the most senseless ditty.

Josie was thrilled to realize that Koster and Bial's wanted her but she knew what the Four Cohans had wrought to come as far as they had. They were probably the finest four-act in vaudeville, needing only proper recognition to come into their own. For this reason and because she sensed George's acute disappointment over his failure to win recognition at Keith's, Josie decided not to split up the act. This was the one thing that George needed to understand that Koster and Bial's was what Josie deserved. He withdrew his objections and Josie opened at the home of vaudeville's top acts to great acclaim and the offer of an indefinite stay. Later in the season she was booked into the prestigious Imperial Music Hall and remained the entire winter at a salary double anything the Four Cohans had yet received.

Josie was well on her way but George felt immured. He tried all the booking offices to no avail, his only consolation the scant one that Jerry and Nellie were not doing so well either. It was a considerable shock years later when they admitted to him that they failed to work that winter by turning down engagements as a two-act purely to preserve George's inner harmony. The love of the Four Cohans for one another was the most substantive part of their lives, and their interdependence through their years of hardship was a deeply annealing experience.

George's frustration during the winter of 1893 was relieved only once. He had been writing songs since his tenth year. Typical of these was his first effort, "The First Floor Front":

There's a French girl named McCarthy,
Her first is Mary Ann.
Her mother is her father's wife,
Her father he's a man.
Though Mary's very homely,
She has a pretty face.
And the flat that Mary occupies
Is a most exquisite place.
She has a grand piano,
It makes a fearful noise.
It's pounded every evening
By a gang of girls and boys.
Assembled there at Mary's
For fun they needn't hunt.

They find a whole lot of it
In the first floor front.

CHORUS: There's Kate and Nancy
Billy, Clancy, Dan and Mike Magee.
There's Pat O'Day and Hughie Fay,
All loaded down with glee
There's Jimmy Grogan, Johnny Logan,
Both so big and blimp,
At number three the boulevard,
The first Floor Front.

This is hardly deathless verse but it is awfully good for a ten-year-old. The song contains elements that are to characterize many Cohan songs: the Irishness, the nonsense strain, the jingly exuberance, the "listen." George wrote many of these songs and in 1893 while Josie was gathering glory at Koster and Bial's, he applied himself to writing a song which he hoped would bring him even a small measure of fame.

In the nineties when home self-entertainment was a vital factor in American life, the sale of sheet music was very big business. George had known music from infancy because Jerry wrote pleasant songs for the shows he had appeared in, and later wrote more for the Four Cohans. George's songs were much like Jerry's but, in general, had cleverer lyrics. Almost always written in a major key, they were spiritedly happy, using simple, natural progressions like a person's speaking voice. They did not emphasize flats or sharps, and they were sparing in the variety of notes. "As a composer," Cohan was to say later, "I could never find use for over four or five notes in my musical numbers."

In 1893, George wrote his first professional song, "Why Did Nellie Leave Her Home?" The theme he drew from close to home: "The Nellie I got from my mother's name. Everything about mothers is usually all right. Then I heard her talking with women friends about girls leaving home and wondering why they left such a thing if they had it.

From this I constructed my song." He took the "Nellie" song and four others on a tour of the music publishing offices. His reception was cool, and in a gambler's throw he tried M. Witmark and Sons, the leading song publishers in the country, whom he had heretofore avoided because of their pre-eminence. He gave his card to the receptionist and waited briefly, certain that nothing would come of it. To his shocked surprise, M. Witmark himself came out to see George and greet him with hand extended. Mr. Witmark, it seemed, had a fondness for Jerry, having seen him several times when he played New York with Nellie. George was taken into the office of the oldest Witmark boy, Isidore, and left there with parental instruction to do all that was possible for Jerry's boy. George played the five songs for young Mr. Witmark who decided that only the "Nellie" song had merit. He gave George $10 and a promise that the song would be published on the usual royalty basis.

After the first glow of family congratulation subsided, George went out into Union Square a few days later to congreet new show business friends in the song-writing field. This was his first acquaintanceship with "pros," a word he was now keenly aware of and one which henceforward he would bestow only as an accolade.

From the ragtag group of song-writers and song-pluggers who loitered up and down 14th Street, George had received heavy kidding for his cheekiness in considering himself a pro. It was to this group that George had been singing "Why Did Nellie Leave Her Home?" for several weeks eliciting not a single laugh for what was in the author's view an irresistibly comic song. Now, with the Witmark acceptance, George was going to show the pros, and literally. Stopping in at Witmark's the day "Nellie" saw print, he walked out in a glow with several copies, and stopped on the corner to read his song. What he saw stunned him. The music was his, but his glib, funny, jingly words were gone. The song had been turned from a vaudeville routine to a sentimental ballad. Not a single word was his. The terrible shame was that he could not now boast of his work because every song-writer on the street knew the previous lyrics. As he looked at the newly imprinted song, one detail struck him. There was no reference to another writer. At the bottom of the sheet it read, "Words and Music by George M. Cohan." He walked in among the pros all day, casually showing the song with an earnest request for an opinion as to its worth in revised form. The boys agreed that it was now a much better song. Their acceptance of George was complete, and with their approval came the realization that indeed the new lyrics were better than his.

He concentrated on his songs all that winter, polishing up "Venus, My Shining Love," which he had begun at North Brookfield the summer previous, and writing twenty more. He sold "Venus" and a few others and writing seized him forever. "I scribbled parodies and patter for comedians, comic songs and extra verses for serio-comics, and even took a shot at a couple of afterpieces for burlesque shows," he said. "After a while, I got to writing sketches for variety teams, and orders came in so fast that I found it impossible to supply the demand. With parodies in every pocket and sketch manuscripts under my arm, I was soon the envy of all the pencil pushers in the variety branch of the theatrical game."

This work was to serve as laboratory for his work as a playwright. Arthur Hobson Quinn in *A History of American Drama* points out that Cohan's dramatic works are based "on the principle of the variety show, the deliberate planting of the remark for the sake of the answer." This, with certain exceptions, was indeed to characterize much of the early Cohan dramatic form. By 1894, George was perfecting his skills as writer of vaudeville sketches and songs which jingled. Jingling, too, were his pockets. If Josie was at least pro tem the star of the family, George was its principal source of income. He not only contributed to living expenses the lion's share, at his proud insistence, but before his sixteenth birthday he had over $1100 in the bank.

But Josie did not want to be the star of the family. She knew what the Four Cohans meant to each of its members and she determinedly rose to the need. She told George that in her view the Four Cohans should stick together, offer themselves as a unit and be so booked or leave New York vaudeville forever and take out their own road show. This was a great personal sacrifice for Josie but then, as her brother said frequently, "There never was anyone just like Josie." The four-act was reconstituted but had trouble getting sustained booking. For a time it seemed that re-forming the act was a bad idea when a sudden stroke of luck came to them in the person of the well-known Dutch comedian, Gus Williams, who signed them for character roles in the 1895 tour of his play, *April Fool.* Williams was never a Broadway figure but he had a great road following. The Cohans were pleased to be prominently cast in a play which had received audience acclaim across the United States, but when George read the play he thought it inadequate and at first rehearsal offered to improve it. Williams's angry refusal and Jerry's vexation quieted George but later he assured the family that he honestly knew ways in which the play could be improved considerably. Jerry was not able to understand why George did not have the patience as well as the courtesy to keep his mouth shut but in later years Jerry recalled two facts about George at the time—he was seventeen, and he had more talent than the man who hired him.

George deferred to Jerry's wishes and left well enough alone. The play went on tour. But George could never leave well enough alone. He was frustrated by instructions to play the role just as his predecessor did, a young man named Midgely. On opening night George played the first act as he always wanted to but never dared to in rehearsal. After a spectacular verbal battle between the acts highlighted by Jerry's first swing at George in his life (it was ducked), George promised to play it Williams's way and apologized to him in front of the company. George played the show for what he called "thirty-five of the longest weeks of my life," agonizing over doing something that he knew in his bones he could have improved by some simple changes in dialogue and stage business. He said, "Even then, as a seventeen-year-old trouper, I solemnly swore to myself that never again, if I could possibly side-step the issue, would I follow any man in a part he had created." This vow he kept until an emergency, the death of a leading actor in one of his plays, twenty-five years later. It was also the cause of his deep-seated preference to act only in plays that he had written. After he became famous, he acted only in three plays written by other men, and in each instance there was an inevitable amount of acrimony and dissatisfaction.

After the Williams engagement (he let the family go after George had a roaring argument with the company manager), the Four Cohans went to the town they knew would always welcome them, Buffalo. Here, in a one-week engagement at the Court Street Theatre, George accidentally created the dance step which was to make him the most imitated vaudeville dancer at the turn of the century. In the four-act, George did an old dance called the "essence" which was an undemanding little step done to the tune of "Coming Thru the Rye" played in six-eight time. At rehearsal George asked the orchestra leader for another tune and was assured it would be forthcoming at the performance. During the show as George's dance began, he discovered to his horror that the music was indeed different but different also was the tempo, now an agonizingly slow two-four time no longer fitting the "essence" steps. Desperately he went into a buck dance, and dragged out the steps in order to accommodate the slower tempo, leaping from one side of the stage to the other instead of remaining center stage as was customary. Laughter stimulated him to exaggerate the steps, and he did a scissors-grinder movement with his arms and legs as he threw his head back in an extravagant gesture of comic strain. His hair, worn long, flew back and forth in ridiculous punctuation to the movement. The audience erupted in hilarious excitement and, after the show, an old friend and well-known dancer, Lucy Daly, came back in ecstasies. In her highly professional opinion, it was the most superb eccentric dance she had ever seen. It did, in fact, revolutionize buck and wing dancing and became an applause milker for hoofers down to the present day.

The success of this simple dance step did more for George than holster the four-act. It made him conscious of a phrase that was to dominate his self-opinion until the day of his death. The term "song and dance man" was never to attain anything like artistic respectability until Cohan wrote a play with that title years later. A song and dance man was regarded in turn-of-the-century vaudeville as a pleasant act not much above the trained seals or the Swiss bell ringers. George knew at seventeen that he was essentially a song and dance man, and that song and dance men rarely became headliners. He also knew that his performing abilities at that time were not remarkable. His singing voice was just a cut below ordinary (years later when warned that his voice was being strained, he answered, "I don't care if I lose my voice. Nobody will know the difference."), and his dancing was really only good in eccentric routines. But being a song and dance man was fun, and George valued that commodity highly. Even when he received wide praise for his acting in late years, his personal identification as a song and dance man was unremitting. In 1938 at a testimonial dinner given for him by the Catholic Actors Guild, he spoke as always with little preparation. In pointing out that he really should have prepared a substantial speech, he added, "but of course that's asking a great deal of a song and dance man. (*Laughter.*) Especially a song and dance man who tried so hard not to be a song and dance man. (*Laughter.*) [Cohan had written a series of non-musical plays for himself.] And then had to go back to being a song and dance man in order to earn a living! (*Laughter.*)" (He was then romping his way through *I'd Rather Be Right* as a song and dance Franklin D. Roosevelt.)

George realized early that although he was a song and dance man he was not withstanding committed to the entire package; he was a total man of the theatre: playwright, director, producer, composer, and actor. And unlike Bottom who wanted to play the lion too, George did it all not from inflated self-esteem but because he had learned that if a thing was to be done in just the way he wanted it, the best way was to do it himself. He did not fancy being at the mercy of cloddish stage managers, hack playwrights, and dictatorial producers.

In 1895–96 the Four Cohans traveled extensively and disastrously. On a Chicago tour, on a Southern tour, on a tour through Ohio and a subsequent one on the Eastern seaboard, they joined companies which closed in every instance two weeks after auspicious openings. The only cheery note was struck in Chicago where they were invited to a picnic given for the employees of Armour & Company.

The secretary to the company's president was Julius Tannen, a gifted amateur mimic, who haunted the variety halls to study the performing idiosyncrasies of many popular performers. During an impromptu amateur show at the picnic, Tannen delighted George by doing an imitation of him. Tannen received great applause for his effort and for a bow-off, he ad-libbed in Cohan nasality, "My mother thanks you, my father thanks you, my sister thanks you, and I thank you." Tannen was to become an actor and one of the first monologists in vaudeville, and decades later worked for Cohan.

This kind of pleasant interlude was rare. For the most part the Four Cohans' tours at this time were frustrating, and George began to feel strong regret that Josie had sacrificed her career as a single by returning to the four-act. They returned to New York for weeks of idleness and the decision that Josie should indeed become a single again.

Suddenly their luck changed and the Four Cohans replaced an act unable to play its date at Hyde and Behman's Theatre, at that time the most sophisticated vaudeville playhouse in the United States. To succeed there was to reach the heights in the world of variety entertainment.

The Four Cohans were told brusquely that they were to open the bill and Jerry was astounded when George smilingly assured the manager of the theatre that the Four Cohans would rather open the show at Hyde and Behman's than to be next to closing in any other house. George had an instinct that something might happen. *Goggles Doll House* was a seventeen-minute act. Here at this great Brooklyn theatre, before the most demanding vaudeville audience in the country, the act ran twenty-six minutes due to added laughs and encores. The Cohans ran offstage and went to their dressing rooms breathlessly. They knew they had made a hit because they took four curtain calls but they were almost frightened when the stage manager came to order them peremptorily back on stage. The audience was still applauding.

As they stumbled onstage to take the extra call, the Four Cohans for the first time in their lives heard the cry that most performers hear only in their secret dreams: "Speech! Speech! Speech!" Jerry was incredulous, unnerved, and when George turned to him, he waved the boy to the footlights. George was almost at a loss for words but as he walked toward the audience, he remembered the mock curtain line Julius Tannen improvised in Chicago a year before. Bowing low, George said, "Ladies and gentlemen, my mother thanks you, my father thanks you, my sister thanks you, and I thank you!" Loud applause and laughter, and George had found a memorable and durable curtain speech. He never used another.

The Four Cohans had peaked. In a very real sense, all that came to them now—the money (they were shortly to receive a standard $1000 a week, unheard of for most acts at the time), the critical acclaim, above all the faithful audiences—all of these, glorious as they were, meant not half so much as that golden moment on Hyde and Behman's stage when they crossed the threshold into what was known even then as the big time. It was the turning point in their life, and George's pushy assertiveness the family now saw as a needed primer charge for their progression. George, to Jerry's relief, became the manager of the Four Cohans.

Broadway after Hyde and Behman's was to take five more years but they were bright substantial years with ample rewards for the family. George was newly in demand as a song-writer. "Venus, My Shining Love" was becoming a standard in the repertoire of Broadway café orchestras. May Irwin, the bouncy vaudeville singer, had bought a Cohan song, "Hot Tamale Alley," and made it the high point of her act. This song was of that curious genre known as "coon songs," purporting to represent the lazy charm and lovable eccentricity of Negroes. Repulsive in their implications today, at the turn of the century these ditties were wildly popular and Cohan wrote the Irwin song as well as "You're the Warmest Baby in the Bunch" to meet the demand. Most of his songs were comic, usually called "novelty" songs, and invariably with jingly titles like "Hugh McHugh, You Mick You."

The Four Cohans, riding the top of the wave, savored every minute. They became the top-salaried four-act in vaudeville, and all booking worries were over. B. F. Keith was riding a wave crest, too. By the late nineties he was the uncrowned king of vaudeville; any act that wanted to reach the top rank was virtually forced to work for him. He was a cynic and not a very nice man: one of his favorite expressions was, "I never trust a man I can't buy." The Four Cohans worked for him indefatigably through the hard years and of the family only gentle Jerry felt anything like respect for Keith. George was not impressed by vaudeville's dictator; he worked for him only because Keith offered the best chances to appear in first class theatres. The affiliation with Keith came to an end in a burst of hearty acrimony. In 1938 Cohan told the story in dialogue form to Douglas Gilbert for his definitive history, *American Vaudeville:*

> We [the Four Cohans] signed a contract with B. F. Keith to play eight weeks a season during the years 1897, '98 and '99. We had played twenty-two of the twenty-four weeks and had lived up to the contract religiously. In the meantime our outside bookings had been popular and profitable, so much that we came to Boston to play the remaining two weeks our salaries had risen to three times that called for in the Keith contract. Well, when we got in I went over to the theatre and took a look at the bill: we were bottom-lined. Previously we had been headlined and our contract called for that billing.
>
> I went at once to the house manager, a man named Bryant, and complained, told him it was impossible to play under that billing and he told me to see Keith, which I did. And Keith said, "Well, I'm sorry. It's some mistake, some press agent's or sign painter's mistake, some press agent's or sign painter's mistake not mine."
>
> COHAN: It isn't mine, either.
>
> KEITH: What are you going to do?
>
> COHAN: What would you do in my position?
>
> KEITH: If I'd been associated with a man as long as you people have with me, I'd certainly go through for him.
>
> COHAN: Well, Mr. Keith, I haven't any particularly fond memories of you. The only thing I can recall in the early days of Keith is a lot of hard work, a lot of extra performances, a lot of confinement, six and seven and eight shows a day, running up eighty and ninety steps to the dressing rooms, and a million rules and regulations hanging all over the place. Any time you wanted to smoke you had to go into a little tin closet. So the nice little speech you just made to me, inviting me to go through with the broken contractual conditions, doesn't

mean much. Besides, Mr. Keith, I remember a little incident in Providence on a Saturday night. You didn't have enough to meet the payroll. And you came back to ask us if we'd mind waiting until the following Tuesday or Wednesday. And my father, Jerry, said, "Why, no, if you're short, and maybe we could lend you a little money and how much do you want?" And you said about $600 and we let you have it.

KEITH: I don't remember it.

COHAN: Another thing; you probably don't realize, Mr. Keith, that we are getting a whole lot more money in outside booking than we did when we signed this contract three years ago.

KEITH: Oh, that's the idea. You want more money.

COHAN: Yes, a whole lot more.

KEITH: I understand now; it's a shakedown.

COHAN: Call it what you like, Mr. Keith, but just because of that crack, I'll make you a promise right now—that no member of the Cohan family will ever play for you again as long as you are in the theatrical business.

And they never did.

This account of the Keith break-up reveals two interesting Cohan characteristics. First is his habit, natural to a playwright but one which Cohan carried to extraprofessional lengths, of expressing himself in dialogue. Throughout his life, in the writing of many letters, articles, and newspaper stories, he used the spoken word. He believed firmly that direct, colloquial American speech was the best way for Americans to communicate. And also, speaking for himself, he was the first to admit that his own vocabulary was small and was limited to direct colloquial American speech in any case.

The second Cohan characteristic the Keith incident reveals is the Cohan anger, still volatile forty years after the event. Douglas Gilbert says of Cohan that throughout his long career "he fought with everybody at one time or another" which, if not quite true, is close to the mark. This deep-seated belligerence was mostly pragmatic in origin, as has been noted. In his autobiography, Cohan says, "My father was a very timid man and always seemed to me to have a holy terror of talking business, especially with theatrical managers. His quiet, gentle manner, and the way they used to take advantage of his let-well-enough-alone way of going along, was a thing which taught me that aggressiveness was a very necessary quality in dealing with the boys who were out to accumulate the nickels and dimes." The Cohan carapace of brash self-confidence began as a defensive growth, but it could be the essential Cohan when, as with Keith, he felt the sting of injustice.

After the split-up with Keith, the Four Cohans were almost forced to set their sights for Broadway; it was the only part of show business they had not yet conquered. They had become the most famous four-act in vaudeville, and George was responsible in large measure for their attainment. He drove himself unrelentingly. In addition to performing with the act and booking it, he was composing songs and writing sketches for other vaudevillians. The sketches did not merit much tangible reward over-all. In an interview given to Ashton Stevens, the drama critic, in 1905, Cohan described why writing for others grew to be a burden:

> The way they used to pay me was the funniest joke in vaudeville. A fellow would owe me $500, and one week I'd get $35, the next week $10, the next $5 and the next nothing. After two years of writing sketches I quit. You might as well give them away. In fact, I did give one away to Filson, of Filson and Errol. I made him a present of it because I liked him. He wrote to thank me, and I wrote back and signed myself "Your private playwright." He must have taken it seriously, for pretty soon, when I fixed an act for somebody else, he said, "Ain't you going to give me the first chance at the stuff

> you write?" Yes, he was indignant. Hadn't he given me my first chance to show what I could do in the way of writing for somebody else? Hadn't he permitted me to write a piece for him for nothing? And hadn't I been an ingrate in selling the next one?

There was now every reason for reaching into the legitimate theatre, and the Four Cohans prepared for it by playing material provided by George. He took over all writing for the four-act at Jerry's insistence, and *Goggles Doll House* was put in the trunk forever. The four-act began to play acts George wrote, *Money to Burn,* a lively one-act about a spendthrift, and *The Professor's Wife,* a farce. Next came several one-act sketches, *Running for Office* and *The Governor's Son,* which George was later to expand full-length into the first legitimate theatre productions of the Four Cohans. George tried to book the sketches with touring comedy troupes bearing national reputations like the Vesta Tilley Company and the Harry Williams Vaudeville Company. It was during the run with the latter group that George's personal life took a strong new direction. He had experienced the usual backstage flirtations which gave him pleasant and impermanent companionship. He was too busy a young man to think of anything but his prime duty to the theatre and the four-act. Then, shortly after he became twenty, he met Ethel Levey at an after-theatre party in a suite at the Hotel Morrison in Chicago.

Ethelia Fowler, born in San Francisco in 1881 of a Scottish father and an Irish mother, was a bright-eyed young singer with an exuberant personality. At the time she met George she was playing Chicago with a Weber and Fields company under her professional name, Ethel Levey, her surname derivative from her Jewish stepfather, Sol Levey. She could play the piano, dance with style and sing with a piquant vitality which made her a likely candidate for stardom on the musical stage. Her skills as a comedienne were marked, and this aspect of her strong personality first attracted George to her. He respected her professionalism and was intrigued by her temperament. Ethel always stood up to George if she thought he was wrong, and this was not infrequent. He had met his match literally. When he returned to New York after the Chicago engagement he corresponded with Ethel as she toured the country, and her letters he found most diverting. They met very little in ensuing months but this failed to hinder their growing affection. They announced their engagement in early 1899, to the mild disapproval of Jerry, Nellie, and Josie. The three Cohans were not sanguine about a marriage which seemed to be built primarily on correspondence. Nevertheless, they were present to wish the newlyweds well at the marriage in July 1899 at St. Nicholas Roman Catholic Church, in Atlantic City, New Jersey. There was a honeymoon in California and the young couple returned to New York for two exciting events—the turn of the century and the debut of the Four Cohans as stars in the legitimate theatre.

5. BROADWAY

The American theatre before 1900 was to large degree a theatre of revival, import, and adaptation. Its potential in respect to native drama was enormous—it had hardly anywhere else to go but up. Native American drama advanced a little with the arrival of Augustin Daly on the scene just after the Civil War. Daly has been called the father of modern American drama and, comparatively speaking, this is true. Before Daly, most American playwrights tended not to proclaim their nationality. Daly helped to alter that but it was almost all he altered. The substance of his work, like most of America's leading playwrights, remained eighteenth-century melodrama or farce in new attire. The greatness of American drama was to lie dormant—despite the efforts of bright talents like Clyde Fitch and Percy MacKaye—until the smoldering genius of Eugene O'Neill ignited during World War I. Broadway at the turn of the century, says Brooks Atkinson, was "provincial and parochial . . . artistically trivial [but] it had charm and a kind of disarming simplicity."

Nowhere was this simplicity more marked than in the American musical theatre. In 1900 there was little that was indigenous or creative about what was to become in our day the most vigorous of American dramatic forms. The musical stage has properly been called pure and total theatre. Certainly, at its best, there is no more memorable way to call forth that indefinable human affirmation we call sentiment, the *plus pur du sang* of entertainment as has been definitively demonstrated in recent years. Great American musical theatre is a newcomer to the arts in that it has principally evolved within the life-span of men still with us.

George M. Cohan was a significant part of that evolution. When he came to New York in 1900, American musical theatre lacked definition. New York theatregoers had their choice of three basic forms of musical shows: operettas heavily European in flavor, musical vaudeville, and musical farce. The operettas were endlessly self-imitative, following plot formulas as undeviating as they were unimaginative. Musical vaudeville and its close kin, burlesque, had abounding vigor and little artistry. Much of it was American in tone, robust in its assertiveness and unsparing in its ridicule of ethnic groups newly come to the United States. Musical farce was not much more sophisticated in its treatment of the immigrants but it frequently tried at least for authenticity in costume and décor when presenting these minorities on stage. Irish-Americans were regarded as especially colorful types and they became a focus of Harrigan and Hart's musical gallimaufries of life in New York's Five Points section. Also popular at the century's turn were the plays of Charles Hoyt who wrote resolutely American farces laced with songs from many sources.*

It was to this combined Harrigan-Hart-Hoyt tradition, the farce-based, roughly vigorous American play with music, that Cohan looked for inspiration when he first began to write for Broadway. Harrigan had a particular fascination for him. In 1914, Cohan wrote: "Edward Harrigan was a fine artist, a great writer of human comedies and one of the grandest men it has ever been my pleasure to meet. Hoyt could always tickle the funny bone of the American

* Hoyt's stage manager and director, Julian Mitchell, later directed a number of Cohan's musical shows.

theatregoer, but Harrigan turned the same trick and got to the old heartstrings at the same time. Harrigan inspired me when I applauded him from a gallery seat. Harrigan encouraged me when I first met him in after years and told him of my ambitions. I live in hopes that some day my name may mean half as much to the coming generation of American playwrights as Harrigan's name has meant to me."

Cohan was to reshape Harrigan, and in turn, other playwrights were to take Cohan's sometimes inchoate musical plays and refashion their fundamentals into such enduring American works as *Oklahoma!*, *Guys and Dolls*, and *Pal Joey*. One of these playwrights and a Cohan admirer was Oscar Hammerstein II who wrote in the New York *Times:* "Never was a plant more indigenous to a particular part of the earth than was George M. Cohan to the United States of his day. The whole nation was confident of its superiority, its moral virtue, its happy isolation from the intrigues of the old country, from which many of our fathers and grandfathers had migrated." The year 1900 was clearly a happy time to be alive, and if in looking back it is not easy to forgive rampant social injustices, it must be remembered that this was America in adolescence. Who could fail to be euphoric, living in what seemed literally to be the home of the free and the brave? The songs of the country at the century's turn reflected this exultation unendingly, and in Hammerstein's words, "Cohan's genius was to say simply what everybody was subconsciously feeling." To which Brooks Atkinson, adds, "Cohan's songs, both words and music, were sublimations of the mood of their day. They said what millions of people would have said if they had Cohan's talent."

The twenty-one musical plays of George M. Cohan are crude by today's standards but they have a joyous vitality which far transcends their years. Their books are bland and frequently obvious but there is much authentic American humor in them. Above all, there are the songs, most of them still as rousing and freshly vibrant as they were many decades ago.

Cohan's first legitimate theatre audience saw a production which had been well tested in embryo on the road. *The Governor's Son* began life as a sketch for the Four Cohans in 1899 and as George's New York ambitions grew, he added extensively to its plot complications until he had a vehicle for the family and twenty-five other actors, including a role for his wife whose obvious talents as a singing comedienne needed accommodation. Cohan's writing of the show in the summer of 1900 was interrupted happily by the birth of a daughter, Georgette. In every way, he was primed for success in his debut as a New York playwright.

The Governor's Son, financed by Lou Behman of the Hyde-Behman partnership, opened February 11, 1901, at Hartford, Connecticut, coming to New York's Savoy Theatre on 34th Street two weeks later. Cohan was in fighting trim. A feisty twenty-two, already a show business veteran, he knew he had attained maturity because at this point in his life the managers and agents and producers who had called him "Georgie" were now referring to him as "Cohan" or "Mr. Cohan." He had reached his full height, five feet six inches, averaging between 135 and 140 pounds, and without giving the impression of smallness. His eyes were piercingly blue and his jaw was strong and pugnacious. His mouth was sensitive, and he tended to hide this by deliberately twisting down the left side of his mouth (a habit he picked up from comedian Joe Leslie), keeping his face immobile, thereby adding a wry nuance to his appearance. The critic for the *New York Dramatic Mirror* in reviewing *The Governor's Son* commented: "He is like William Collier in his delivery, making the most ordinary lines seem unusually funny, and that without a change in expression." What Cohan was doing, at a very early age and at a time unaccustomed to it, was underplaying. On the stage both Cohan and Collier (they were later to become great friends and co-star in a Cohan revue) projected pert blandness, an ingratiating comic reserve.

The Governor's Son was mildly appreciated by the critics.

The *Dramatic Mirror's* man summed up the general opinion: "The story is familiar to vaudeville patrons. It was better condensed than in its elongated condition. The fun is rather primitive, and some of the jokes are none too new. A score or more of musical numbers are pleasing enough, though of the simplest character. But the life and soul of the performance are the Cohans, or rather the two youngest members of the family."

The mild praise was not enough. The play closed after only thirty-two performances. Some of the music from *The Governor's Son* is still vital: "Push Me Along in My Pushcart" was one of the brightest numbers in the recent production, *George M!*, and "Nothing New Under the Sun" said something about Broadway musicals then which could profitably be said about Broadway musicals up until recent times:

> Same old songs about the same old moon,
> Few new words but the same old tune;
> Dashing on before us,
> We see the merry chorus,
> And everything they do you know's been done;
> You hear the same old jokes,
> That make the same old hit,
> The scenery's just the same
> But it's been painted up a bit;
> You can ask most any showman,
> Inquire of Charley Frohman,
> And he'll say there's nothing new beneath the sun.

The paradox of this song is that it was the only new thing in *The Governor's Son.* Cohan might have been describing his show; indeed he *was* describing it. The song did the service of at least letting the audiences know that Cohan knew the cliché aspects of the production. Moreover, the song began a Cohan habit of consciously referring to theatrical device within his plays, a habit which was to persist throughout his playwriting career. Perhaps no Broadway author has taken as much delight in simply *talking* about the theatre in his plays as Cohan did.

The plot of *The Governor's Son,* as one Boston critic put it, is "as destitute as a jellyfish of coherent outline," but it is good fun, if minor good fun, for all of that. The setting is a resort inn, and the action consists primarily of couples divided, united, redivided and reunited through unsubtle confrontations with each other's putative paramours. (And if that sentence seems involved, it is clarity itself compared to the intricacies of the plot it tries to describe.) Jerry and Nellie played a mature couple one day married who have had exactly one hundred and twenty-four fights within that period because of his jealousy. George as Algy Wheelock, the bright, brash son of the governor of the state, did little but dash on, dance, and dash off. One critic praised his "clever, capable legs that prance uniquely with apparent disregard of other members." He was pursued by a man-hungry widow (She to George, "I hope to see more of you!", and he answers, "I'm going in bathing tomorrow.") and a high-spirited soubrette, Emerald Green, (Ethel Levey). The key situation does not resolve around the governor's son at all but a runaway husband, Dicky Dickson, pursued by his wife, appropriately referred to in full throughout as Mrs. Dicky Dickson. This was Josie's role and she brought to it beauty and great comic dignity. (A Boston critic was irresistibly reminded of Ethel Barrymore.) At one point, Mrs. Dicky Dickson encounters Curtis (Jerry) whom she astounds with the erroneous news that Mrs. Curtis (Nellie) is really Dicky Dickson's wife:

CURTIS: Dicky Dickson's wife!

MRS. DICKY: If you're her husband, how can she be my husband's wife?

CURTIS: Your husband's wife!

MRS. DICKY: If you're her husband and she's my husband's wife, then you must be my husband's wife's husband. (*Going*) I'm going to protect my husband. Your wife shall never harm my husband even though she is his wife. (*Exit*)

CURTIS: (*Bewildered*) I wish I could wake up. She threatens to kill me. Now she's got another husband, and he's got another wife. I wonder what relation I am to my wife's other husband's other wife?

Which is where one had better leave active analysis of *The Governor's Son.*

As disappointing as it was for the New York run to be cut short, the show did not die, finding a great success on tour in places where the Four Cohans were well known. On his return, Cohan, now a known New York entity, was meeting most of the people at the top of his profession. One day, he was standing at the bar of the Gilsey House, Broadway and 29th Street, when his companion introduced him to the idol of his youth, Nat Goodwin. Cohan said, "Pleased to meet you, Mr. Goodwin." "Hell—I'm not Mr. Goodwin. My name is Nat." With uncharacteristic diffidence, Cohan said, "I'm sorry, but you're Mr. Goodwin to me." Goodwin said, "Well, if you can't call me Nat, call me Hector and I'll call you Ralph." Those were the names they used for each other the rest of their lives.

Josie's great personal success in *The Governor's Son* brought her into sight as one of the most desirable young ladies in New York with stage door Johnnies three deep. In June 1901 she was married, predictably within her profession, to Fred Niblo, highly talented young comedian and monologist, who was shortly to take a part in managing the Cohan business operations.

The Cohans spent most of 1901, 1902, and the spring of 1903 with *The Governor's Son* on tour, George adding and revising. The extended tour was undertaken principally to make a little money and to allow George to take another of his Four Cohan vaudeville sketches, *Running for Office,* and expand it into full-length musical farce. The plot was perfectly symmetrical: John Tiger (Jerry), widower, married a widow (Nellie) whose son (George) falls in love with Tiger's daughter (Josie). Both Mr. and Mrs. Tiger for no better reason than that the young people's getting together too soon would end the play before the first act is over, keep the knowledge of their children from each other. The young people become engaged not knowing that their parents have married. Inevitably all disorder is ordered but at such a gallop that the usually placid reviewer for the *Dramatic Mirror* was slightly dazed: "One situation follows another with such amazing rapidity that the spectators have scarcely time to draw their breath between laughs." The unrelenting speed of the Cohan shows is typified in a stage direction in Act II (*From this point on, the action must be very fast*). In rehearsals Cohan seemed obsessed with the rapid entry and exit of all characters, particularly the chorus people. In an interview after the opening night, he defined the basic element of his musical shows as "Speed! Speed! And lots of it. That's the idea of the thing. Perpetual motion!" He had seen too many musicals with a staging tempo influenced by operetta and its languid flow from one number into another. Cohan's alteration of stroll pace to a running tempo was one of his permanent contributions to American musical theatre.

Running for Office also began the Cohan habit of infusing his already colloquial dialogue with current slang. This habit was to scandalize at least one leading drama critic of the day but it was a delight to New York audiences who rarely encountered this flavor in any kind of theatrical offering. *Running for Office* was replete with this kind of language: "bird" for "girl," "soak" for "hit," "coco" for "head," and a phrase still current, "getting loaded" for "getting drunk."

The critics were kinder to Cohan this time. They would never fully warm up to him but as the critic for *Theatre Magazine* put it: ". . . the play is not high art, but it is excellent of its kind and superior to many of the more widely advertised and showy productions on Broadway." It was just those showy productions Cohan aspired to, and during the national tour of *Running for Office* in the 1903–4 season, he began to set his plans for not only Broadway (his first two New York productions had been produced at small theatres downtown) but personal stardom for himself. There was increasing evidence that Josie planned, unwillingly, to leave the Four Cohans. Ethel Levey was Mrs. George M. Cohan, and although she did not have Josie's talent, George was teaching her many things. An inevitable tension grew between the two young women. Josie, too, was married and her husband had ambitions for them both.

On the 1903–4 tour, Cohan began to ponder just what kind of vehicle he could write which would give him a distinctive role, smartly, contemporaneously American and suitable for him physically. One day he read a glowing account in a newspaper of the talents of Tod Sloan, the famous jockey, and it struck Cohan that a jockey hero would be type-casting for a man of his stature, bursting with energy. The idea for *Little Johnny Jones,* his first starring vehicle, was germinated. All it needed was sustenance.

This came in the form of Sam H. Harris, native New Yorker, former newsboy, delivery man, and cough-drop salesman. Harris fitted George M. Cohan like a boxing glove to a fist. A vital man with a great love of the theatre, he felt he belonged in it but had no talent for or interest in performing. He was to serve as Cohan's buffer against many of the workaday worries of play producing in his capacity as the partner with the keenest sense of business. But Harris was more than a businessman; he had an almost uncanny sense of what would play well on the stage. More, he and Cohan were perfectly paired temperamentally. Both were quietly gregarious, both could not live without the theatre and both had strikingly similar senses of humor. Cohan has left an account in dialogue of their first meeting at the

Words and Music Club's annual picnic on Staten Island in the spring of 1904:

> Sam Harris was one of the wittiest men I've ever known. When I first met him he was manager of the fighting little Terry McGovern who had just lost the lightweight championship to Young Corbett. Our first conversation was something like this:
>
> HARRIS: You bet against Terry, didn't you?
>
> COHAN: How did you know that?
>
> HARRIS: Remember the fellow you won the money from?
>
> COHAN: Sure.
>
> HARRIS: He was my betting commissioner.
>
> COHAN: Oh, I see. Does Terry know that I bet against him?
>
> HARRIS: No, and I'm not going to tell him. He likes you too much.
>
> COHAN: How do you know he likes me?
>
> HARRIS: He told me so.
>
> COHAN: Do you control his likes and dislikes?
>
> HARRIS: (*Chuckling*) I'm his manager, ain't I?
>
> (*A few days later I ran into McGovern.*)
>
> TERRY: Say, you bet against me, didn't you?
>
> COHAN: Harris promised me he wouldn't tell you.
>
> TERRY: He didn't tell me. I told him.
>
> COHAN: You told him?
>
> TERRY: Sure.
>
> COHAN: How did you find out?
>
> TERRY: The fellow you bet with is my cousin.
>
> (*The next day I met Harris again.*)
>
> COHAN: See here, Harris, you and McGovern ought to rehearse your stuff a little better.
>
> HARRIS: (*Interrupting with a chuckle.*) I know what he told you, and believe me, it was all very well rehearsed. We've been pulling it on everybody that bet against us.
>
> COHAN: What's the idea?
>
> HARRIS: Well, didn't it hand you a laugh?
>
> COHAN: Not exactly.

HARRIS: I'm sorry, but you see Terry gets a lot of fun out of it, and I want to keep him in good humor for the return match with Young Corbett.

Cohan and Harris had an unfailing facility to keep each other in good humor. Their first shared enterprise was the production of *Little Johnny Jones,* and it was one of their most successful. They had little money to begin it. At a dinner honoring Cohan years later with a chuckling Sam Harris at his side on the dais, Cohan spoke of the preparations for their first show:

> This Harris man, by the way, is a very surprising person. Full of surprises. I know he's handed me many a surprise. I don't mean by that that I didn't know he was always a great showman—a great judge of plays, and all that sort of thing, but I mean really he's a surprising man. I remember the first time he surprised me. Of course when Sam and I went into business together, I naturally thought he had a lot of money. We didn't talk about that until we were in the middle of rehearsals for our first show, and then when he told me he was broke, that was my first surprise. And he seemed to be just as much surprised as I was when I told him I was broke too! And the members of the company were very much surprised when they found out we were both broke!

Actually Cohan had a bit of money in the bank from his recent tour but there were times when the payroll was late or barely met during rehearsal. There was a lot riding on *Little Johnny Jones:* the future of Cohan and Harris as a producing organization and Cohan's future as a playwright. There was one artistic deficit even before rehearsals began. Josie announced to her family tearfully that she and her husband were accepting jobs in another Broadway musical show, *The Rogers Brothers in Paris.* The family shared the tears but there was an inevitability about the decision which eased the pain of loss.

Little Johnny Jones opened in Hartford on October 10, 1904, and delighted its audience. There was more of a substantial plot than in previous Cohan shows, which is saying very little, and it was the first of the real flag-waving Cohan productions, a flag-waving unqualifiedly sincere. Most of the play is set in England and permeating the proceedings is the unspoken and sometimes spoken sentiment that dear old Blighty cannot hold a candle to the good old U.S.A. One character is asked, "What makes the Americans so proud of their country?" and the quick reply is, "*Other* countries." The personification of this American pride was Cohan as cheeky Johnny Jones. Midway in the first act, enjoying himself during the excitement of pre-Derby days in London, Johnny is surrounded by girls anxious to meet him even though he has proclaimed his engagement to an American girl. He asks the girls if they want a tip on the race and when they clamor for one, he replies, "Pawn your jewelry, go in hock, and play Yankee Doodle to win!" which is prelude to his singing, in the penetrating Cohan twang:

I'm the kid that's all the candy,
I'm a Yankee Doodle Dandy,
I'm glad I am.
GIRLS: So's Uncle Sam.

JOHNNY: I'm a real live Yankee Doodle,
Made my name and fame and boodle,
Just like Mister Doodle did by riding on a
pony.
I love to listen to the Dixie strain,
I long to see the girl I left behind me;
And that ain't a josh,
She's a Yankee by gosh!

GIRLS: Oh, say, can you see
Anything about a Yankee that's a phoney?

JOHNNY: I'm a Yankee Doodle Dandy,
A Yankee Doodle do or die;
A real live nephew of my Uncle Sam's,

Born on the Fourth of July.
I've got a Yankee Doodle sweetheart,
She's my Yankee Doodle joy.
Yankee Doodle came to London,
just to ride the ponies.
I am a Yankee Doodle Boy!

The audience was electrified. They had never heard a song like this—patriotically stirring, yet funny, and fitting integrally into the farcical plot. Audience interest focused strongly on Johnny Jones but Cohan wisely did not offer too much of himself. The comedy came first. The best lines in the play belong to a jovial drunk, actually a private detective named Whitney Wilson, a role played by a former blackface comedian well known on Broadway, Tom Lewis. Lewis, fat, funny, and florid, received the biggest laughs and the greatest number of exit "hands" during the run of the play. His drolleries and the caperings of Ethel Levey took over much of the play which is essentially musical melodrama. Ethel played Johnny Jones's fiancée, Goldie Gates (a San Francisco girl) who must assume two disguises in the play, a Parisian midinette and an English lord (sic). Tom Lewis had the lines which more than any other reveal the vaudeville flavor of early Cohan dialogue. In one scene, Lewis playing Wilson enters, says the stage direction, "*with a bun on,*" and kids the waiter who hovers over him solicitously:

WAITER: Do you feel like a cup of tea, sir?
WILSON: No. I don't feel like a cup of tea. Do I *look* like a cup of tea? . . . 23! ["Skidoo" understood.]
WAITER: What, sir?
WILSON: 23!
WAITER: Who, sir?
WILSON: You.
WAITER: No, sir. 36. Is there anything else I can do, sir?
WILSON: If there was, you wouldn't be a waiter . . .
WAITER: Shall I call you a hansom, sir?
WILSON: Call me anything you like.

These jokes, it must be noted, were rather new in 1904 and are not too bad even today. Jerry Cohan, instead of playing his usual amiable self, was the villain of the piece, the man who framed Johnny Jones and had him barred from both the English and American turf on the charge that Johnny threw the Derby. Jerry had only one decent laugh line all evening (speaking of the wealthy widow he is engaged to: "I am not marrying Mrs. Kenworth because she has twenty million—I'd marry her if she had *forty* million!"), and some of the critics were nonplused by his debut into perfidy. Nellie played his wealthy fiancée.

Johnny Jones had two other great moments in the show. The first came at the end of Act II following his disgrace when after fighting off a vengeful mob with a pistol, Johnny is at Southampton Pier, preparing to board ship for home. But, dispirited though he is, Johnny decides to stay in England and vindicate himself. His faithful pal, Wilson, assures him that evidence can be found which will prove Johnny's innocence. It is agreed that the signal for the evidence's discovery will be a rocket fired by Wilson from the ship when it passes Lizard Island out in the bay. As Wilson boards ship, Johnny waves to him and sings plaintively:

Did you ever see two Yankees part upon a foreign shore,
When the good ship's just about to start for old New York once more?
With tear-dimmed eye, they say good-bye, they're friends without a doubt;
When the man on the pier shouts "Let them clear" as the ship strikes out?

A steward returns Johnny's bags from the ship, and as Johnny receives them he sings softly, with infinite sadness:

Give my regards to Broadway,
Remember me to Herald Square;
Tell all the gang at Forty-second Street

That I will soon be there.
Whisper of how I'm yearning
To mingle with the old time throng;
Give my regards to old Broadway
And say that I'll be there, ere long.

The ship, only its rear deck visible, pulls away and then follows the kind of device much loved by Boucicault, a "transformation." Johnny walks sadly into the shadows of the darkening stage and for a few moments the lights dim slowly to indicate passage of time. Then, in miniature cut-out against the ocean backdrop, the ship appears in the distance, moving in the harbor, its lights softly twinkling in the gloom. It progresses slowly and at just the moment when tension must be relieved, there suddenly arches up from the boat a shivery, sparkling white rocket. Whereupon the orchestra thunders into a spirited, happy-tempoed chorus of "Give My Regards to Broadway" with Johnny singing and exulting in every phrase. Curtain. The opening night audience broke into wild applause and would not be satisfied until Cohan bowed and said a few words of thanks.

Cohan's one other stirring moment in the play was a quieter one. In the third act, Johnny's reputation is restored, the villain foiled and love comes to all against the picturesque setting of San Francisco's Chinatown. At mid-point in these frenzied proceedings, Johnny has a moment of respite—a most unusual thing for Cohan in any of his productions—in which he delivered a little philosophical homily, set to lively music, but a homily for all of that. Between rapid excursions of fleeing Chinamen and the blowing of police whistles, the stage is left empty and suddenly there are no noises off as Johnny comes on to tell the audience that there isn't a corner of Chinatown he has not searched for his kidnapped fiancée, ". . . and what a study it all is. By golly, life's a funny proposition, after all." Johnny half-speaks, half-sings the verse:

Did you ever sit and ponder, sit and wonder, sit and think,
Why we're here and what this life is all about?
It's a problem that has driven many brainy men to drink,
It's the weirdest thing they've tried to figure out;
About a thousand different theories, all the scientists can show,
But never yet have proved a reason why.
With all we've thought, and all we're taught, why all we seem to know is,
We're born and live a while and then we die.

He spoke-sang the refrain more slowly:

Life's a very funny proposition, after all;
Imagination, jealousy, hypocrisy and all;
Three meals a day, a whole lot to say;
When you haven't got the coin, you're always in the way.
Ev'rybody's fighting, as we wend our way along,
Ev'ry fellow claims the other fellow's in the wrong;
Hurried and worried, until we're buried and there's no curtain call;
Life's a very funny proposition after all.

This would be unbearably sententious if it were solemnly delivered but solemnity was as foreign to Cohan as it was to Bernard Shaw. He gave the lines in pleasant bemusement, as if unaccountably intrigued. The audience was bemused as well. This song or recitation (Ed Begley spoke it beautifully on the Johnny Carson Show for his last professional appearance before his death) has in it what was to become a fundamental Cohan theme—mystery, or more deeply, the comedy of mystery. Cohan was to find in the naturally dramatic tensions of mystery more of laughter than of fear; the unexpected, for him, always had in it seeds of the ridiculous. In "Life's a Very Funny Proposition After All," Cohan meant "funny" in the sense of "odd" but even more he meant it as "amusing."

Little Johnny Jones was a tremendous success in Hartford. It was not quite a failure in New York at the Liberty

Theatre on 42nd Street, but it only played fifty-two times in its first showing. The reviewers of the non-theatrical papers were unenthusiastic; the trade papers, the *Dramatic Mirror* and the *Clipper*, enjoyed the production although they were a bit off-put by the new Cohan. He had (they both commented) written a role for himself in which he sang no really comic songs, and the *Mirror* felt it ". . . a pity that he has decided to take such a serious view of his abilities."

The only serious thing about Cohan after reading the reviews was an angry determination to take what he knew was a first-rate show, tour it, strengthen it, and bring it back to Broadway to make a lasting and favorable impression. Which he did. But on the road, his febrile temper was again aroused by a review which disturbed him more deeply than he cared to admit. In his home town of Providence lived many relatives and friends, and when he had the chance to take *Little Johnny Jones* there, he did so eagerly. It was a mistake from one point of view. A local drama critic gave the play an airily supercilious appraisal. Calling it a "musical offense," "an ill-assorted combination," the reviewer sneered at Cohan's singing as well and said that although musical comedies were common, this was, alas, the first attempt at musical melodrama. Cohan now had two more things to add to his list of more or less permanent antagonisms—critics (he had taken critical disfavor easily enough before this), and Providence, Rhode Island.

He took *Little Johnny Jones* back to Broadway not once but twice within the next year and he accomplished two important things. He became an established Broadway figure and he made a great deal of money. He wanted the latter principally to sustain the former.

6. THE MAN WHO HAD TO OWN BROADWAY

In 1905 Broadway was owned, as it is today, by businessmen. For the most part the theatre has always had to exist as a business. In these sad days when Broadway's destinies are almost irretrievably in the hands of real estate operators, one looks back to 1905 with something like nostalgia. Although there were those then who were fully as sharkish as many profit-circumscribed theatre owners of our time, there was a difference. With few exceptions, the men who owned or controlled the theatres at the turn of the century were men who loved the theatre.

One of the few exceptions was a cold, ferret-eyed producer named A. L. Erlanger—the A.L. representing his wildly inappropriate forenames, Abraham Lincoln. Together with five partners, he formed in 1896 the Theatrical Syndicate which held a virtual monopoly over the American theatre for sixteen years. Erlanger was the dominant member of the group which, in consequence of its investments, could dictate the booking rates of almost every Broadway and provincial theatre. The members of the Syndicate made a curious mélange. One of Erlanger's partners, for instance, was a man much loved in the theatre, gentle Charles Frohman. It was a classic example of the words from Isaiah, "The wolf also shall dwell with the lamb, and the leopard shall lie down with the kid." If Cohan was to be the kid, in several senses, he was not to do business with Erlanger as an underling.

Erlanger knew that *Little Johnny Jones* with its exuberant rhythms and lively American spirit was the wave of the musical future. Here was Harrigan and Hart sophisticated, updated, and holding the mirror up to its principal audience, the American middle class. Erlanger had under contract a delightful comedienne, Fay Templeton, who for years had been principal soubrette for the Weber and Fields Music Hall. Erlanger, whose previous business with the Cohans had been the bestowal of roles in one of his shows to Josie and her husband, came to Cohan and asked bluntly, "Do you think you could write a play without a flag?" The prompt reply was, "I could write a play without anything but a pencil."

In constructing a play, Cohan not only heeded the Boucicault traditions of sentiment, laughter, song, and scenic excitement but also remembered the lesson he had learned from watching *A Gilded Fool*'s genesis. He knew to a fine shade the acting personalities of the performers in his plays: the bubbling, Oliver Hardy-like Tom Lewis; quiet gentlemanly Jerry Cohan; the lady-like Nellie Cohan with an infectious grin ever-ready to crack her façade; spirited, graceful Josie. Cohan used the living personalities of actors and the life and situations about him as the raw material for his work. He was hardly a realist but he gave his public what they saw—or thought they saw—about them, and he served it up, as he was later to tell Spencer Tracy, always with a little dressing. Frequently a lot of dressing.

The raw material of his play for Erlanger was a mixture of two attractive stage personalities and a locale. The locale was New Rochelle, New York, the home of an actor friend of his, T. Harold Forbes. One day Forbes bragged to Cohan that the wonderful little town he lived in had all the delights of bucolia yet was only forty-five minutes away from New York by rail. The two stage personalities Cohan built his play around were Fay Templeton and Victor Moore. Fay was something of a multi-talented Sophie Tucker. She could sing almost any kind of song in a resonantly warm contralto and she was cheery, jolly. A clue to her personality can be found in her contribution of the memorable phrase, "stuffed shirt," to colloquial American speech. In 1899 she threw the epithet at John Gates, a haughty actor who pretended to great wealth and who, it was rumored, padded his shirts to improve the appearance of his physique. Victor Moore was a beamish broth of a boy, with a wistful toughness that permitted him to play ruffians with hearts of gold. Moore was the kind of actor Cohan loved—the deeply sentimental wise-guy. Just such a person Cohan regarded himself, justifiably, and it was this kind of role he wrote for Moore.

From these ingredients Cohan fashioned *Forty-five Minutes from Broadway,* the greatest musical comedy success in New York since *The Black Crook* in 1866. It was delightfully easy for the audience to identify with this, their own world, or their world as it ought to be. Mary (Fay Templeton), a spunky, intelligent housemaid has nursed a crotchety old millionaire with compassionate skill until his death, and the townspeople of New Rochelle confidently expect her to be his heir. The old man does not leave a will and his money goes to the heir-in-law, a nice young man who arrives to claim his due in the company of an affected actress fiancée and her nasty mother. The heir-in-law has picked up a tough-talking secretary, Kid Burns (Victor Moore), who feels uncomfortable any distance away from his beloved Broadway. The fiancée's mother, in rather ostentatious villainy, attempts to steal the fortune and is duly thwarted by Kid Burns who finds the missing will which indeed had left the estate to Mary. To round out a very well-rounded plot, Mary and Kid Burns obligingly fall in love but the Kid says that he cannot marry a girl with money lest it be thought that he . . . whereupon Mary caps the cliché with an even showier one by tearing up the will five seconds before the beginning of the finale.

Forty-five Minutes from Broadway still exudes the life that captivated its first audiences. For all the sophistication of its title song and its condescending references to "jays," "reubens," and other assorted hicks inhabiting New Rochelle, it is a play which pretty much upholds the values of the hay-whiskered types Kid Burns kids. And in the end, the Broadway wise guy falls in love with the New Rochelle girl. She was some girl, *is* some girl. At times Mary sounds like a retired vaudevillian:

> ANDY: I've known you for a long time, Mary. You know I knew your father, Mary.
>
> MARY: You mean you knew my mother, Mary. My father's name was Oscar . . .
>
> ANDY: Don't you think Tom's secretary is an odd fellow?
>
> MARY: He may be a 32nd degree Mason for all I care . . .
>
> ANDY: Say, Mary—
>
> MARY: You want me to say "Mary"? "Mary."

And later the Kid engages her in dubious verbal battle:

> BURNS: How would you like to fall in with a millionaire?
>
> MARY: I wouldn't mind if I had on my bathing suit.

and so into similar joke clusters which are essentially pace-changers from the melodramatic thrusts of the plot. Mary was played by a lady who could do vaudeville routines with ease, and switch quickly to weightier material and a display of her ampler powers as an actress. The *Dramatic Mirror*, restraining itself, said, "It is always a temptation to write a treatise on Fay Templeton's artistic economy of gesture, her ability to get large effects with little motions, her strange power to make a modest droop of the eyelids, so to speak, re-echo through the whole house, and her magnificent control of comic repose."

Forty-five Minutes from Broadway opened in Columbus, Ohio, in September 1905, with Cohan, as was always his custom, seated in the back row of the theatre. He took a day off from the national tour of *Little Johnny Jones,* then in Louisville, to see his production for Erlanger bloom into flower. Erlanger had not been hopeful during rehearsals. He opposed the play's original title, *Mary,* and had insisted, probably with justification, that it be named after the most vigorous song in the show. He admired Cohan but felt that too many precedents were being broken. Cohan admitted that the show had new concepts—just a few basic sets and only eight girls. Erlanger felt the public would never accept a musical show with only eight girls, and his usually parsimonious soul was perversely outraged by the sparseness of the costume bill. The largest single item was twenty dollars for eight calico dresses and to him it epitomized the essential drabness of the production. What Erlanger failed to appreciate was the very fact of the show's ordinariness. Most audiences loved it because they saw themselves. *Forty-five Minutes from Broadway* succeeded because it was *not* a show about Broadway, because it was about a town just safely far enough away from the big city.

From Columbus, the show went to Chicago for an extraordinarily successful twelve weeks before moving to the New Amsterdam Theatre in New York on New Year's Day, 1906, where it was equally well received. The time on the road had altered one emphasis; Fay Templeton no longer dominated. Her charming singing of the two splendid songs, "So Long, Mary" and "Mary's a Grand Old Name" and her versatility as an actress had somewhat overwhelmed Victor Moore initially, but he worked very hard and in New York came into his own. There both stars were in full professional harmony and Fay, delighted with his success, gave him a signet ring which Victor Moore wore to the day he died more than fifty years later.

There had been rumors on the Rialto that Cohan was not a very methodical playwright and this was made public in an interview given to the Chicago *Post* in 1906 when he revealed for the first time his creative processes: "I don't make plays according to Hoyle. I can't sit down and deliberately make out a skeleton of what it is going to be. My plan is to collect half a dozen characters, make them well acquainted with each other, and with me, put them down on paper and then just let them run along. Whenever they want to say anything I let them say it. After I have finished one act I haven't any more idea than you have what the next one will be. I write my plays after midnight. I get back to my apartment after the theatre and have supper—a big one, too: a pound of beefsteak, a large collection of fried potatoes and a pot of coffee. Then I go to my room and write steadily until nine in the morning. At such times I never touch stimulants other than coffee, for I find they unnerve me and muddle me when I am keyed to a high pitch. It's like throwing sand on a hot bearing."

This habit of night writing was to become engrained. Rarely did he complete a play before the first rehearsal and in any number of cases, he did not finish the last act until mid-point in the three- or four-week rehearsal period for straight plays and the five or six weeks needed for musicals. There was the excitement of challenge in announcing that a certain play would open on a certain date when he knew he had only the vaguest idea of theme or characters. Frequently these were real-life characters he had met or only read about, like Tod Sloan for *Little Johnny Jones.* A number of the characters in *The Governor's Son* Cohan had observed while attending a Tammany picnic, and *Running for Office* was stimulated by Cohan's interest in "Big Tim" Sullivan, the colorful Tammany leader.

The comedy role of Wilson so hilariously brought to life by Tom Lewis in *Little Johnny Jones* was patterned after "Big Tom" Foley, the former Sheriff of New York County. The model for Kid Burns was a clerk Cohan had met in the coroner's office at the Criminal Courts Building.

An excellent example of how a little incident could trigger the Cohan imagination occurred when he was riding in a funeral entourage with a Civil War veteran who was holding a folded flag in his lap. The old man spoke of his part in Pickett's charge at Gettysburg and of the ideals for which he and all his comrades fought so desperately. "And it was all for this," the old soldier said, stroking the flag softly. "She's a grand old rag." The phrase would not let Cohan alone and by the end of the ride he had composed the first verse and the refrain of a march which he felt in the depths of his mind and heart:

There's a feeling comes a-stealing,
And it sets my brain a-reeling,
When I'm list'ning to the music of a military band;
Any tune like "Yankee Doodle" simply sets me off my noodle,
It's that patriotic something that no one can understand.
"Way down south, in the land of cotton!"
Mel - o - dy untiring;
Ain't that inspiring?
Hurrah! Hurrah! We'll join the jubilee,
And that's going some, for the Yankees, by gum!
Red, White and Blue, I am for you;
Honest, you're a grand old rag!

You're a grand old rag, you're a high-flying flag,
And forever, in peace, may you wave;
You're the emblem of the land I love,
The home of the free and the brave.
Ev'ry heart beats true, under Red, White and Blue;
Where there's never a boast or brag;
But, should auld acquaintance be forgot,
Keep your eye on the grand old rag.

It was an unusual creative sequence for him to write a song before the rest of the play; he usually wrote his songs after he had structured at least a vague plot or created some characters to make sure the songs had some organic connection with the story. But in this case, the "Grand Old Rag" song begot the play. It focused his thinking inevitably along patriotic lines and what could be more patriotic, he reasoned, than Washington, the man *and* the city, set somehow into a modern context. He decided to put the first scene at Mount Vernon on the front lawn in consonance with what was becoming the First Law of the Cohanic drama: always make the scene interesting and, if possible, warmly familiar. The story centers around a bright, brash young man whose first name is George, another forward step in the growing Cohan self-identification with his leading roles. Johnny Jones was George M. Cohan as a jockey but George Belgrave in *George Washington, Jr.* is Cohan virtually as Cohan. George Belgrave, is an aggressive lad born in Providence. (". . . but don't blame the state on me," this George says. "From Providence, are you?" "No, Providence, R. *I*," is the answer.)

The defensive cockiness of Cohan's youth had firmed into a dramatization of himself, off and onstage, as the outsize egoist with impertinent manners, firecracker wit and heart of gold. The reviewer for *Theatre Magazine* who saw *George Washington, Jr.* was baffled at the striking popularity of the stage Cohan: "His ideas are good but his manners atrocious. He is thoroughly flippant and common, not vulgar, but the spirit of juvenescent enthusiasm is so assertive that the actor has it all his own way."

George Belgrave is told by his rich and conniving senator father (Jerry) that an English lady of title has been picked out for him to marry but George is in love with a charming Southern girl, Dolly Johnson (Ethel). Father, a roaring Anglophile, is insistent, George persists in his refusal, and upon his father's disowning him, disowns his father: "The only father I know is the father of my country. I'll take his name!", carrying patriotism about as far as it can go. The English lady and her brother are ultimately revealed as detectives in the employ of another dastardly senator who wants to compromise George's dad. The detective-mystery element which was present in *Little Johnny Jones* is even more marked in *George Washington, Jr.* and continues as a strong thread through most Cohan comedy. Belgrave's story is set against a Washington background with various patriotic highlights, one of an old veteran coming out to hand George a tattered flag which elicits the comment, "Gee, it's a grand old rag, isn't it?" followed by the song. The comedy at times is reminiscent of an old friend of Cohan's, Will Rogers:

GEORGE: The Senate is the finest body of men that money can buy.
DOLLY: Do the senators get a big salary?
GEORGE: That's all according to the corporations they represent.
DOLLY: There are no female politicians, are there?
GEORGE: There are lots of old women in the Senate.
DOLLY: Honest?
GEORGE: No, senators.

Later, the Senate is described as a body of men surrounded by Standard Oil. There is a more or less stereotyped black comic character, Eaton Ham, who is, however, given much of the best humor in the play and not of the condescending type his name suggests. At one point when he is trying to beguile a silver dollar out of some tourists, he tells how the father of our country threw the coin clear across the river, and adds philosophically, "Well, a dollar used to go much further in those days than it does now." The book, then, is not unfunny and the music is thumpingly bouncy and melodious. Ethel Levey had a particular hit in "I was Born in Virginia" and George got much laughter on a topical flight of fancy, "If Washington Should Come to Life":

He'd soon discover we're no second raters,
I know he'd sing the "Yankee Doodle Boy."
I wonder if he'd visit our theatres
I wonder if he'd laugh at Eddie Foy.
I wonder if he'd try to dope the horses
I wonder what he'd think about Broadway,
He'd buy the New York Journal first
And then he'd call on Willie Hearst
If Washington were alive today.

But the great moment of the evening was "You're a Grand Old Rag," electrifying both audience and critics. It carried all before it except one disgruntled journalist two evenings later who, Cohan said, was angered because he had not been sent seats for opening night. This reporter professed to be horrified at the profanation of the flag and its supposed relegation to the dust bin. A commotion broke out in public print and Cohan hastily changed "rag" to "flag," a distinct dramatic loss. The whole point of the song as sung in the play was that the flag carried out by the old veteran *was* a rag, splendidly tattered after valiant service, its raggedness emphasizing its proud durability.

George Washington, Jr. was a conspicuous success and for the next few years Cohan played it, *The Governor's Son,* and *Little Johnny Jones* both on Broadway and the road. He was now one of Broadway's most interesting personalities, very popular and widely reported in the New York press. For all of its reservations on the brashness of his theatrical approach, the critical fraternity agreed generally with the *Dramatic Mirror* which said, after *George Washington, Jr.*, that perhaps the ". . . true secret of Mr. Cohan's unprecedented success, too permanent for more theatrical luck, consists of his admirable stagecraft. In the art of presenting musical comedy Mr. Cohan is apparently without a peer . . . Cohan seems to have fully established his theory of the melodramatic musical comedy." Boucicault would have been proud.

One who was not proud of Cohan's presence in the American theatre, one who represented the critical few who saw in Cohan a threat to the integrity of the American drama, was James Metcalfe, drama critic for *Life* (the old *Life*, pre-Luce). After seeing *George Washington, Jr.*, Metcalfe erupted. There is something verging on the psychotic in his lofty tirade which betrays some of the anti-Semitism which frequently marked his magazine's editorial viewpoint. This remarkable fulmination deserves to be printed in full:

An Especially Awful Example

> It certainly takes all kinds of people to make a world, and in no way can an intelligent person be better convinced of the fact than by a consideration of the pecuniary success attained by Mr. George M. Cohan with his curious theatrical entertainments, the latest of which, entitled *George Washington, Jr.*, has recently been produced at the Herald Square Theatre.
>
> Mr. Cohan's personality and accomplishments are quite worth notice as a peculiar evolution of our theatrical situation. He is apparently quite a young man. Quite a large part of his stock in trade is an absolute lack of bashfulness as to himself, his family and his doings. One curious feature of his career is that his real name is said on good authority to be Costigan. [Nellie Cohan's maiden name, of course.]
>
> It is not unusual for a Hebrew to exchange a patronymic which betrays his race for one which will conceal it, but for anyone bearing a good old mouth-filling Irish name as Costigan for a distinctively Hebrew appellation is strange indeed. However, Mr. Cohan is very shrewd in a business way and, considering present conditions in the theatre in America, he was perhaps wise in his choice. He has amplified this appeal to one interest by adopting as a bait for another the soubriquet of *The Yankee Doodle Comedian.* To some persons of discernment this might appear a trifling and, in a way, belittling epithet, but Mr. Cohan evidently finds it a

valuable asset in attracting the attention of persons of some kind or other, as he never permits it to be lost sight of.

Metcalfe's sniffs become almost audible:

Mr. Cohan is a sort of universal genius. He writes plays, he writes the words that are set to his combinations of music to his words. These combinations of music are curious things, consisting mainly of several bars of well-known patriotic or sentimental songs strung together with connecting links of lively and more or less original musical trash. The words fitted to these curious contraptions are of the kind of unmetrical stuff that children compose and call poetry, and are for the most part mawkish appeals to the cheapest kind of patriotism. *George Washington, Jr.* is a fair example of his play-writing. It hinges on the Anglo-maniac tendencies of an American father, which are strongly disapproved of by his intensely American son, who goes so far in his intense patriotism as to renounce the paternal name and assume that of the father of his country. On this is based a crude and silly plot, giving opportunity for the Cohan musical sundries as well as for the chorus and show girls now indispensable to the success of anything on the American stage.

Mr. Cohan is naturally the highly patriotic youth who is the hero of the piece, and trades on the national regard for the name of George Washington as a dollar-catcher. His most successful effort in the song line is a similar use of the American flag, which he dignifies in the oft-repeated refrain as "the grand old rag." In this character which he has created for himself, he presumably typifies his ideal of American young manhood. He makes him a vulgar, cheap, blatant, ill-mannered, flashily dressed, insolent, smart Aleck, who for some reason unexplainable on any basis of common sense, good taste, or even ordinary decency, appeals to the imagination and apparent approval of large American audiences. As a living character in any American town or

> village, it is hardly to be conceived that he would not be driven out as a public nuisance and a pernicious example to the youth of the community. The rounds of applause which greet the efforts of this offensive personality must convey to the minds of ignorant boys a depraving ideal for their inspiration and imitation.

Metcalfe then realizes it may reasonably be conjectured that he doth protest too much:

> It may seem strange that so much space should be devoted to a theatrical attraction which, from any artistic importance, should be passed over in contemptuous silence. But it deserves notice. It is one of the most recent and emphatic proofs of the continuous downward tendency of the American stage and the American audience. Mr. Cohan is not to be blamed. In fact, from the American viewpoint that money-making is the test of real success, he is highly to be commended as a successful American. If he can bring himself to coin the American flag and national heroes into box-office receipts, it is not his blame, but our shame. If he hasn't any higher education or ideas than his cheap vulgarities, he is not to be blamed so much for exhibiting them as are the people who go to see them.
>
> *Life* recommends its readers to go to see Mr. Cohan's performance. There could be no stronger appeal for the betterment of the American stage—no fiercer commentary on the debased condition of the intelligence of a large part of the theatre-going public.

The public took Metcalfe's advice. It went to see Cohan, in increasing numbers, and in ever-increasing numbers it continued to see him.

Stung by the Metcalfe attack and further annoyed by the snipings of Rodney Lee, critic for the Toledo *Blade*, who had taken potshots at what he considered the incredibly vain Cohan self-appraisals found in *The Spot Light*, Cohan counterattacked. *The Spot Light* was the Cohan-Harris house organ, a newsletter, four pages of lively intramural gossip, feature stories on Cohan-Harris actors, photographs from the productions, occasional poems by Jerry and a personal column by Cohan consisting mainly of one-line comments on the shows, critics, performers he liked, towns he disliked, future productions and himself. The entire flavor of his column was so studiedly cheeky that it is hard to imagine anyone being provoked into accepting it literally, but Mr. Lee was clearly a man easy to upset. Calling Cohan a "youthful egotist . . . an over-inflated would-be playwright . . . for whom the personal pronoun 'I' was the only letter in the alphabet," Lee hurled himself into Metcalfe's corner.

Cohan, for the only time in his career, deigned to answer critical attack seriously. This he did in a front-page riposte to Lee and Metcalfe in *The Spot Light*'s Birthday Number, 1906. It is an interesting document psychologically. It shows that Cohan could be hurt, that he was aware at an early point in his career that his fullest interests were with management rather than with labor, and that he was, above all, damned good, damned proud of being damned good, and damned well aware of his certitude on these matters.

Birthday Number

THE SPOT LIGHT

New York and Chicago,
July 4 1906 Vol II, No. 3

AM I AN EGOTIST?

Some penny a liner, who writes syndicate articles, has taken it upon himself to call me an egotist. I'd love to wager that the young man doesn't know the real meaning of the word. I trust no one will imagine that I am—as the saying goes—"trying to square myself." Far be it from me, for the opinion of any one man will never make or break any ordinary person, let alone me.

If an egotist is a man who believes in himself, is not afraid of himself, and knows his true value, then I am an egotist. If an egotist is a man who over-estimates his ability, takes himself seriously, and figures any and everybody out of the running, I am not an egotist. My idea of an egotist is one full of self-commendation, vanity and conceit. This pen slinger's idea of an egotist is a successful man who fails to advertise himself as a lucky man and whispers the lie that his achievements are purely accidental and due to circumstances and opportunity.

In this little sheet, for the past thirteen months, I have scribbled squibs and bits, poking fun at different people, papers and towns, and have tried to say little things that would please the very persons at whom I poked the fun. Any sane man would never have taken me seriously. All of my friends and acquaintances know me well enough to know that I have never taken myself seriously.

But, for the benefit of some damned fools I've met, let me say that my success comes from the fact that I know and have studied the business in which I manage to knock out a very good livelihood. I write my own songs because I write better songs than anyone else that I know of. I publish these songs because they bring greater royalties than any other class of music sold in this country. I write my own plays because I have not yet seen or read plays from the pens of other authors that seem as good as the plays I write. I produce my own plays because I think I'm as good a theatrical manager as any other man in this line. I dance because I know I'm the best dancer in the country. I sing because I can sing my own songs better than any other man on the stage. I never hang out with actors because I think they know so little of the business they're in. My companions are men of great standing in this profession. I'm always with them, because there's money in them. They're with me because there's money in me. I publish this paper because it reaches certain desks where certain men sit who have scissors to clip and are

1. Jerry, Josie, Nellie, and George M. Cohan, 1884.

2. George as "Hennery," the title character in *Peck's Bad Boy*, 1891.

V. & S. HALL, EAST BROOKFIELD, WEDNESDAY EVENING, JULY 31, 1895.

In a new and sparkling Comedy, in two acts,

"A YOUNG LADIES' SEMINARY."

CAST OF CHARACTERS:

Prof. Mooney, a light hearted music teacher, JERRY COHAN
Sammie Knary, the seminary's solitary male pupil, GEORGE M. COHAN
Anna Kondher, a charmer fair, an interesting pupil, JOSIE COHAN
Mora Enmore, } Mexicans, MARGARETTA COSTIGAN
Salza Worder, } Mexicans, ALBERT M. CHILDS
Minnie Apolis Jones, assistant preceptress, a theosophist, HELEN F. COHAN

Incidental to the Play, the following Specialties and Songs.

New Girl Coming, - - - - - - - - - - SAMMIE
"Broadway Girl," (by G. M. Cohan) - - - - - - - - - ANNA
Sarah Kews and Sammie, double Song and Dance, - - - - - - SAMMIE and ANNA
New Dance, "The Keating," - - - - - - - - - - ANNA
Mr. Walker, (original) - - - - - - - - - - - SAMMIE
The Dancing Lesson, - - - - - - - - - - - PROF. MOONEY

OVERTURE, PROF. J. WILLIS MILLIGAN.

Concluding with THE FOUR COHANS' Original Specialty Farce,

"GOGGLES' DOLL HOUSE."

Introducing novel and enjoyable situations, concluding with the wonderful

DANCING DOLLS.

A Special Train will leave North Brookfield at 7.42 p. m., returning from East Brookfield after the show.

Admission, 25 Cents. **Reserved Seats, 35 Cents.**

Seats on sale at Pepper's in North Brookfield, and at Vizard's in East Brookfield.

3. Billing for a comedy sketch written by Jerry Cohan for his family.

4. The Four Cohans, 1896.

HAPPY NEW YEAR, 1899.

People's Theatre.

Week Commencing Sunday Matinee, JANUARY 1.

Matinees—Sunday, Monday, Tuesday, Thursday, and Saturday.

H.W.Williams' Own Company

(Also Gay Morning Glories Vaudevillers.)

Under the Direction of SAM A. SCRIBNER.

JOE O. ZIEFLE .... MANAGER
GEO. M. D. WALKER..... TREASURER | W. M. BYLES............ PROPERTIES

"THIS BEATS THEM ALL."

The Original Comedy Trio,

EMMONDS, EMERSON and EMMONDS,

In their Farcical Sketch, "Only a Joke."

"Ladies' Night," Friday Evening.

The Eccentric Character Comediennes,

SISTERS ELINORE,

In their Original Creation, "The Irish 400."

England's Most Daring Aerialists,

THE THREE POLOS,

In their Latest European Novelty, "The Human Trapeze."

"Ladies' Night," Friday Evening.

CLARICE VANCE,

The Southern Singer.

THE FOUR COHANS,

JERRY, GEORGE M., JOSEPHINE, HELEN,

In George M. Cohan's Latest Success, "RUNNING FOR OFFICE."
Specialties introduced by Josephine and George M.

"Ladies' Night," Friday Evening.

WATERBURY BROS. and TENNEY.

Mirth and Melody.

IRVING, BURT, SADIE,

JONES, GRANT and JONES,

Originators and Authors of "Get Your Money's Worth," "Take Your Clothes and Go," etc.

"Ladies' Night," Friday Evening.

WEBB and HASSAN,

Marvelous Hand to Hand Acrobats and Head to Head Balancers.

DON'T MISS THIS ACT.

Compliments of

JOE O. ZIEFLE.

Cincinnati, O., January 1, 1899.

5. Billing for the "four-act" vaudeville tour.

6. (a) George M. Cohan and Sam H. Harris, 1904. First photograph together.

6. (b) And their last photograph together, shortly before Harris's death. *(Photograph: Museum of the City of New York)*

7. Cohan and Ethel Levey.

8. Cohan as the literally bouncy juvenile frightening the female chorus, Act II, *The Governor's Son*, Savoy Theatre, 1901. *(Photograph by Byron. The Byron Collection of the Museum of the City of New York.)*

9. The Four Cohans in *Running for Office*, Fourteenth Street Theatre, 1903.

10. On the porch of Haddon Hall, Atlantic City, New Jersey, during 1903 tour. Standing below: Josie. Above: Unidentified stage manager, Ethel Levey, George, Nellie, Jerry.

11. Cohan as the title character, *Little Johnny Jones*, 1904.

12. The "transformation" scene ending Act II, *Little Johnny Jones.* Its spectacular lighting effects are completely erased by the crude stage photography of the time.

13. Fay Templeton and Victor Moore, Act I, *Forty-five Minutes from Broadway,* New Amsterdam Theatre, 1906.

14. The Four Cohans in their usual exuberant mood.

15. Cohan directing Thomas W. Ross in a scene from *Popularity*, Wallack's Theatre, 1906. The first Cohan failure.

16. Cohan and Sam Harris with Victor Moore, the star of their production, *The Talk of New York*, Knickerbocker Theatre, 1907.

> in a position to get my name in other papers. I write these little stories because I think I write them better than other writers of stories. I play the leading parts in most of my plays because I think I'm the best actor available. I pay myself the biggest salary ever paid a song and dance comedian because I know I deserve it.
>
> But believe me, kind reader, when I say, I am not an egotist.

Cohan never again replied to press criticism. In time his eminence in the theatre would be ample insulation against critical disfavor, and this eminence was growing rapidly in 1906. By then he had set a new standard in his musical plays, and their impress on the American musical theatre was to be deep. In Cecil Smith's incisive view: "Whatever the merits of their content, Cohan's musical comedies introduced a wholly new conception of delivery, tempo and subject matter into a form of entertainment that was rapidly dying for want of new ideas of any kind. Brushing aside the artificial elegances based on English and German models, he reproduced successfully the hardness, the compensating sentimentality and the swift movement of New York life, which, except for surface sophistications, has not changed much between then and now."

The day after his twenty-eighth birthday, Cohan revealed to his friend, Tom Lewis, that the Metcalfe attack had helped focus his ambitions. "Tom," he said with a deceptively modest smile, "I'll never be really happy now until I own a part of Broadway. Just a little part, mind you. The top part."

7. THE MAN WHO OWNED BROADWAY

A few touches of adversity, personal and professional, came to temper Cohan before he reached his goals.

The paradox of Cohan's personal life in maturity is that never was there a more devoted family man, and never was a man less able to fulfill this role. In his early years he was part of a devoted family in which there was no dividing line between personal and professional life. The Four Cohans were four theatre people who worked together superbly and who had the added sustenance of being mother, father, daughter, and son. Cohan could never remember a time when this relationship did not exist, and in a real sense this luxury of rich fulfillment in every aspect of life was to spoil him for conventional family existence.

Ethel Levey was a good wife to Cohan. She had the necessary gifts of art and nature to be the working consort of a master showman. An attractive singer-dancer-actress of real ability, she became the fourth Cohan after Josie's departure, but only in name. Had she been less her highly individualistic self, she might have become the fourth Cohan in fact, but Ethel Levey was too much like George M. Cohan to ever remain Mrs. George M. Cohan. She was too volatile, too opinionated to complement him, and it is likely she felt that in a very real sense no one but Josie would ever be the fourth Cohan.

As rumors of troubles besetting the Cohan marriage were flooding Broadway, the rumor that Cohan had gone straight theatrically was authenticated. As if to further confirm his reputation for unadulterated cheek, Cohan announced that his first Broadway play without music, *Popularity*, was to be produced in October 1906. He disclaimed any attempt to join the ranks of Ibsen and Pinero, making the point that he was an entertainer, first, last, and always. The reviewer of the *Dramatic Mirror* taking note of this disclaimer said that under that proviso *Popularity* was almost good, and principally because of the playing. Cohan, then starring in *George Washington, Jr.*, gave the leading role in his new play to Thomas W. Ross, a personable young comedian. The plot of *Popularity*, fortunately, can be put in a sentence: a wildly popular young actor, despite a jealous intrigue against him, ultimately marries a millionaire's daughter who loves him to distraction. Robert Rand, the protagonist, is modeled very clearly on Cohan: he is brash, vastly interested in himself and overwhelmingly in love with the theatre. As usual in Cohan plays, the female characters are not fully drawn, and their principal roles seem to be that of loving and uncritical admirers of forthright manhood. The play is melodrama, some of it very badly written, but it has one Cohan characteristic which all his rapid and slipshod writing hardly ever dampened—life. For all its dramatic crudities (characters eavesdropping just out of sight, etc.) the play's vitality is found in several sources, the natural use of slang—some of it astonishingly still current as in the approval of a man's sophistication: "You're hip!"—and in its forthright handling of theatricalism. Cohan knew two things better than most playwrights of his time, vernacular language and the theatre itself. He used both lavishly.

The entire second act of *Popularity* takes place in Rand's dressing room which is cut away to reveal the backstage of a theatre, and in this instance it was the actual backstage of Wallack's Theatre where *Popularity* was produced. This was an absolute novelty at the time, as was Cohan's use of the audience to create a theatrical highlight. In the program for the play was an inelegant note requesting the audience ". . . to holler for Rand when the lights go out during Act II." Most of the audience did, stimulated by "plants," thereby creating an effective climax to a scene in which Rand comes out to address "his" audience which has supposedly been waiting impatiently for him. This use of theatricalization within the play as a device of entertainment is prototype for much of Cohan's work to follow. No other playwright in the American theatre was to use the theatre itself so consistently as a stratagem of entertainment and, ultimately, as a symbol for life itself.

Popularity failed. Most of the critics were irritated by the unrepentant insouciance of the leading character, a role that needed its creator to bring it to life. It was Cohan's first outright failure and its coming at a time when his personal life was troubled gave him his first real frustration. Troubles, disappointments, he had encountered but for the first time he was up against irreversible odds. He allowed Ethel to obtain a divorce in Chicago on arranged grounds of unfaithfulness. Four months later, on June 29, 1907 he married Agnes Nolan, a dancer and singer who had first worked for Cohan in the chorus of *Little Johnny Jones.*

When Cohan's troubles with Ethel were simmering, he met and developed a warm friendship with the three Nolan sisters who had come down from Brookline, Massachusetts, to audition for the Cohan shows. They came from a remarkable family. John F. Nolan, a mail carrier, and his wife, Mary, were the parents of eighteen children. Agnes Nolan, in auditioning for Cohan, was not impressed by his eminence as a producer. When he told her the going salary for dancers, she insisted on $3 more or she would not play. Intrigued by her spunk, he gave it to her. When the three Nolan girls had obtained jobs in *Little Johnny Jones,* Nellie

Cohan took them under her wing and after she told George the size of the Nolan family, he took another look at the girls. He loved big families and was very impressed with the news that Theodore Roosevelt had given a medal to John Nolan for having the largest family in Massachusetts. (*Sic tempora mutantur!*) In marrying Agnes Nolan, Cohan inherited a Brobdingnagian clutch of relatives and he delighted in them. He bought the Nolans a larger home as well as a summer place in Nantasket across the street from another large brood of Irish, the Joseph P. Kennedy clan. Cohan insisted that his father-in-law retire and when the Cohan productions opened in Boston, as most of them did, old John Nolan was picked up by chauffeur, delivered to the theatre where he reveled in the show and invariably took a number of the chorus girls out for a beer later.

With the sting of *Popularity's* demise and his divorce soothed by his remarriage, Cohan went ahead on a well-plowed path to concentrate on the new musical form which he had fashioned. He rewrote *Running for Office,* added new music and some topical gags about football and the then distinctly unthreatening prohibition movement, and retitled it *The Honeymooners,* with a pointed subtitle, "The Summer Song Show." It is light material indeed but as he paced its tempo, the audience found that hard to tell. Rennold Wolf, critic for the *Morning Telegraph,* complained, "If Cohan would play fair and give his audience a chance to catch its breath it might make a few unkind remarks." The now Three Cohans played in *The Honeymooners* while George tried to think of an adequate sequel to *Forty-five Minutes from Broadway,* a project which had been on his mind for some time. The new play had to take its direction from the availability of Fay Templeton and Victor Moore, and when it was clear that only Moore was free to do the show, Cohan gave the burden of plot activity to Kid Burns. The result was *The Talk of New York,* a successful musical froth which opened in December 1907. In it the Kid wins a fortune, foils a racetrack intrigue and settles down forty-five minutes from Broadway in the town he once professed to scorn. He sings:

> "After the dead cold New York crowd,
> Gee, ain't the jays just grand . . .
> I'm very strong for the old green fields,
> I'm for the small town thing."

The Cohan self-identification is again clear; Kid Burns reveals that Jerry is a name he loves because it's his dad's name, and at one high point the Kid grabs both the American and Irish flags and waves them vigorously.

The autobiographical also leaps out of the next Cohan effort written the same year as *The Talk of New York*. In *Fifty Miles from Boston*, Cohan was returning directly to the happiest scenes of his childhood, North Brookfield, where he spent most of his summers while the Four Cohans were resting before the autumn tour. The play is set in North Brookfield and despite its rather obvious melodrama has the warmth of a variety of small-town types come to life. The best song in the play is still sung and was something of an "in" joke because, although it fitted naturally into the plot, it was a tribute from Cohan to one of his idols, Edward "Ned" Harrigan, whose long career in bringing American musical farce to New York had just ended. The Harrigan in the play, like his namesake, is a charismatic old Irishman, proud of his heritage and his career. Ned Harrigan did not see the opening night performance but a few weeks later he was in the audience and tears were in his eyes as he heard:

> "Who is the man never stood for a 'gadabout?
> Harrigan! That's me!
> Who is the man that the town's simply mad about?
> Harrigan! That's me!
> The ladies and babies are fond of me,
> I'm fond of them, too, in return you see.

Who is the gent that's deserving a monument?
Harrigan! That's me!
H - A - double R - I - G - A - N spells Harrigan.
Proud of all the Irish blood that's in me,
Divil a man can say a word agin me.
H - A - double R - I - G - A - N, you see,
Is a name that a shame never has been connected with,
Harrigan, that's me!"

While *Fifty Miles from Boston* was attracting good audiences in the months following the New York opening in February 1908, Cohan was concocting an even more personal musical statement. He prevailed on Josie to reunite the Four Cohans and she was delighted to return. In planning a vehicle for the family he was influenced by the successful essentials of *Little Johnny Jones*. Where else better to highlight the popular Yankee theme than again in scenic old London town and who better to disport in patriotic highjinks than a coterie of wise-cracking Irish-Americans? All of these aspects were presented frontally in his new script, with joyous unsubtlety, and the Four Cohans sang, danced and mugged their way happily through the proceedings. The theme of *The Yankee Prince* is imbedded in the title—a prince of an American ("That's what they call a good fellow where I come from") is better than an English earl any day. The earl, of course, wants to marry an American girl for her money, but the girl, despite the urgings of her snobbish father, loves, cannot help but love, the Yankee prince. Nellie and Jerry were the girl's parents and George the prince as ever was. Nor was he shy about it. In a move deliberately calculated to curl the toes of his critics, Cohan billed himself: "George M. Cohan and His Royal Family in *The Yankee Prince*." Cohan was told that *Life*'s Metcalfe was seen drumming his fingers savagely on the arm-rest of his seat as he read the offending theatre program.

The Yankee Prince displayed what were by now essential

attributes of the Cohan musical play: settings which were pleasurable in themselves (Windsor Castle's exterior); a humorous character who turns out to be a detective; adept and funny vaudeville patter; and the conscious demonstration of theatrical device. In subsequent pages, the adjective "intratheatrical," and the noun "intratheatricality," will mean Cohan's directing of attention to the very fact of theatricality itself—to remind the audience that they are not only watching a play but to point out that a particular usage they are seeing (plot development, acting technique, character type, technical effect, etc.) is interesting, or obvious, or different, or conventional. Basically this is using the calling of attention to theatrical device as a device of entertainment itself. It also served the purpose of allowing Cohan to disarm criticism of his use of old theatrical techniques by his candid and kidding reference to their cliché aspect.*

For example, in *The Yankee Prince*, the two villains sing a song, "Villains in a Play," which sets forth quite clearly who they are and what they do. They admit they ". . . always do the dirty work/And blame it on the jay . . .", and this revelation is placed within the outlines of a realistic plot. One of the reasons why Cohan's audiences found these plays so refreshing is because of the sheer novelty of these intratheatrical references. The jokes in *The Yankee Prince* got the same treatment: "I know how to run an elevator. I was raised on an elevator. That's a joke—it's one of last year's jokes."

The success of *The Yankee Prince*, which opened at the Knickerbocker Theatre in New York on April 20, 1908,

* This concept bears some resemblance to "metatheatre" and "metaplay," words coined by Lionel Abel. Mr. Abel defines metaplays as "theatre pieces about life seen as already theatricalized," and he calls the metaplay the necessary form "for dramatizing characters who, having full consciousness, cannot but participate in their own dramatization." Metaplay, however, is not applicable to Cohan for several reasons: it concerns essentially serious drama only, and is an ontological concept set specifically in the realm of idea and theme. Except in a very limited sense, this is hardly Cohan's realm.

caused Cohan to think that yet another variation on Americans abroad would do well. Ever since the great reception given the "Harrigan" song, he had been thinking of Ned Harrigan and the fascinating Ned Harrigan and Tony Hart shows which had flourished in New York in the years after the Civil War. Most of these boisterously American pieces featured a crusty Irishman named Mulligan and his pet enemy, an equally gruff German, Lochmuller. They were united in detestation of each other and in the Romeo and Juliet connection of their children. Cohan took this base and extended it. Mulligan and Lochmuller become Sullivan and Budmeyer, retired millionaires on a jaunt abroad, and each of these twain have two children of both sexes with inevitable and symmetrical pairing despite parental opposition. Cohan called the play *The American Idea* which is, as one character defines it, to "work all winter to get enough to spend the summer in Paris." The mandatory flag-waving is at its most piquant when one American demands a cocktail with a tiny American flag in it. There are several good near-vaudeville routines, including one between a lady and her former husband which ends:

HE: Do you understand that I never did you a wrong since the day we met?

SHE: (*Sobbing.*) Yes, yes. I know, Steve. It's all my fault, I'm to blame.

HE: Then will you ever forgive me?

SHE: (*Sternly.*) Never! I'm here in Paris to grab for myself a title . . . I'm sorry, Steve, but it's all cold. Goodbye!

HE: Goodbye!

SHE: (*Music swells.*) Don't you dare come to the door of my room!

HE: I don't even know the number of your room.

SHE: Don't you dare come to room 502. (*Music swells.*) It's all over, Steve, it's all over! You go my way and I'll go mine!
(*Exits sobbing.*)

HE: (*To audience.*) I'm glad *that's* over.

An intratheatrical and wholly original manner of introducing the usual Cohan mystery figure is found in having the character speak his own stage directions, which he simultaneously executes:

> *A man enters right.*
>
> MAN: He was a man of medium height, say forty years of age. He arrived in Paris Thursday morning and was driven directly to the Elysee Palace Hotel. As he stepped from the cab and approached the Court Portal, a bell-boy appeared and said:
>
> BOY: Baggage, monsieur?
>
> MAN: Yes, he replied, and handing the boy his suit-case and hat-box, he followed on in a careless manner. He seemed very interested in the surroundings. Not a single object escaped his piercing glance. He seemed to be looking for something—somebody.
>
> *Girl appears, crosses in front of man. Suits action in words: "She stopped" etc.*
>
> At that moment, a pretty girl emerged from the side door and passed him by. She stopped, she looked and softly whispered to herself:
>
> GIRL: It can't be—no, surely I'm mistaken.
>
> MAN: And she turned and slowly disappeared from view. (*Girl exits.*) And he passed on into the hotel. (*He does so.*)

The American Idea opened a few eyes. *Theatre Magazine* which had usually been aloof to the Cohan shows was intrigued by Cohan's "light satirical touch" which they seemed to have missed before, and it was noted that although the play did not measure up to Arthur Wing Pinero or Augustus Thomas standards, there really was no reason why it should: "Mr. Cohan has every right to set up his own standard as a theatrical purveyor. He is young, he is exuberant, he is American, he is Manhattanese."

What he also was was rich and growing richer. In the space of two years, Cohan and Harris had brought to New York six productions, *The Yankee Prince, Fifty Miles from*

Boston, Winchell Smith's *The Fortune Hunter* starring John Barrymore, *The American Idea, The Man Who Owns Broadway,* and *The Cohan and Harris Minstrels.* The *Minstrels* did not last long, and with jokes like "I was engaged to a girl with a cork leg, but I broke it off" one can see why. Of all these productions, it was *The Man Who Owns Broadway* whose success most pleased Cohan. It was exhilarating to know that his only failure to date had been reworked into a hit. He took *Popularity* and built it into a sparkling musical commentary on the theatre and on the kind of entertainment he was helping to institutionalize.

The leading character in *The Man Who Owns Broadway* is one Sydney Lyons, again clearly Cohan, a bustling, wisecracking, whimsical actor who, as in the original play, winds up with a millionaire's daughter—the implication strongly being that it is the least he deserves. The play abounds in intratheatrical device. The juvenile wants a pair of troublemakers arrested at once, but Sydney stops him with, "What do you want to do—spoil the plot? My boy, the villains are never handcuffed 'til 11:00. That's been going on for years and years."

When the young man is distraught, Lyons consoles him: "Remember, my boy, you're only in the middle of the second act. I'll bet you that everything ends happily . . . If it doesn't, the author's crazy." The young man asks Lyons, a musical comedy star, if he will ever be a serious actor. "No," Lyons says, "I'll leave that to [David] Warfield. I'll stick to musical comedy as long as George Cohan will write them for me." Lyons also speaks stage directions which various characters enact. These things are done only by Lyons and within the framework of totally serious action. The intratheatricality acts as comic relief which not only entertains on its own level but offers a distancing effect relieving one from accepting the melodramatic dialogue and situations without, at the same time, forcing one to disbelieve them.

Cohan made sure that the leading role in *The Man Who*

Owns Broadway was played by a man of his own quality. Lyons was created by Raymond Hitchcock, a star with the Cohan graces as a performer and a bright, cheeky charm.

The play was acclaimed by *Theatre Magazine* as ". . . a real Cohan show, with bustle, business, snap and ginger as its salient qualities . . . All is activity, all is earnestness and beneath it all is an element of contemporaneous significance and humorous expression that never fails to work laughter of the most spontaneous and comprehensive character." Part of the contemporaneous significance is the discussion, sketchy and inconclusive, but a discussion nonetheless of the theatre's value. The millionaire whose daughter loves Lyons is questioned by his new son-in-law. After explaining that he could never give up the stage ("It's my life, it's all I know—all I care to know.") Lyons asks the old man why he doesn't like actors. The old man is not sure why. Lyons smiles, and speaking for Cohan the Entertainer, says, "Yes, actors are a pretty bad lot. These clowns have no calling except to amuse, make you forget, ring happiness out into the world, promote charities and swallow the insults of the very people for whom they make life worth living. Yes, actors are a bad lot."

With *The Man Who Owns Broadway,* Cohan assumed that title by proprietary right. There was no more popular audience figure in New York. He and Sam Harris were building and buying theatres, and their production company was earning the reputation, rare for the time, of being unfailingly fair and generous to actors. And even one young drama critic, George Jean Nathan, had astonished his colleagues by asserting that in the construction of plays Cohan was easily the equal of Euripides and Calderon.

Cohan, in Brooks Atkinson's words, had become the king of Broadway. "Broadway" for Cohan and compeers meant more than the theatrical Rialto: the word embodied ultimate professionalism. To be first rank Broadway was to attain a showman's eminence. Something in addition to his dazzling virtuosity as a theatre man had placed Cohan at Broadway's pinnacle. Quite simply, no one thought more, spoke more or wrote more about Broadway, and for good reason—no one loved Broadway more. Among other things, Broadway for Cohan represented the essence of entertainment, the giving of holiday for those who needed it at a price they could afford. In his view, it was the greatest bargain any buyer of happiness ever had. And his identification as the man who did this more often and better than anyone else of his day sealed his love of the street forever.

Many years later, when it seemed that Broadway was passing him by, he could still write with undiminished love a lyric:

> Broadway will always be
> Broadway to me.
>   No matter what they say
>   Of the old Broadway
>   Or the new Broadway,
>   I'll take it any way,
>   I'll take it any day.
> It was,
> It still
> It always will
>   Be *my* Broadway.

8. THE THREE COHANS

As Cohan gained his ascendancy in the theatre, the pattern of his non-theatrical life emerged. In a boyhood which he spent principally backstage and in travel, Cohan had to forgo many youthful pleasures including skill at baseball —a game he always yearned to play well. His occasional games with his summer friends in North Brookfield only whetted his appetite for it. When he was very young, Jerry took him to a professional game in New Jersey and said, "Son, this is a game that I want you to love." He did, unswervingly, to the day of his death and it was his only passion outside the theatre. When he lived in New York he went to the Polo Grounds and Yankee Stadium at least twice a week and frequently every day for months, when not in rehearsals. Taking a seat far in the upper stands, he would pull his inevitable black fedora over his eyes in order not to be recognized and watch the nine innings without a word to his companions. In the taxi homeward he would review the game, almost play by play.

One of the binding connections between Sam Harris and Cohan was their mutual love of baseball. As early as *Little Johnny Jones*, every actor auditioned by them was asked if he played baseball and it was not an idle question. A Cohan and Harris team was recruited from actors in their shows, and Cohan himself would pitch occasionally, with indifferent success. They played teams scrounged up from other shows, anticipating by decades the now well-established Broadway Show League. Baseball was a very real experience in Cohan's life because the national pastime was for him what it is for most men, the vicarious experience of conflict under controlled conditions, which is also a basic definition of drama. In watching baseball he was seeing a theatre game, and a man's game, played by men principally for men.

Cohan was all of his life a man's man, a phrase unambiguous in its day. Devoted to his family, he saw little of them because when he was not working his usual long hours rehearsing, directing, and performing, he was out with his pals—at the ball park, at his two clubs, the Lambs and the Friars, and later in life at a table in the northwest corner of the Oak Room of the Plaza Hotel.

His closest friend for most of his years at the top was Sam Harris. Harris was a perfect partner for him; Harris could handle all the prime business details at the same time he helped select plays which merited production. As a pair, they had solid ability to spot a winner, a process always marked by the same sense of pawky humor. Oncc when Cohan came into Harris's office and found him reading a manuscript, Harris handed it to him and said, "Put it up to your ear and listen." "Listen to what?" "Just listen, that's all, George, and tell me if you can hear any laughs in it." One playwright sent Cohan and Harris a play accompanied by a thirty-page closely typed letter explaining how and why the play should be produced. "This guy's so enthusiastic, I'd like to let him down easy," said Harris. "What are you going to say to him, Sam?" "I think I'll write him," said Harris, "and tell him that we've decided to produce his letter." The two men even had parallel taste in wives. A year after Cohan married Agnes Nolan, Harris married her sister, Alice, thereby firming a firm partnership even firmer.

Male friendship dominated Cohan's social life. He was not a cocktail party or night-club man. He was, to use an old-fashioned word about what may be an old-fashioned thing, gallant toward women. Women tended to be secondary in his life although his courtliness toward them was deeply felt and instinctive. He usually placed them on a pedestal which in large measure accounts for the bloodless, one-dimensional female characters in his plays.

In many ways William Collier was the actor closest to Cohan in style and temperament, and their friendship, despite occasional strong disagreements, was to last to the end of Cohan's life. Collier was hired by Warner Brothers during the making of *Yankee Doodle Dandy* to act as technical adviser of the Cohan biography but he was not represented in the film, more's the pity. Collier had a fine wit. One night in a Cohan revue, *Hello, Broadway!*, Collier spoke a line and Cohan said, "A little louder, Willie." Collier replied, "I can't speak any louder with the material you've given me" which promptly broke Cohan up. Another time after Cohan had returned to the Lambs Club after a disagreement with the officership, he was invited to participate in an act with Collier for the annual Lambs Gambol. The act was done before a drop representing the Lambs Club and when Cohan made his entrance he received a great ovation. In bowing to the audience, his cane hit the backdrop and Collier said, "You haven't been back in the club a day and already you're knocking it."

It was Collier who was fond of repeating his pal's favorite theatrical anecdote when Cohan was not around to tell it. Significantly, the story, a true one, was about a man of Cohan's temperament. Not long after Cohan's death, Collier recalled the story with great gusto. "George," he said, "could tell this story much better than I. I think he loved the story so much because it was about a man who was as contentious as he was. Anyway, the hero of this tale was the late Charles Couldock, an old character actor who flourished before the turn of the century. He was a man noted for his bad temper. During one scene of a play he was in, Couldock had a vital few lines with a character representing his father. One matinee performance, the actor playing the role of the father became ill, so the stage manager got the inspired idea that he would sit the assistant stage manager in the father's chair, put a white wig on him and turn the chair so that the 'old man' was facing the fireplace, and then the stage manager would read the 'old man's' lines through the fireplace and the audience wouldn't be any the wiser. A very good idea—except that no one remembered to appraise Couldock of this arrangement. Performance time came and the assistant stage manager was duly installed with the white wig before the fireplace. Couldock came on and began the scene. Regrettably, the stage manager had completely forgotten about reading the lines through the fireplace and was off about other business. Couldock, as I say, not knowing anything at all about this, delivered his first line to his 'father,' a searching question. No reply. Couldock rephrased and asked the question again. Silence. Couldock ad-libbed a cover-up and then asked another, even more vital question. Silence. Couldock began to grind his teeth in rage but he finally controlled himself with a great effort and again ad-libbed himself out of a very bad spot. And now he had to ask a question on which the entire progress of the plot depended, a question which simply *had* to be answered. So Couldock threw the question at that old white head behind the chair. A profound silence. At this, Couldock wheeled, walked down to the footlights and with a voice crackling in rage, said, 'Ladies and gentlemen, as you will observe, my father is an old man. A very old man. In fact he is so godamned old he can't even *talk!*' "

Collier and Cohan loved tasteful practical jokes in which they could employ their very considerable acting talents. They particularly enjoyed ribbing Louis Mann, a fine comedy actor who tended to seriousness offstage. One night at the Friars, Cohan and Collier prearranged a card game, making sure Mann was kibitzer. The set-up was that Cohan would begin to lose heavily and, as his losses grew, he was to become desperate and increase the size of the bets to recoup. This plot progressed merrily and during the game Mann grew more and more nervous as the Cohan "losses" stockpiled. Cohan began to play with a fine show of barely controlled desperation, and Collier openly displayed an avarice which shocked Mann beyond comment. He watched, closely, as his two best friends worked themselves into an intense game which threatened their entire futures. Cohan "lost" thousands of dollars until his bank account was depleted. Then, in a superb simulation of passionate anger, he said, "Very well, Collier, if that's the way you want to play the game—to the very end—so be it. I bet you the Cohan and Harris Theatre!" Mann looked on aghast as Collier replied with steely glance, "I've had enough of your boasting and bragging, Cohan. I take you up. On the next turn of the cards, I bet you all that I've won against your theatre!" Mann pleaded with his two friends but they were adamant. Cohan in a frenzy began to bet all of his properties, including his home, and Collier inexorably "won" them. Mann's despair at Cohan's self-destructiveness was not to be contained, and he pleaded, argued with the two men. At last, Cohan slumped back in his chair, and glared at Collier. "All right, all *right,* you swine," he shouted. "I'm going to do it. You've taken it all except one thing—and after I wager this, I am cleaned out. Cleaned out, do you hear?" Collier looked at Cohan with incredulity, and stammered, "You mean—you mean—?" "Yes!" roared Cohan. "Yes! I'll bet you Sam Harris!"

As Cohan and Collier collapsed into laughter, Mann took himself away in injured dignity.

But Mann was capable of a good comeback on occasion. One afternoon when he went to the Polo Grounds with Cohan, he was cheering on his beloved Giants who were beating Chicago handily. It was the ninth inning, score Giants 10–Chicago 0, when Cohan turned to Mann and offered the odds on Chicago. "I'll take it, George," Mann said. "You can't bluff me."

Cohan's friends were principally theatre people, most of

whom belonged to at least one of the three New York actors' clubs. There is a still-current definition of the three which Cohan always enjoyed telling. "The Players is a group of gentlemen trying to be actors, the Lambs is a bunch of actors trying to be gentlemen, and the Friars is a bunch of guys trying to be both." At one time or another Cohan expressed fondness for each club but he went principally to the Friars because it was the only theatrical club that Jerry Cohan ever joined.

A great joy came to Jerry in 1910. He was told that the Friars, in an unprecedented move, had selected his son as the guest of honor at a very special banquet to celebrate his emergence as a major Broadway figure. On the evening of April 3, over 1500 men and women prominent in the theatrical, business, and political life of New York met in the grand ballroom of the Hotel Astor for a spectacular meal featuring four brands of vintage champagne, memorable entertainment and genuinely witty after-dinner speeches. The principal comments of the evening were made by A. L. Erlanger who, for all his toughness, possessed wit and an indestructible regard for the guest of honor. Highlights of his speech give a clear idea of the prevailing mood of the evening and of the regard in which George M. Cohan was held by the most powerful individual in the American theatre. Erlanger said:

> Some weeks ago, an article by Charles Frohman appeared in the New York *Herald* crediting the foundation of the Theatrical Syndicate [Erlanger's organization] to John Shakespeare's son. I can say in all frankness that I wish the wonderful son of that same John Shakespeare had been alive the last fifteen years so he could have faced the censure of his glory. [The Syndicate had been under attack for its monopolistic policies.]
>
> When asked to act as the advance agent for Jerry Cohan's son, I gave the matter much consideration, knowing how difficult it was to please the son of Cohan, and I realized that, no matter how great my efforts to

bring him reknown, he would take them with the firm conviction that my subject, and not my work, gave me my great opportunity.

Now, I want all of you here tonight to act as reporters, and spread broadcast throughout the land the merits of Jerry Cohan's boy. I know you will give it the widest publicity because my advance work will warrant it.

The son of John Shakespeare wrote plays to please Queen Elizabeth. The son of Jerry Cohan writes plays to please the Queen of Mirth. Both had the same purpose in mind—money.

John Shakespeare's son wrote some of his plays over a butcher shop. Jerry Cohan's son writes all of his plays over his wrists on his shirt cuffs. He has handed me in plays at times that covered two closely written shirt cuffs. Of all the plays John Shakespeare's son wrote, I like *Julius Caesar* best, for the reason that it gave me the keynote for my work in advance of Jerry Cohan's son. Shakespeare's son tells us that Mark Antony delivered an oration at the funeral of Julius Caesar. Well, I will be his Mark Antony tonight . . . to address you as he did, "Friends, Romans and countrymen: I come to bury Caesar, not to praise him." It was on account of that sentence I accepted my job tonight.

A dinner to Jerry Cohan's son is incomprehensible. His accepting the invitation to eat free is worse. There are just three working men in this country who are not entitled to eat free dinners—Jerry Cohan's son, J. Pierpont Morgan, and John D. Rockefeller. They can afford to buy their own dinners. There is only one logical reason why Jerry's son is eating here tonight . . . Everyone around a theatre knows that give a musician the slightest excuse to leave the theatre and he will rush to the free lunch counter . . .

We were first introduced to Jerry Cohan's son as a composer of ballads when he was the envy of all modern Romeos and gave the world that tuneful, passionate song, "Venus, My Shining Love." Watch his versatility. His next was "I Guess I'll Have to Telegraph My Baby." What a deception! He was only fourteen when he

> wrote that song, and not the father of a baby anyone knows anything about. If he had written the song at twenty-one everyone would have looked up his baby—and I speak within the strictest rules of propriety . . .
>
> Then he started his real career of parting the public from its money. Too young, although ambitious, to be a governor, he wrote *The Governor's Son.* There was a lot of money in that play. I know that to be a fact because I put a lot of it in myself.
>
> Strolling down Fourteenth Street one evening—all theatrical managers stroll when they leave Broadway—I passed by the Fourteenth Street Theatre and read an electric sign *Running for Office,* and I said to myself, "That is Jerry Cohan's son. He always wants to run something." I watched the performance and heard Jerry's son sing . . . and later when he brought me *Running for Office* under the title of *The Honeymooners,* I discovered that the man who had inspired the line "All that glitters is not gold" must have had his own sad experiences.

After reviewing his initial connections with Cohan in the preparation of *Forty-five Minutes from Broadway,* Erlanger said that the guest of honor

> . . . wrote the first act the same day, brought it to me on a shirt cuff the next morning, read it standing up and tried to make me believe he was a bad businessman. I asked him to bring around the other two cuffs as soon as he got them out of the laundry. When he delivered them to me he told me he didn't want to lose any money on the play, so he would take half the risk. Well, he took half, and $250,000, just to show me he wanted to treat me on the square!

Erlanger then gave a humorous history of all the Cohan plays sequentially (including the statement, "We will draw the veil of charity over *Popularity* which won the storehouse prize . . ."), discussed Cohan's new-found manner of freebooting—the purchase of theatres—and concluded with a request to the audience that it become a jury to condemn the defendant:

> Jerry's son is guilty of a crime that no intelligent jury can disregard. He must be convicted. His crime has made him enemies, and as the years roll over his head, will make him more and more enemies. Your verdict must be "Guilty without reservation." I charge him with being guilty of the crime that no one can dispute—he is the possessor of super skill in everything he undertakes.
>
> In conclusion, gentlemen, I want to say that my mother thanks you, my father thanks you, my wife thanks you, my sister thanks you, my baby thanks you, and I thank you.

After loud, long cheers, Cohan got to his feet in the unexpected grip of the most profound stage fright of his life. But he rallied and charged Erlanger with having robbed him of the only speech George M. Cohan ever made, and after suggesting that his life to date might make a pretty good comic opera, Cohan pointed out how kind everybody was to him:

> The managers tell me I'm a good actor and the actors say I'm a bully manager. The musicians tell me I ought to write nothing but plays and the playwrights tell me I should confine myself exclusively to music. Why, no man could help getting along with so many people saying these encouraging things to him. One critic out in Seattle wrote about me that he had been informed that I could write a play in twenty-four hours and that after seeing *The Yankee Prince* he had no reason to believe otherwise.

After reminiscences in similar vein, and offering deep gratitude for the honor of this unusual evening, Cohan concluded with:

> I have only one request to make of you tonight, and that is, wherever you are, whether it be Lynn, Massachusetts, or in the wilds of Africa, that you please mention my name as much as possible.

He sat down to applause and cheers, and Erlanger's partner, Marc Klaw, was called on for a few words. Klaw surprised everybody by saying a few words. One of his phrases contained a potent metaphor in its reference to the most powerful auto engine of the times:

> Jerry's son represents the spirit and energy of the twentieth century—a concentrated essence, four-cylinder power—a protest against and apology for the elimination of the palmy days of the drama. Who would want to go back to the *Uncle Tom's Cabin* days when the scene in the last act with gates ajar and the red fire burning was a fine representation of hell with a label "Heaven" on it, when you can get Georgie Cohan, with banners flying, drums playing and fifes blowing to the merry tune of "The Grand Old Flag" or "Yankee Doodle Dandy"? . . . I have sat in a restaurant on the Strand in London and in the boulevard cafes in Paris—and felt my mind go lovingly across the sea as I heard the musicians playing "Give My Regards to Broadway" and "Mary Is a Grand Old Name." This youngster struck a universal chord in his songs and plays, and that is why we know and love him and that is why we are here to do him honor tonight.

This was the peroration and point of the evening.

The audience included such notables as John and Ethel Barrymore, Willie Collier, Raymond Hitchcock, Al Woods, Channing Pollock, DeWolf Hopper, four justices of the New York State Supreme Court, and an obscure young man named Samuel Goldfish only three years away from his name change to Goldwyn. This audience, well warmed by the speeches and the champagne, reacted with particular delight to a vaudeville act featuring a knockabout comedian named Keaton, his wife, and their fourteen-year-old son with highly bendable bones and the intriguing nickname of Buster. Victor Moore created a particular triumph for himself by forcing one man literally out into the aisles gasping with laughter in response to the Moore monologue of an amateur reciting "The Wreck of the Hesperus." He could only have been topped, and was, by the man Erlanger correctly identified as America's greatest comedian, Bert Williams, who sang his supremely inimitable "Nobody." Another master showman arose and gave a lively speech in which he announced both his retirement from "the show business" and his deep pleasure in having the opportunity to pay tribute to "one of the most remarkable young men this country has produced. I should like to state that in my double identity," he said, "as Buffalo Bill and Colonel William F. Cody. That will perhaps establish the emphasis I mean."

In an evening of climaxes it was not in the order of things to have a topper but it happened spontaneously when one exuberant Friar yelled, "Jerry—you and Georgie. A song, a song!" The crowd picked up the chant, and Jerry, as one man described him forty years later as "glowing, glowing," stood up, beckoned to his son and led him by the hand to the platform before the dais. He began the song and Georgie chimed in:

"I'm called the Lively Bootblack
For my style and occupation,
When work is done I like to play
By way of recreation . . ."

and then into the dance of eighteen years before. Jerry did his old waltz clog, George scrambling hard to keep up, but it was Jerry who won the biggest hand. Nellie and Josie blew them kisses at the bow-taking and wept without shame.

The New York *Telegraph* put the dinner in its proper

perspective: "Nothing Like It, Theatrically, Ever Given Before . . ." was the article lead. At thirty-one, for Cohan to have won the high praise of Broadway's top professionals and the imprimatur of the redoubtable Erlanger was singular accomplishment. Only a few months earlier, on a guided tour of the Erlanger mansion by the lord-patron himself, Cohan, in walking through the gorgeous master bedroom, said, "Mr. Erlanger, some day I'm going to have a big bedroom like this, so I can walk up and down and figure out how I can take somebody." The cream of this jest was that when Cohan did get the big bedroom, he walked up and down thinking of ways to give people more entertainment than they paid for.

From about his thirtieth year, Cohan began to display very actively three faces of his essential personality. These aspects, each at perfect ease with the other, were Cohan the Pro, Cohan the Egoist, and Cohan the Pal.

Cohan the Pro was the truly dedicated theatre man, fully giving of his time and energy to the work at hand—acting, directing, composing, playwriting, and producing, frequently in combination of these activities with a large group of creative people. Cohan the Pro was courteous but demanding, pleasant but totally committed to the thrust of his work. He expected similar involvement from fellow workers. Peggy Wood recalls:

> One rehearsal at the Astor Theatre, he had laid out some dancing that he wanted for the chorus boys, and one boy was to do a certain thing in the number. When it came time for the boy to rehearse that part, he couldn't do it. He had either forgotten it or hadn't worked at it. Cohan stopped the rehearsal in a rage and said, "You haven't got a damned thing to think about when you leave the theatre. You shut the stage door and you cut the theatre out of your mind and go off on some footling thing. You don't even remember what you were told yesterday because you don't even think of the theatre. I never *stop* thinking of the theatre!" He

> proceeded with the rehearsal. He had marched down the aisle in a fury talking to that boy, and he was *right* to be furious. That boy was supposed to be a professional, to do what he was supposed to do.

In this, Miss Wood remembers a key facet of Cohan the Pro, the man Cohan was mostly. He never stopped thinking of the theatre, and under working circumstances, his temperament can best be described as affably stern, utterly lacking in the star or boss complex, totally given over to work.

Cohan was not an egotist in the usual sense; he was inescapably an egoist, this in large measure deriving from his life pattern and full commitment to the theatre. A standard dictionary definition of "egotist" is "A conceited, boastful person." An "egoist" is defined as "A self-centered or selfish person." The words which describe Cohan accurately are "self-centered" which he was at times to almost appalling degree. In his early years this was decidedly abrasive in effect. Gus Williams, the German dialect comedian for whom the Four Cohans had worked one season, told Cohan after an argument over billing, "There's one thing I can say about you, George. You have convinced me that capital punishment is absolutely necessary." Cohan's egoism was born of the need to succeed and it was nurtured by the circumstances of his taking on the duties of a man and a manager while he was still a boy, a boy forced to miss much of his boyhood. As he matured and his talents proliferated, his egoism, not surprisingly, grew proportionately.

In his plays, "old pal" was Cohan's unvarying phrase for a close friend. Cohan the Pal was the gentlest, warmest of men, much like his father. Charles Washburn who was Cohan's press agent for many years said after Cohan's death, "George was really a sensitive, bashful guy. He probably didn't have ten really close friends." These friends were of the theatre with the exception of Steve Reardon who was to become his closest friend after Cohan began to see less of Sam Harris. Reardon was a bookish ex-detective of private means who gave Cohan the companionship he needed most pulling him away from work pressures when they became stringent. Cohan's autobiography says, "Reardon hasn't worked in years and solemnly swears he never will again. Can you imagine a man who not only refuses to work, but goes about advocating the idea, hanging around with me? Well, it's a fact. Reardon and I string it out together. We get many a laugh, too. He always refers to me as "'The Slave' and my pet name for him is 'Hobo.'"

Reardon provided another worthy if largely ineffective service for Cohan. He tried to curb him of his impulsive generosity. For Reardon and other close friends, Cohan had only one defect—he totally embodied the phrase, "generous to a fault." Cohan could never resist a hard-luck story, particularly from anyone in the theatre, and old actors learned to take advantage. Frequently, from the height of his fame until his last years, Cohan walked from his Fifth Avenue apartment near the Metropolitan Museum to his office on 42nd Street. His preparation for the walk was unvarying. He filled one pocket with fifty-dollar bills, another with tens, and yet another with fives. From the first block past his home to the elevator going up to his office, he was stopped periodically until the pockets were empty. Reardon and Cohan intimates told him there was no sense in giving away *all* his money. After he died, it was found that he had indeed given away much of his considerable fortune, not in street handouts, but in various ways including an unofficial pension list of people who had worked for him, sometimes only once. Most of this money went to members of a profession he was supposed to scorn—actors.

Chester Morris, an actor in three Cohan plays of the 1920s and whose father before him had been a Cohan actor, said that there was never a more intriguing man. "Behind his back, Cohan was always the Little Fellow or the Little Guy to those of us who worked for him," Morris said. "But that was only a reference to his physical size. He was a giant, really—and Spencer Tracy and I loved him and respected him, and used to discuss him for hours. Spence and I decided that the Little Guy was a mystery man in a lot of ways. Cohan was never terribly fond of actors as a group but he loved them individually. He would drive you hard as hell in rehearsal but always like a kind of father—as if he were doing it for our own good, and it *was* for our own good. He was cocky—but he had all the reason in the world to be, and his cockiness was never offensive. And when he complimented you, which was not frequently, you glowed all over because the smartest guy in show business had patted you on the back. Cohan was a lot of things—tough, tender, cocky, aloof—and a great friend."

Cohan the Pro, the Egoist, and the Pal showed these faces to many people and none of these aspects was a mask. Many people who knew him briefly saw only one of these sides of him and assumed that this was his essential self. Most people who worked with him in the theatre saw only the Pro with occasional glimpses of the Pal. At times Cohan would instantly disidentify as the Pro or Pal and congeal into the Egoist. This happened less as the years went by.

Perhaps the only interesting thing about Cohan's personal life is that he had so little of it. His family life was circumscribed by his continuing presence at rehearsals, performances, production duties or all-night writing sessions. Socially for the most part, he sought needed relaxation with male companionship over drinks at the Friars, Lambs, or the Hotel Plaza's Oak Room. There were a few extramarital connections. His wife's growing invalidism, stemming from three difficult births, gradually phased out their physical relationship, and Cohan, like any man of strong sexual attractiveness, found it difficult to resist some of the many fascinating actresses interested in him. These affairs were few and consummately discreet. Primarily, Cohan's personal life was given over to a small group of men pals, and he needed these few friends. But he needed something else much more—the theatre, a theatre on which his professionalism was increasingly leaving a deeper imprint.

9. THE BEST OF BROADWAY

As Cohan and Harris went into the second decade of the century, their substance grew apace. Before the decade ended, they had acquired part interests in the Grand Opera House, the Astor Theatre, the Gaiety Theatre, the Bronx Opera House, Cohan's Grand Opera House in Chicago, and they owned outright their own playhouses, the Cohan and Harris Theatre and the George M. Cohan Theatre. For a few years during this period, Cohan and Harris were the busiest producers on Broadway, not only presenting Cohan's plays but others very much in the Cohan tradition of light comedy —*The Fortune Hunter, The Girl in Waiting, The House Next Door,* and *Officer 666* featuring such expert farceurs as Douglas Fairbanks, Wallace Eddinger, Laurette Taylor, and John Barrymore.

A high proportion of Cohan and Harris productions went on the road, almost always profitably, and to every area of the country. An amusing little poem of Cohan's about box-office possibilities on tour gives an excellent idea of the amazing range of the towns and cities covered. Two of the poem's terms may need translation today: "jay" means "hick" or "rustic"; "ten, twent', thirt'" means popular priced melodrama, available at ten, twenty, and thirty cents.

A stands for Albany, good for one night.
B stands for Boston, for two weeks all right.
C for Chicago, big money, no yaps.
D stands for Denver, break even, perhaps.
E stands for Evansville, Sunday night stand.
F is for Frisco, you must have a band.
G for Grand Rapids, for ten, twent' and thirts.
H is for Houston, and getting there hurts.
I Indianapolis, fills in on the tour.
J stands for Johnstown, capacity sure.
K Kansas City, big coin for the West.
L Louisville, just one night at its best.
M Minneapolis, as good as St. Paul.
N for New York, the jay town of them all.
O for Oswego, they always come late.
P is for Pittsburgh and Phillie—both great.
Q is for Quebec, gross 389.
R is for Rochester, S.R.O. sign.
S is for St. Louis, for big shows O.K.
T for Toledo, ain't played it, can't say.
U is for Utica, taking a chance.
V is for Vicksburg, sold out in advance.
W, Washington, always a doubt.
X is for Xenia, get in and get out.
Y is for Youngstown, the management cheap.
Z is for Zanesville, you'll stand 'em ten deep.
Not one stands for Providence—none in the lot.
I wouldn't insult the proud capital "P."
I can't stand for "Prov." and it can't stand for me.

The partnership of Cohan and Harris flourished and was much sought after by playwrights. Scripts poured in, and when an author's reputation was such that a personal interview seemed desirable, Cohan and Harris would ask him to come up to their offices and read the script to them. At these sessions Harris usually asked the author to sit at the desk while the two partners sat at the other end of the room. If Harris got bored with the reading he had a habit of walking slowly about. On one occasion a very forthright young man arrived with his manuscript and began his reading rather brusquely.

After ten minutes, Harris got up from his chair and walked around the room a bit, sat down, then got up again later. At this the author said, "Listen, Harris, I wish you wouldn't keep pacing up and down the room like that while I'm trying to read this play. I should think you'd have more respect for a playwright. You act like a damned jumping jack." "What do you mean?" asked Harris. "You've got me nervous, that's what I mean," replied the author. Harris assured the man that he only *thought* he was nervous. The exasperated author asked if he wanted to hear the play or not. "No," said Harris, "I'm too nervous." The author stalked out in high indignation and shouted that this would positively be the last manuscript he would ever bring to this office, and when Harris asked if one could depend on that, the author bawled out, "Mark my words, you'll be sorry!" "So will you," yelled Harris after him, "if you ever produce that play."

Cohan and Harris were noted for their amiability with all their clients whether of high or low degree, and both men were especially proud of their treatment of actors. In a day when actors' contracts were more honored in breach than observance, the word of Cohan and Harris to an actor was bond. Cohan and Harris assumed that the reverse would always be true but on one occasion at least it was not. The punch-line of this frequently repeated anecdote has usually been attributed to Cohan; it actually belongs to Harris. Shortly after the opening of a Cohan and Harris show, one of its leading actors was offered a bigger salary by another management and promptly left for the new job. Harris asked his partner what he thought of this and Cohan said angrily, "One thing he can be sure about. The son of a bitch will never work for this office again." "The son of a bitch sure won't!" said Harris. He paused. "Not unless we really need him."

The classic instance of this situation was Arnold Daly,

one of the English-speaking theatre's finest actors and well-known for his acting in and championing of Bernard Shaw's plays. Daly accepted the lead in a Cohan-Harris production, *The Penalty*, by Henry C. Colwell. An uneven melodrama about a child who learns of an idolized mother's immorality, it was as removed from Bernard Shaw as air from iron. Daly took the role because he needed the excellent salary. The play opened in Philadelphia the first week of April 1910, and its opening night Cohan was never to forget. In a 1935 broadcast interview by John B. Kennedy, he recalled the occasion:

> The first audience was kind enough to like it very much. They were cheering at the end of the first act. Harris and I were doing a jig of delight in the box-office when Daly stepped between the curtains to make a speech.
>
> "I've been to Philadelphia before," he said in that meaty crispness of his—his diction always reminded me of good bacon. "But never," he said, "never have I been received so enthusiastically."
>
> "Hooray!" shouted Harris, and I echoed it.
>
> "Now I understand you perfectly," Daly smiled at the audience—a poisonous Daly smile. "When I came here in good things you stayed away in large numbers. And now you rave at this bit of bilge. I'm glad to know what you like."
>
> Harris broke out of the box-office and ran down the aisle. "Where are you going?" I said. "I'm going to kill him," barked Harris. And I think he'd have done exactly that if we hadn't caught up with him.

The Penalty lasted only six weeks on the road, then died, and Daly never worked for Cohan again—until ten years later when he was needed.

In their search for plays of quality, Cohan and Harris spread their nets wide. It became apparent that Cohan, for all his fecundity, could hardly be expected to come up with a new hit every year nor were there that many scripts about which fitted the Cohan-Harris entertainment specifications. The partnership decided that dramatic adaptations of popular magazine material were bound to have a measure of success. For some months in 1910 Cohan noticed that a number of stories in *The Saturday Evening Post* were sending the magazine's circulation to new heights. These were the Get-Rich-Quick Wallingford tales by George Randolph Chester. Cohan bought the dramatic rights and set about to make the series stageworthy. There was drama inherent in the protagonist of these stories because he was a rogue with a gift of gab, and resolutely, uniquely American. J. Rufus Wallingford is a confidence man, possessing many of the attributes of Jeff Peters, O. Henry's con man hero. It is noteworthy that at the turn of the century there were two very popular American fictional characters whose basic experiences consisted of robbing other people for personal gain, thereby delighting thousands of readers.

Wallingford became something of a minor American folk hero in 1908–10 because he blossomed at a time when American interest in big business and its growth was at a high peak. The first collection of Chester's stories was titled "Get-Rich-Quick Wallingford, a Cheerful Account of the Rise and Fall of an American Business Buccaneer." There is rather more rise than fall in these stories, and Wallingford is a genial and attractive man, a minor Falstaff—rotund, bluff, and much disposed to gourmandizing. He is given the sympathy factor of a loving wife and of an interesting fellow rogue, personable "Blackie" Daw, smooth-talking confidant and co-worker. Wallingford is ultimately laid low by the backfire of a massive swindle he instigated, but the man swindled unexpectedly turns a profit on the enterprise and hires Wallingford for future advice, readily forgiving him because, in his words, Wallingford ". . . is only the logical development of the American tendency to 'get there' no matter how." A tidy justification, if not exactly a moral one, but one that probably explains why Wallingford was so popular.

Cohan in taking this material and "Cohanizing" it (a word he thereafter used for revisions of any script submitted to him) was initially daunted by Wallingford's immense physical appearance, an appearance well established in *The Saturday Evening Post* illustrations. When Cohan wrote a leading man's role he always structured it for his immediate or eventual playing, and as a slim 5′ 6″ he did not conform in any way to the popular image of Wallingford. The only thing to do under the circumstances was to ignore the popular image completely and make Wallingford a slim 5′ 6″ with an engaging way of talking out of the corner of his mouth. Moreover, make him an intensely patriotic American with egoistic tendencies. Wallingford at his first entrance in the play registers at a hotel desk and engages the clerk in quick interchange: "Do me a favor?" "Certainly." "Don't sell this autograph." The stage Wallingford insists that his hotel suite be decorated profusely with American flags. Cohan was once birthday-surprised by his cast decorating his dressing room in extravagant patriotic bunting; thereafter, for years, flag decoration was standard for his dressing rooms.

The play, *Get-Rich-Quick Wallingford,* dispenses with Wallingford's wife in order that a continuing love interest can be maintained, and the plot follows Chester's most interesting story in which the protagonist comes to a small town and perpetrates one of his biggest swindles only to discover that his chicanery redounds to the town's financial gain. Cohanizing in this instance included the comparative purifying of the characters of Wallingford and Daw. The critic for the Cincinnati *Commercial* noted with relief that Cohan had ". . . cleared away the original dross of downright, commonplace evil . . . He has separated Wallingford and Daw from the low fellowship of the Wallingford stories; he has brought them into the atmosphere of decency and the companionship of virtuous women and honest, though humble, folks."

The humble folks Cohan piles on with a vengeance, and quite successfully. He fills the play with small-town characters—the gossipy rural hotel clerk, the crusty, vain rich man, the pert office boy, and the wise-cracking waitress. Their vitality is authentic and, as usual, Cohan made sure that the scenery did some acting too. One of the stage effects audiences of the time reveled in was an illuminated object in miniature perspective (particularly a train) moving slowly along the backdrop. Cohan duly incorporated a lighted trolley car effect in the distance which was received with rapturous applause.

When the play opened in New York on September 19, 1910, with urbane Hale Hamilton in the leading role abetted by Edward Ellis, an actor's actor, as "Blackie" Daw, it was an immediate hit. Some critics complained that the plot was not substantive and that its resolution was melodramatic but the public responded with ardor. Again, Cohan was giving them what they wanted—themselves. The lighted trolley car effect helped, too. Years later, George Jean Nathan attributed a good amount of Cohan's success with these slight plays to his ". . . ingenious trick of applying the invariably successful Cinderella theme to the scenery. Popular playwrights for many years had been reaping their rewards from revampings of the Cinderella story in terms of character when Cohan came along with the novel and doubly profitable notion of transferring the Cinderella idea from the character to the painted canvas. The public, become a bit surfeited with the kind of play wherein the poor, abused, little orphan country girl of Act I became the bride of the handsome young millionaire from the city in Act III, jumped over to Cohan en masse when he craftily gave them their favorite Cinderella hokum in terms of stage settings by changing the poor orphan into a shabby drygoods store that came into its brilliant own in the last act or into a down-at-the-heel villa that was eventually metamorphosed into a prosperous and lively town whose glittering electric signs and puffing power plants could be seen through the windows upstage." This scenic refurbishing became an elemental part of Cohanizing in *Wallingford* and a number of other Cohan plays of middle-class life.

Nor did Cohan neglect the power of music in *Wallingford.* He inserted a stirring town band at one point, and at another a song emphasizing a theme dear to his heart which went in part: "Dear old pals, jolly old pals,/Give me the friendship of dear old pals!" These were all pals making small-town talk in such a way as to bring the critic of the Boston *Transcript* to the opinion that Cohan was indeed grass roots America whose characters were "Americans, keenly observed, shrewdly put to speaking themselves in their own idiom."

With *Wallingford* his first great success in the straight play category ("Not really a straight play, come to think of it," he said later. "A crook play."), Cohan debated the propriety of continuing in the vein but his love of music won out as it almost always did. At the same time, he did not want to repeat his standard formula for musicals and in the search for something different, he came up with something almost different. *The Little Millionaire* is the mixture as before in that it has a flourish of flags, the jingly tunes with patter lyrics and intratheatrical device in which the villains of the play identify themselves as such: (". . . Bad all through,/We create the hero by the dirty work we do."). What is different about the show as Rennold Wolf of the *Morning Telegraph* was interested to note is the total absence of music in one of the acts. Act Two is devoted entirely to the book which concerns a father (Jerry) and a son (George) who, in consequence of a capricious will, need each other's permission to marry their respective ladies. George is the eponymous hero, not at all afraid to refer to his lack of height in either art or life. He gets his girl (Josie not being available, the role was played by Lila Rhodes, a cousin), and Jerry comfortably, predictably, winds up with Nellie. Rennold Wolf looked on the demusicalization of the second act as a welcome break from musical comedy tradition, and he was equally pleased that the best song in the show, "Oh, You Wonderful Girl," was unprecedently assigned to the villain. Such diversions if extended might have made *The Little Millionaire* something striking but at base it is the old Cohan formula even down to amiable Tom Lewis once more playing a bibulous hanger-on. It was, nonetheless, amply good for the Broadway of 1911 and had a respectable run. Cohan and Harris had now entered the ranks of top-flight Broadway producers with this, their fourteenth production.

They had remained free of the great Broadway battle between Erlanger's monopolistic Theatrical Syndicate and the up and powerfully coming Brothers Shubert. Speaking of his friendship with the tough boys of Broadway, Cohan said, "Lee Shubert and J. J. Shubert are my friends, and Klaw and Erlanger are my friends also. If a man is nice to me, I will be nice to him. If I cannot choose my own friends and conduct my business as I see fit, and be a regular fellow to all, why, I will get out of the theatrical business altogether. I would rather be a regular fellow on $5 a month than be dictated to as somebody's white haired boy on $50,000 a week."

Cohan knew what kind of money-grubbing opportunists the Shuberts and the Erlangers were, and he was candid with them after their own fashion. Ward Morehouse tells the story of Cohan's chatting one evening with the stage manager of Hammerstein's Victoria Theatre on the north side of 42nd Street, generally recognized as the Shubert side of the street. Erlanger, from his side which was dominated by his New Amsterdam Theatre, crossed over during the conversation and said, "George, how can you stand on the same street so close to those rats, the scum of the earth, the Shuberts?" Cohan looked carefully at Erlanger and said, "And what are you, my good friend?"

In casting his lot with the managers, Cohan was guilty of

no disloyalty to the acting profession because, at base, he did not consider himself an actor. During his career, he announced his retirement as a performer on at least ten different occasions, and he meant it every time. The thing that brought him back to acting was usually the need to be active in the theatre during fallow periods as a writer and composer. He was always at heart a song and dance man who loved to write. He enjoyed acting because he did it well and he knew he did it well, but if he wanted to be remembered for anything, he said, it would be as an author and composer. He learned early that the best way to maintain his work before the public was to be his own manager and producer. He was, moreover, chary of most actors as a breed.

In a revealing article, "The Actor as a Business Man" in the September 3, 1910, issue of *The Saturday Evening Post,* Cohan asserted that the current Broadway actor had "little creative genius. He lacks imagination. As a matter of fact, he seldom suggests a distinctive way of playing a part. He almost never invents lines." For most playwrights, the latter quality would be high virtue but Cohan was a man who encouraged his actors to improvise in rehearsal. One episode in his early career had soured him on actors who introduced new bits of business after the performance had been set. "I shall never forget," he said in the *Post* article, "the distress that an actor once caused me. I had written a vaudeville sketch. It was all right—clean as a hound's tooth—made a big hit. But the horseplay actor who had the leading part wasn't satisfied. The laughter wasn't vociferous enough for him. He was doing the part of a plumber when he introduced this bit—without consulting me, I assure you. When he entered the room he stood looking around for a minute; then, as if his eye had fallen on something, suddenly darted across the stage, picked up a cigar-butt out of the cuspidor, lighted it and proceeded to smoke. The thing created a howl of laughter, but lots of people were disgusted and blamed me for the exceedingly vulgar bit."

The *Post* article is documentation of Cohan's growing distrust of actors as a body, a distrust which was to flower into the most disturbing episode of his life, the actors strike in 1919. He wondered, in 1910, "what the result would be if a party of actors were left to themselves to put on a play. It would be a lot of small boys trying to sail a ship. They'd all want to be commanding or steering . . . and if one were chidden he'd do the regular simian sulking act. In this respect the actor always seems to be under the delusion that he is being discriminated against . . . just as if it weren't to the manager's interest to push the actor ahead!"

As individuals, Cohan loved actors. As a body, he grew to distrust them, and their unreliability as he saw it was never more concretized than in an episode which he was fond of telling in later years. During the Broadway run of one of his musicals, he went on the road with another show and was gone for some months. In such circumstances he left his assistant director, Sam Forrest, in charge of maintaining the New York production's quality. Forrest, an amiable soul, was never a disciplinarian. Cohan, on returning rather unexpectedly from the tour, did not announce his presence at the Broadway production that night. He watched the performance and then asked the stage manager to assemble the cast onstage after the final curtain. Smiling broadly, Cohan stood in front of the group and said, "Congratulations, congratulations!" The company beamed proudly. "That was quite a different production tonight from the one I saw when I left. There certainly are a lot of improvements in the show. So—we are going to have a rehearsal at ten o'clock tomorrow morning during which we will remove all the improvements!"

In 1912 Cohan remarked to a friend that the playing of the lead role in *Get-Rich-Quick Wallingford* (he stepped in briefly during the Broadway run), gave him the idea that perhaps he might be acceptable to the public as a "legitimate" actor. In any case it would be fun to experiment. To that end he wrote a straight play for himself in which the leading man is a genial, wise-cracking Broadwayite set down distinctively in the alien corn of small-town America, hardly a novel Cohan concept. The plot of *Broadway Jones*, observed *Theatre Magazine*, "is so simple that it is almost juvenile. But Mr. Cohan is a true observer of men and conditions, and applies the little comic and pathetic touches of life in a way which makes his completed fabric something distinctly vital and real."

Jackson Jones, known as "Broadway" because of his playboyish predilection for that street, spends his patrimony and is being forced to marry for money when he is relieved by the inheritance of his uncle's gum factory in rural Jonesville. He goes to the town and is about to sell the plant to the gum trust when the plant's charming secretary argues that the sale will endanger the livelihood of the town. Jones inevitably elects to keep the plant, defeat the gum trust in its machinations to subvert the local product and winds up with the charming secretary. Because Josie Cohan was not able to appear in the play (she was on tour with her husband), Cohan included her by naming the secretary Josie. Jerry and Nellie had what the *Dramatic Mirror* called "congenial parts"; all in all, save for the lack of music, a typical Cohan production. Even the Cohan infatuation with Broadway is glanced at briefly in a bit of dialogue which came very much from its author's heart. Near the end of the play Jones is catechized by Josie:

JOSIE: What is Broadway?
JONES: Broadway?
JOSIE: A street?
JONES: Sure, it's the greatest street in the world.
JOSIE: Some people say it's terrible.
JONES: Philadelphia people.
JOSIE: And some people say it's wonderful.
JONES: That's just it. It's terribly wonderful.
JOSIE: I don't understand.
JONES: Nobody understands Broadway. People hate it

and don't know why. People love it and don't know why. It's just because it's Broadway.

JOSIE: That's a mystery, isn't it?

JONES: That's just what it is, a mystery.

As indeed it always was to Cohan. To the very last of his life he was never fully able to explain what Broadway meant to him beyond that it represented most of what he wanted and loved. It was something more than money, power or prestige. Success on Broadway was of course the ultimate recognition of his function as a creative person, and it was the world's best entertainment bargain. But it was something more. "I guess Broadway, for me," said Cohan, "was everything in life I've never had: my education, and the friendships, games, adventures, and just plain fun of boyhood and growing up."

With *Broadway Jones*, a vital phase of Cohan's life closed. When the company went on tour, Jerry and Nellie during an affectionate, tearful discussion with George told him they were retiring from the theatre. "It's been a long run, son," Jerry told him. "Mother and I have had all the fun in the world, but one's got to learn how to bow out and when to bow out, and for us, this is it." George was deeply moved but also, he found, somewhat pleased. What better occasion for his retiring, too, as a performer? They would take their last curtain call together. On the evening of January 31, 1914, Jerry's sixty-sixth birthday, they did just that in a Detroit theatre. Cohan announced to the audience that three of the Four Cohans were now permanently retired from acting. That same evening in their hotel, George gave Jerry a letter making him a half-owner of all Cohan enterprises present and to come. "Jerry could never read that letter even halfway through without breaking into tears," Nellie recalled later. "He always said it was more than a gift, it was a blessing to have a son like that."

Prior to the *Broadway Jones* tour, Cohan offered Broadway a play which dilated his love of mystery to the fullest.

From his earliest days he had been taken by plays with mysterious strangers in black drifting in and out of the night. These staples of melodrama thrilled Cohan as a youngster and he never outgrew an affection for them. He often said that there was no more striking contrivance dramatically than the mysterious stranger, and his plays reflect his love of the device. As a peg to hang not one but an entire spectrum of mysterious strangers, Cohan took Earl Derr Biggers's novel, *Seven Keys to Baldpate,* Cohanized it and came up a rich winner.

The novel had been a great success and Cohan saw no reason why a dramatization of it should not merit the same acclaim. Certainly it was a work calculated to win his own attention. It was melodrama and it was mystery, the two things Cohan always found of abiding interest dramatically and the novel was full of incident triggered by a situation much to Cohan's liking. The hero, Billy Magee, is a writer of melodramatic novels of the popular variety. He goes to a summer hotel, Baldpate Inn, in the dead of winter for the solitude necessary to complete a really fine novel his pal, Hal Bentley, bets him he cannot write in two months. By a series of coincidences possible only in melodramatic novels, Magee finds that his key to the inn, supposedly the only one, has been duplicated six times, each key representing a person who is looking either for refuge or gain at Baldpate. The novel's catalyst is a package containing $200,000 which is maneuvered in and out of the inn's safe to the tune of shots in the night, screams, a mysterious suicide, and echoes of scandal in high place. The Billy Magee of the novel, Cohan found to his delighted surprise, *was* Cohan—a pert, wise-cracking popular novelist (playwright) whose entertaining books (plays) were scorned by the critics but loved by the public.

The play retains the essential thread of Biggers's novel. Magee comes to the inn out-of-season to write a novel on a bet, with one difference. In the play, Magee's novel is to be written about Baldpate itself and within the span of twenty-four hours. Again, the bundle of $200,000 is established as the desideratum of the six other key-holders, one of whom turns out to be Billy's dream girl. Like the novel, the play abounds in incident: mysterious phone calls, revolvers brandished and shots outside, people locked in rooms, crooks confronted and confronting, and the breaking down of doors. The ending of the play, however, is a sharp departure from the Biggers's novel. In the novel Billy Magee with his newfound love and a gang of rascal politicians securely apprehended comes back to the city and a bright, new life. Cohan's play almost reaches this point but suddenly comes Billy's encounter with a bizarre contradiction of order: the sheriff called in to arrest the chief villain turns out to be a crook himself and seizes the $200,000 for his own use. Shots are heard outside, and the owner of the seventh key comes in. He is Hal Bentley, the owner of the inn and the man with whom Billy had made the bet. Hal announces coolly that he has killed the two policemen outside because they refused to allow him to pass. Astounded almost to the point of trauma, Billy babbles of the incredibilities he has seen this night, and assures Hal he has won the bet. "Why, I couldn't write a book in twenty-four hours in a place like this. My God, what a night this has been!" Which is cue for the smiling Hal to say that it is a night totally manufactured. All the characters at Baldpate Inn, Hal explains, are just that—characters devised to bedevil Billy in a rigadoon of melodrama, characters played by actors from the local stock company hired for the job of creating this evening of lively errors. Hal tells Billy, "I wanted to prove to you how perfectly improbable and terrible those awful stories you've been writing would seem if such things really and truly happened." Billy, chagrined but pleased, turns to his "girl" and asks, "Well, Mary, the shots in the night, the chases after fortunes, and all the rest of the melodrama may be all wrong, but will you help me prove that there really is such a thing as love at first sight?" She agrees and the company smiles approvingly as Billy takes her in his arms. Curtain. A perfectly enjoyable twist ending—except that it is not the end. The twist has a twist.

The curtain goes up again for a brief epilogue in which it is revealed that all the foregoing, all of the play except for the brief prologue which showed Billy coming to the inn to be locked in for the twenty-four hours of the bet, has been the plot of the novel Billy has just written. The epilogue concludes with the caretaker assuring Hal Bentley by telephone that Billy has been working uninterruptedly for the past day and night, has indeed just now finished a manuscript, the title of which, *Seven Keys to Baldpate,* the caretaker carefully reads to Bentley. The bewildered caretaker tells Billy that Hal is laughing: "He says there's only one." Billy takes the telephone and jubilantly tells Hal that the job is done indeed, the bet is securely won, and in words that reflect Cohan's heartfelt feelings on a few matters, ends the play:

> . . . some title, isn't it? Wild, terrible, horrible melodrama as usual, the kind of stuff you always roast me about. Treated as a joke, however, this time . . . and say, I'm the hero . . . This thing's going to sell over a million copies . . . The what? The critics? (*Laughs*) I don't care a darn about the critics . . . This is the stuff the public wants . . . Yes, I'll meet you at the 44th Street Club tomorrow. (*Adlib as the curtain falls. Slow curtain.*)

It was the stuff the public wanted. *Seven Keys to Baldpate* was a roaring success. The critics in the main were impressed and comment by a few of them that the play was basically a trick is justified. The play *is* a trick, a trick that works. This play which delighted Broadway playgoers in 1913 is still very much a living organism. Its unquenchable vitality is grounded in the rapid onrush of continual surprise. Just when one has become accustomed to a situation and before one can recognize its inherent improbability, Cohan does one of two things: he either has Billy allude to the moment as melodramatic which eases the incredibility, or we are precipitated into a new situation so actionful and diverting that attention is sustained. The play, a triumph of sheer theatricality, was Cohan's best play to that date, and is worthy of revival at very least off-Broadway as a specimen of magnificent melodramatic farce.

An amusing incident stemming from the success of *Seven Keys to Baldpate* concerns a prominent playwright of the day, Augustus Thomas, who saw the play and was shocked to the depths of his formalistic soul. His sense of playwriting decorum was outraged because Cohan had broken all the well-established rules of play construction. Attempting to be polite but unable to disguise the disapproval dripping from his tone, Thomas asked loftily, "On what lines do you construct your plays, Mr. Cohan?"

"Principally on the New York, New Haven and Hartford —and once in a while on the Pennsylvania," came the reply.

After the success of *Seven Keys to Baldpate,* Cohan brought into focus an idea which had been lurking in his subconscious for over two years. He had been thinking of writing a serious play but a concept or basic plot eluded him. A few days after the *Baldpate* opening, he read a magazine story, "None So Blind" by Frank L. Packard, which intrigued him, and from it he constructed his only serious play, *The Miracle Man.* Working slowly for the first time in his life (he took an unprecedented ten weeks to write it; *Seven Keys to Baldpate* took ten days), Cohan wrote the story of a patriarchal healer whose goodness puzzles, then finally converts a gang of confidence men who had planned to use him. Cohan's writing here generally eschews oversentimentality and he makes the confidence men vibrantly humorous, but the miracle man himself is uninteresting. Cohan was too much in awe of him. On the night of its opening, Cohan told George Jean Nathan that although he felt pride in the play, it would probably fail. "I have a hunch it's not what the public wants," he said to

Nathan, "but I'm going to take a chance and see if my hunch is wrong." His hunch was right.

Pivotal to the plot of *The Miracle Man* is a crippled fourteen-year-old boy whose miraculous cure is the principal event of the play. The role was played by young Percy Helton who went on to a distinguished career on Broadway as an adult. As an actor who worked in three Cohan productions over a five-year period, the late Percy Helton had an excellent opportunity to see Cohan the Pro and, to a lesser extent, the Pal. In recent years one of Hollywood's best character actors, Helton's extensive career gave him ample authority to speak of his world. He had vivid memories of his old mentor.

"George M. was a wonderful man, always," said Helton. "My dad, my sisters, and I had been cast in *Fifty Miles from Boston*, and during the show's second year on tour, I read in the *Dramatic Mirror* that Mr. Cohan was going to dramatize Frank Packard's story which I happened to have read, and which I knew had the role of a boy in it. I was sure that I could play that role, so with my dad's encouragement, I saw Mr. Cohan, and I reminded him that two years before when we first began playing *Fifty Miles from Boston*, he had told me to go after anything I wanted to do and *always* to say, 'I can do it!' That time two years before is an interesting story. In the early days of *Fifty Miles from Boston*, Donald Brian had to drop out of the leading role because he had the chance to appear in the new comic opera, *The Merry Widow*. That made a star of Donald, and of course Mr. Cohan, being the nice man he was, let Donald go without a murmur. The difficulty was, however, that the understudy was not able to dance like Donald (who danced like Cohan) in this one particular great number, 'The Boys Who Fight the Flames.' So Mr. Cohan said, 'All right, we'll cut the number.' But my dad, always on the lookout for a chance for me, went to George M. and said, 'Boss, why don't you let the kid do that number? Put it down a couple of keys and he can do it. He knows the number cold.' So

George M. sent for me, and I hadn't known anything about their conversation. Mr. Cohan set me up on his knee, and he said, 'Percy, do you know "The Boys Who Fight the Flames"?' And I said, 'Yes, Mr. Cohan.' And he said, 'You know the dance?' and I said, 'Yes sir.' Then he said, 'Could you do the number?' and I looked at him and said, 'Well, I don't know. Maybe.' And with that, he slapped me right in the puss, right in the face. Tears came to my eyes, I was hurt all right. And the second after he slapped me, he threw his arms around me in contrition, because he knew he had hurt me. Then he said, 'Now, wait a minute, Perce. I want to tell you something. You're in the theatre and I know you're going to stay in the theatre. And *if* a director, *if* a producer, *if* an author, *ever* asks you if you can do something—I don't care if he asks you at your present age if you can play Shylock in *The Merchant of Venice,* you tell him *yes,* because if he didn't think you could do it, he wouldn't ask you. Now. Can you do "The Boys Who Fight the Flames"?' and I shouted '*Yes,* Mr. Cohan!' I did the number for the rest of the tour, and I remembered that lesson for the rest of my life."

The Miracle Man was a flyer into serious drama which Cohan was never to repeat. The lesson was well-learned; the rest of his life he forbore messages. But after *The Miracle Man,* he was in an artistic quandry—where to now? By 1914, his lively, all-American musical shows with their simplistic plots, ragtag vaudeville dialogue, and non-stop action were becoming predictable in format. Something new was clearly needed; he seemed to be at a dead end. Music and humor were in his bones and to some extent it seemed as if the Cohan talent was all dressed up and with no place to go. But late in 1914 his talent found a natural habitat in revue.

Revue is now rather out of fashion but at apogee it was one of the most engaging of American entertainments. It was begot out of pre-Minsky burlesque, the true burlesque, with its astringent kidding of local and national mores. This burlesque, which lived up to its name precisely, began as a living force in the New York theatre with William Mitchell in 1839 and flourished under John Brougham until the advent of *The Black Crook* (1866) when the female leg was added as a constituent element. The identification of sex with burlesque grew until they are now virtually synonymous, but for long years the New York theatre delighted in authentic burlesque which Walter Pritchard Eaton defined as "the joyous, good-natured parody of serious or classical plays, or of events and characters in history, and the turning topsy-turvy of accepted theatrical values."

Pure (in all senses) burlesque became a vital part of musical revue. Revue had its first surge to great popularity in the initial *Ziegfeld Follies* (1907), and went on to greater strengths for approximately three decades. Cohan by abilities and temperament was uniquely predisposed to the crafting of revue, and he is generally credited with creating the personality revue as distinct from the Ziegfeld glamour displays. Robert Baral, the leading historian of this entertainment form, says, "Cohan gleaned the Broadway shows and parlayed them into snappy skits, scenes and curtain talks. He revamped the burlesque formula into American vernacular."

Cohan's revues—there were three of them—are mostly unplayable today because of their intense cluster of topicalities but their wit is still robust and unquenchable. *Hello, Broadway!* (1914) grew from a conversation at the Friars when Cohan told Willie Collier he was thinking of writing a show, a different kind of thing from his usual, that would have music, sketches, and if possible a personality like Collier to dominate proceedings. Cohan admitted that he, too, as a song and dance man would like to be in the show but he had announced not long before his irrevocable decision to stop performing. "I've sworn I'd never act again," he complained to Collier. "You never *did*," Collier assured him solemnly, and this proved to be the happy justification for Cohan's appearance in this, the first personality revue.

Hello, Broadway! had the benefit of Collier's great experience in old burlesque. He had been one of Weber and Fields' great farceurs in the heyday of their Music Hall when half of each program was devoted to an uproarious take-off on a current Broadway play. At Collier's suggestion, Cohan decided to follow this tradition but with a wider range of target. In consequence, he sent affectionate blasts at twelve current New York shows, including two Cohan and Harris productions. Intratheatrical reference runs rampant from the very first chorus of Broadway cops who admit their fortuitous entrance is an excuse to sing an opening chorus, through devices like a character addressing the audience halfway through the show, "Ladies and gentlemen, so that you may follow the story closely and not become confused, the management requests me to offer you an explanation of the intricate construction of the play. The scene you are about to witness, Scene 6, is supposed to have taken place during the action of Scene 3; that is to say, we are going to prove to you that the things we told you were happening outside the house, really transpired. It is what might be called advance playwriting."

Cohan even kids his own recent flop by having an actor dressed as The Miracle Man do a grotesque dance and appear throughout as a comedy character, Daddy Long-Beard, landlord of the local reform school whose star pupil is little Ruth Chatterbox. Ruth Chatterton was then playing a very verbose role in *Daddy Long-Legs* just down the street. Peggy Wood made her debut in the show as Elsie Workingson, the duplication of a reigning star, Elsie Ferguson. In a scattershot reference to ten shows and one film then in New York, Elsie admits sorrowfully to Collier that she is an *Outcast*. She sighs that she indeed has had *Life* and *Experience*.

COLLIER: Yes, we know. You were put *On Trial* for stealing *My Lady's Dress*.

COHAN: And they claimed you were *Under Cover* with *A Pair of Silk Stockings*.

COLLIER: And they threatened to send you to *Cabiria* if you didn't *Kick In.*

COHAN: But you used *Diplomacy* and were pronounced *Innocent.* We know all about it.

ELSIE: Yes, and all that happened this season.

COLLIER: There's nothing left for you to do now, little girl, but to go into vaudeville.

Hello, Broadway! bears the substitle "A Musical Crazy Quilt Patched and Threaded Together with Words and Music by George M. Cohan," a precise description. Its many songs are specifically theatrical in flavor: it's most memorable a pastiche of all the fragrant locale-flavored love songs of musical comedy history. One of the comediennes, at the end of a comic-melodramatic episode, announces in high anti-climax that she is going to steal away to Buffalo and settle down tranquilly by the Erie Canal. She makes this announcement twice, the orchestra leader standing by with folded arms, until she turns indignantly to the audience and says, "Isn't that the limit? The only decent song I've got in the show and he misses the cue. How those two Jewish boys, Cohan and Harris, ever stand for you, I don't know." She asserts the value of her song as "a sure-fire, pretty little ditty, popular tin pan song." It is still a classic of mock pathos but was incomparably more so to audiences of the time who could summon up a vivid picture of the stagnant Erie Canal waters carrying an endless procession of dreary barges:

Down by the Erie,
There waits my pal,
Though the days are long and dreary,
He declares he'll ne'er grow weary.
Poor John O'Leary,
I'm afraid you've lost your gal,
For I've left you flat, my dearie.
By the Erie Canal.

This gentle satirization was contrasted with a song in which Cohan the Pal and the Pro meet in easy harness, "The Irving Berlin Melodies," a cheery paean of praise from a friend to an up-and-coming young song-writer. Friendship can hardly have been more signalized than this tribute from the older, established man to the younger. Cohan embraced Berlin's work even more fully in *The Cohan Revue of 1918* which included five songs by the newcomer. In a *New Yorker* profile of Cohan by Gilbert Seldes in 1934, Berlin is described as agonizing over the creation of his songs for this revue because he deemed the association with Cohan such an overwhelming experience. Berlin spent nights and days on his lyrics and music, and in Seldes's words, "Cohan, Berlin noticed, would knock out a song overnight, create the dance number for it the next morning, write a sketch between lunch and dinner, in intervals of rehearsing, and was directing the entire production besides. Berlin considers Cohan one of the greatest of American song-writers, and specifically the one who gave new life to ragtime and led it a long way toward the snap and sparkle which ended in jazz. In 1904 and after, when Berlin was singing at Nigger Mike's, the sentimental ballad was the chief item in the repertory; 'but when we wanted to sing a *class* song,' says Berlin, 'we always sang something by Cohan.' "

In keeping with its patchwork format, *Hello, Broadway!* has no immediately observable theme but Willie Collier keeps walking through the bizarre proceedings with a mysterious hatbox thought to contain the script of a Chinese melodrama he is smuggling into the country. (Two of the plays burlesqued in the show had Chinese ambience.) Ultimately Collier is forced to reveal that the hatbox actually contains the plot of *Hello, Broadway!*, and he guards it assiduously. Shortly after, Cohan happily satirizes himself in the song, "Go and Get a Flag," a plea from Collier and others to include a patriotic ditty, even one in ragtime, as box office insurance. This is dutifully followed by a serious song, "My Flag," with beautiful Peggy Wood bravely standing forth attired as a hybrid between Columbia, the Gem of the Ocean, and the Statue of Liberty. Just before the final curtain, Collier's box containing the show's plot is stolen from him and brought before the audience where it is opened to reveal, of course, nothing.

Hello, Broadway! was received with great enthusiasm on all sides. What surprised most of the critics as well as the Broadway professionals, especially writers and producers, was the great amount of humor extractable from American life. It had not occurred to them that a major production could be given to the pungent kidding of the New York scene. Regrettably, Cohan wrote only two more revues, *The Cohan Revue of 1916* and *The Cohan Revue of 1918,* in neither of which he nor Collier appeared. In revue, Cohan had discovered a theatrical form which suited him notably, and he might have brought it to subtler and more interesting forms after World War I had not the direction of his professional life shifted. In 1919, Walter Pritchard Eaton issued a public appeal to Cohan in the magazine, *Shadowland:* "There is only one man in New York today who holds sufficiently the regard of the public, and has the necessary wit and skill to revive this ancient tradition [pure burlesque] and carry it on. But he has apparently abandoned the attempt. It is a great pity."

In this article, Eaton recalled with almost tearful nostalgia the superb burlesque in ragtime rhythms and rhymed couplets of *Common Clay,* a highlight of *The Cohan Revue of 1916. Common Clay* by Cleves Kinkead was a sturdily improbable and very popular melodrama of the day featuring Jane Cowl as a girl, once sinful common clay but now reformed, who is interrogated savagely in court by a censorious judge. The thundering coincidence which climaxes the play is that the judge discovers the girl is his daughter. Cohan took this painful material and made it swing, literally. In the climax of the Cohan version, the girl's mother is brought to the stand where she is sworn in (on the telephone book) in the names of Klaw, Erlanger, and the Brothers Shubert. The actors sing the words to a ragtime beat:

CLERK: The truth and nothing but the truth?
MOTHER: And nothing but the truth.
CLERK: So help you, K. and E.?
MOTHER: So help me, Jake and Lee.

The mother reveals a startling fact: her daughter Jane's name is not Clay, as commonly supposed, but Mud.

JANE: What am I going to do? I don't know where I'm at! How am I going to live with a name like that?
MOTHER: Oh, oh!
JANE: What have you got to tell?
MOTHER: Oh, oh, oh!
JUDGE: Well?
MOTHER: Oh, oh, oh!
JUDGE: Well?
MOTHER: Oh, *oh!*
ALL: Oh, hell!

Mother finally admits that Jane's dad was a man of high degree—Oliver Mud.

JUDGE: Is there a scar on your left hand ear?
JANE: Yes, on my left hand ear, you can see it right here.
JUDGE: My dear!
JANE: What?
JUDGE: I'm here.
JANE: Who?
JUDGE: Your dad.
JANE: You're mad!
MOTHER: No, no, it's so—I can tell by the sty on his left hand eye. Oliver!
JUDGE: Maud!
TOGETHER: My love!

They embrace and talk of their little boy, Tom, who ran away.

> JUDGE: I'll find him sure as sin—I can tell him by the scar on his left chin.

Jane's lawyer, startled, pipes up:

> STEVE: Excuse me, please, If I butt in—but *I've* got a scar on my left hand chin.
> JANE: Where?
> STEVE: There!
> JANE: Oh, is it true, is it you?
> STEVE: Sister!
> JANE: Brother!
> MOTHER: Father!
> JUDGE: Mother!

As mother shouts "Son!", Steve shouts "Ma!", Judge shouts "Daughter!", and Jane shouts "Pa!", they all embrace passionately, sing "There you are, there you are!" and jig vigorously as the curtain descends.

With the creation of his revues, Cohan concretized his reputation as the most distinguished of Broadway's craftsmen, the most professional man in the American theatre of his day. He was far from the best playwright, his singing voice was something of a nasal shout, his acting was confined to light comedy roles and his music, while tremendously enjoyable, did not seem imperishable. But what Cohan was and what Cohan had can best be summed up in Peggy Wood's memory of him at that time: "He was such a joy to watch, and I learned much from him. He never stopped thinking of the theatre and one learned from this, and also learned that that was one of the great reasons for his success. I never saw such concentration in my life. He had a great respect for his profession and he embodied that respect in one word—perfection. That was his keyword. He had the deepest and the most instinctive talent for theatre of anyone in his day." Cohan had become the ultimate professional.

His personal life, too, had rewards. By 1914, Georgette, his daughter by Ethel Levey, was blossoming into attractive young womanhood and seemed to possess the instincts of an actress. The children from Cohan's union with Agnes Nolan were lively, charming youngsters: Mary (b. 1910), Helen (b. 1911), and George M., Jr. (b. 1914). Cohan lived part of the time in Manhattan at the Kingston Apartments, Central Park West, but his home was a beautiful estate in Great Neck, the first in a show business colony that was to include Ed Wynn, Ring Lardner, Gene Buck, and other Cohan intimates.

It was during these years that he suffered his first deep personal losses. On July 12, 1916, Josie died. Although she had been ill for some time, the victim of heart disease in part at least caused by her strenuous work as a dancer, Josie never seemed or looked ill. In addition to her husband, Fred Niblo, she left a thirteen-year-old son, Fred. Jr. During her funeral at Blessed Sacrament Church, on New York's West 71st Street, Cohan collapsed in a paroxysm of grief. Little more than a year later, August 1, 1917, Jerry died, and Cohan was unable to cope with it for a considerable period. His closeness to Jerry can perhaps be fully understood only by one who has been in extended professional partnership with a devoted father. Except when on tour, there was not a day when Cohan did not see his father, and each time they met, Cohan kissed Jerry in a way so natural and warming that even decades later old friends remembered it as ineffably moving.

What has not been fully realized about their relationship is the extraordinary amount of influence Jerry had on his son. Aggressive George and gentle Jerry would seem to be a pattern of dominant son and acquiescent father. This was far from the fact. Jerry gave his son not only probity but a fiercely unremitting love of the theatre which embraced a sense of the past and a low opinion of theatrical labor organizations. Many of George's opinions were solidly rooted in his father's. His dad's loss was the greatest one of Cohan's life. At Jerry's death, Cohan went on the only period of hard and sustained drinking in his life.

In later years when Cohan was on stage, he was startled at certain moments to see Jerry in the wings, smiling approval. Cohan, ever a realist in his personal life, thought of this as his imagination responding to the stimulus of his grief, but then he remembered Jerry had once written of a spiritualistic experience. In his privately printed *Poems and Sketches* (1911), Jerry describes a night when he actually saw persons long dead walking about his room. After rereading this account in his dad's book, Cohan in subsequent encounters with his dad's image found needed comfort. He was convinced that he saw something more than an imaginative re-creation of the man who was, always, his best pal.

Fortunately, Cohan had much to occupy him in the years just prior to American entrance into World War I. In addition to his revues, he Cohanized several profitable Cohan-Harris productions, *Young America*, by Fred Ballard, a comedy featuring Percy Helton and Jasper, a cleverly trained dog; *The House of Glass*, a melodrama by Max Marcin; and *A Tailor-Made Man*, Henry Smith's comedy which made Grant Mitchell a star. In 1915, for his brother-in-law, Fred Niblo, Cohan wrote *Hit-the-Trail Holliday*, a mildly entertaining farce whose hero, a reformed bartender turned into a Billy Sunday type, helps bring prohibition to a small town. Shortly after this production, Cohan made three moving pictures of his plays, *Broadway Jones*, *Seven Keys to Baldpate*, and *Hit-the-Trail Holliday*, principally in a New York studio and all within seventy days. The experience did not impress him. The usual cinematic procedure of shooting the story out of sequence frustrated him and he said, "I am stage-minded, not motion picture minded."

On April 6, 1917, Woodrow Wilson signed the declaration of war against Germany, and show business true to its traditions prepared at once for entertainment service. On that day, Cohan was with his family in his Manhattan apartment. Contrary to a press agent's story, which Ward Morehouse repeats, of Cohan's writing "Over There" on the back of an envelope on his way into the city that morning from Great Neck, the song was actually written in New York City.* April 6 was a Friday and Cohan, like most Americans, took the news of our entry to the war in a mood of spirited determination that all would eventually be well. He pondered Wilson's announcement during his Saturday duties at the office, and that evening shut himself up in his study.

Cohan's daughter, Mary, to this day retains the vividest memory of the following morning. "Early that Sunday," she says, "Dad called us all together—we kids, and my mother. He said that he had just finished a new song and he wanted to sing it for us. So we all sat down and waited expectantly because we always loved to hear him sing. He put a big tin pan from the kitchen on his head, used a broom for a gun on his shoulder, and he started to mark time like a soldier, singing:

'Johnnie, get your gun, get your gun, get your gun,
Take it on the run, on the run, on the run;
Hear them calling you and me,
Every son of liberty.
Hurry right away, no delay, go today.
Make your daddy glad
To have had such a lad.
Tell your sweetheart not to pine,
To be proud her boy's in line.'

* In addition to the press release, Morehouse says he heard the story from Cohan. Cohan at this time divided his time equally between Manhattan and Great Neck and may have forgotten where he wrote the song. In any case, his entire family affirms the present story.

and then [Mary continues] he started to walk up and down, swinging one arm vigorously and singing even more loudly:

'Over there, over there,
Send the word, send the word over there,
That the Yanks are coming, the Yanks are coming,
The drums rum-tumming everywhere.
So prepare, say a prayer,
Send the word, send the word to beware,
We'll be over, we're coming over,
And we won't come back till
It's over over there.' "*

As Cohan marched energetically around the room, Mary became terrified: "We kids had heard, of course, that the United States was at war, and now here was Dad acting just like a soldier. So I began to sob, and I threw myself down, hanging for dear life to his legs as he marched, begging him, pleading with him not to go away to the war. I kept clinging to him until he stopped."

"Over There" became not only the most popular song of World War I but the manifestation of a perdurable American theme as well. As Cohan often said, he had simply dramatized a bugle call, but in its incisive notes and words he had also delineated something elemental in the American character—the euphoric confidence that the coming of the Yanks was the march of the good guys to effect infamy's overthrow. It was a conviction that Cohan did not have to assume.

Cohan's other contribution to the war effort was his participation in the war benefit play, *Out There*, by J. Hartley Manners, author of *Peg o' My Heart*, and Laurette Taylor's husband. An all-star cast including Miss Taylor, Cohan, George Arliss, James K. Hackett, Chauncey Olcott, H. B. Warner, Julia Arthur, and other leading players toured the play in May and June, 1918, for the Red Cross. Because of her connection with the playwright, Miss Taylor was understandably pivotal to the action of *Out There,* an overwrought drama of hospital life on the Western Front. One evening in Cincinnati, Miss Taylor, playing a nurse's aide, abruptly absented herself from the stage during a scene with several wounded soldiers (Cohan among them), a scene in which her presence was essential. Cohan, an adept at adlibbing, covered up for her during an interminable stretch. Miss Taylor returned and picked up the action from the point she left. Cohan assumed she had been ill.

At his exit in the act, Cohan asked the stage manager what happened and learned that Miss Taylor had simply strolled off stage to complain to the electrician that she did not like the lighting. Cohan's professionalism was outraged, and he tried to see her after the performance. She avoided him but finally he cornered her backstage. "Listen, little lady," he said, "don't ever do anything like that again. If you try anything like that again, do you know what I'll do?"

"She looked at me with those big wonderful eyes," Cohan told Ward Morehouse, "and she answered, 'No, what would you do, mister?' 'I'll tell you what I'll do, missie,' I said. 'I'll hop right out of that hospital cot and tell the audience the truth and then I'll go into a little song and dance and I'll waltz myself right off stage and down to the railroad station and I'll take the first train back to New York. And I mean it.' 'I guess you do,' she murmured a little timidly. Well, everything went smoothly for the next few days but there came a night when the lighting *was* definitely bad. Laurette was kneeling at the front of the cot scrubbing the floor and I caught her looking around a little questioningly. I leaned over and whispered out of the corner of my mouth, 'Don't try anything, kid. I've got the cornucopia of sand right under my pillow.' Well, she went off into a peal of laughter which must have been a little puzzling to the audience, but with that laughter, all the resentment I had against her vanished completely."

To celebrate the end of the war, Cohan thought it best to reaffirm old values by slipping into a familar groove. He wrote what one critic called a "typical Cohan drama of regeneration." *A Prince There Was* which opened in New York on Christmas Eve, 1918, shows distinct affinities with *Broadway Jones* and *Get-Rich-Quick Wallingford.* Again the protagonist, a man tending toward a dissolute life (drink, in this case), not only saves himself from near-perdition but improves the lot of everyone else in the play. The hero, a blasé playboy who made too much money too soon and early lost a wife, is charmed by a Barrie-esque child into bringing life and hope to the residents of a cheap boardinghouse.

A Prince There Was, from a story by Darragh Aldrich, began its theatrical life as a play by Robert Hilliard who created it as a starring vehicle for himself. The play proving uninteresting to out-of-town audiences, Hilliard asked Cohan to rewrite. Cohan did with such a vengeance, using his familiar Cinderella theme, that it became a new play, attaining a modest success on Broadway with Hilliard as the lead. The play had an interesting footnote. Years later, Hilliard lost a lawsuit against Cohan in which it was alleged that a contract to rewrite another play had been abrogated. George S. Kaufman, who attended the trial as a drama reporter, tells a savory Cohan anecdote stemming from it: "Mr. Hilliard was then a man in his sixties, white of hair and majestic in appearance. He had been an actor for perhaps forty years. Cohan, despite the lawsuit, was gentle with him. 'A nice fellow' was the way he described Hilliard, 'but stage struck.' "

Writing plays for friends was a Cohan innovation and not a good one. While writing *A Prince There Was,* he was approached by his good friend, the Irish tenor Chauncey Olcott who had made "When Irish Eyes Are Smiling" such a great success. Olcott asked Cohan to fashion a pleasant little comedy with a few songs in it. The result was *The Voice of McConnell* which duly turned out to be a pleasant little comedy with a few songs in it. Opening on Christmas Night, 1918, it ran only a month in New York but Olcott loved every minute. He played the role of a successful Irish tenor possessed of a winning way with both song and the ladies, the sum of every tenor's dream. *The Voice of McConnell*, like *A Prince There Was*, seemed a creative dead-end for Cohan. Repeating himself and writing to order was not a new horizon.

10. EQUITY

The year 1919 was the merriest and the saddest one of George M. Cohan's history.

In the watersheds of life, those moments of crisis when one's destiny is set, forewarning is rare. So it was with Cohan. By 1919 his reputation as one of America's greatest showmen was indelible; financially he was several times a millionaire. Cohan and Harris productions were very successful in New York and increasingly so on the road. The only gap in Cohan's life was that there seemed to be little in way of challenge for him theatrically. Temperamentally indisposed to serious drama, a feeling confirmed by the debacle of *The Miracle Man,* he had more or less traversed creatively the entire range of light entertainment.

He succeeded in making Cohanization of other playwrights' work a fairly pat formula, one which George Jean Nathan described as ". . . prefixing to each of the author's original speeches such phrases as 'By gosh,' 'Gee whizz,' 'I say, kid,' 'Oh baby,' 'I'll tell the world,' and 'You said a mouthful,' of adding a wealth of back-slapping and thigh-slapping to the stage business, of writing in at least one mention of a million dollars and one cheer for the United States, and of deleting twenty or thirty sides of dialogue and substituting pantomime." This is Nathan exaggeration to establish a point, but the point is well taken. Cohan had the gift of reducing a script to lively essentials in accurate American idiom, and Cohan-Harris productions of non-Cohan plays were critically regarded as models of theatrical function, whatever their inadequacies as dramatic art.

In early 1919, Cohanization was to acquire a deeper nuance, almost accidentally. Isidore Witmark who years before had published Cohan's first marketable song, "Why Did Nellie Leave Her Home?", came to Cohan with the manuscript of an operetta. Witmark liked the music but wondered about the book. Would Cohan evaluate the dramatic possibilities? Cohan, that rare professional who enjoyed reading even bad plays ("You can always learn what *not* to do," he explained.), took the script and promised an evaluation within a week. That night he read it and was unable to put it down. *Cherry Blossoms,* as its title threatened, was sheer fluff. It was indeed the worst operetta he had ever read, and its most serious defect was that it was not quite bad enough. *Cherry Blossoms* just missed being the supreme travesty of all Ruritanian operettas. Cohan resolved to rewrite it to suit his sense of robust whimsy and present a completely new play to Witmark. There was aptness in the idea; Cohan remembered how the Witmarks had rewritten the lyrics of his first song for him. It would be great fun to hand an utterly transformed *Cherry Blossoms* to Witmark with the comment, "I've touched it up here and there, Issy." The next morning Cohan called Witmark to say that a few revisions might be in order, and he would be happy to do them.

Cohan set himself six days in which to write a new play and six new songs. What he had to work with as source plot was the hoary tale of a Balkan-type prince in love with the fairest and humblest of his subjects. The prince assumes the disguise of a revolutionary firebrand who is threatening the prince's own kingdom, and at the proper moment, reveals himself and wins the girl. Determined to spare their audience nothing, the authors of *Cherry Blossoms* had not forgotten to install a gypsy encampment nearby the palace. Typicalness could hardly have been carried further, but it was Cohan who now proposed to do so with some merry subversions.

He took this hackneyed matter and, in his words, "twisted the story upside down, poked fun at the whole idea, turned the operetta into a jazzy musical," subtitling it "A Cohanized Opéra Comique." He retitled the play *The Royal Vagabond* after its leading character, Stephan, crown prince of Bargravia, who at the hest of his formidable mother, the Queen, is charged with destroying the republican movement in the kingdom. But Stephan meets the lovely Anitza, daughter of the local innkeeper, and instantly becomes the leader of the rebels in order to be near her. As he says, he came to put *down* the revolution but for her sake, he'll *start* one. Stephan's *nom de guerre* is Ferencz, and his affable tutor, Professor "Hoppy" Hopkins, assumes revolutionary guise under the name of "Horrible Harold." As confidant-raisonneur to Stephan, Hoppy, speaking in lively slang and gagging without let-up, bears an understandably uncanny resemblance to George M. Cohan.

The Queen's strong right hand is Colonel Petroff, head of her crack troops, also charged with the responsibility of hunting down the rebels. Most of the action centers around three couples—Stephan and Anitza, Petroff and the princess Stephan is supposed to marry, and Hoppy and the Queen's lady-in-waiting. The three couples bounce in and out to create the mild complications needed until they all fall into a state of engagement simultaneously. The resolving action of the play is the successful conquest of the Queen's loyal troops—with a large amount of cash.

Hoppy, as the Cohanic wise guy with heart of gold, inevitably has the best lines in the play. Typically, in the third act, he enters arm in arm with his inamorata and is moved to versify his love:

He sipped the nectar from her lips
As neath the moon she sat,
And wondered if ever a man before
Had drunk from a mug like that.

His lady marvels at his ability to think up such things, and Hoppy replies, "It isn't a matter of thinking *up,* but you've got to think *back* a little to get them as old as that." Theatrical and intratheatrical gags proliferate. His girl says that he really should have been an actor, and Hoppy coolly asserts that he was, although not as good an actor, he admits, "as Louis Mann or Corse Payton." (Payton was universally regarded as the worst actor in America.) At one point, when reminded of a Bargravian tradition that the king-elect must play a trombone while he is being crowned, Stephen scorns the idea but Hoppy says, "I'm in favor of it. I know a lot of trombone players that should have been crowned years ago." This is the cue for the pit drummer to make a gallop sound effect and Stephan asks Hoppy if that doesn't sound like somebody approaching on horseback. "Well, not exactly," says Hoppy, "but it makes a pretty good effect at that."

The most interesting thing about Cohan's use of intratheatrical device in *The Royal Vagabond* is that it is never top-heavy or overused. The play begins with it, in an opening number, "Tra La La," which epitomizes all Student Prince opening choruses in operetta history. Seated before the picturesque inn, clinking beer steins, the Boys and the Girls sing lustily:

"Tra la la la, tra la la la
The villagers sing tra la la.
In every comic opera it's got to be sung . . .
The villagers, the Hes and the Hers
Are there when the tra la la occurs . . .
The lyric would make you laugh, ha ha!
For *that* we pay the royalties

They sing in fifty different keys . . .
Here comes Chefchik, the keeper of the inn.
There's got to be an inn . . .
Or a comic opera can't begin."

Fun though this kind of parody is, and it is well sprinkled through the play, it is never obtrusive. The hokey charm of the colorful costumes and the Alt Wien love songs is carefully retained and resolutely honored. Heywood Broun, among other critics, was much struck by this artistic discretion of Cohan's: "To carry the burlesque too far would make it difficult for the audience to feel a sufficient interest in the love affairs of the characters to receive their melodic protestations of love in a sufficiently mellow mood. To have held his satire in check would have impaired the fun of the piece. Cohan has showed no hesitancy in shifting the mood from humorous disbelief to sentimental interest with entire suddenness but this seemed feasible enough . . . Personally we found no difficulty in smiling at the iconoclastic words of an opening chorus and promptly became interested in the question of whether the disguised prince would succeed in winning the beggar maid."

Isidore Witmark was more than slightly overwhelmed by Cohan's reworking of *Cherry Blossoms* but he saw its great potential after an initial period of protest. The script was not flawless when it went into production, and during a road tryout, Cohan had to do hurried rewriting, once while the cast actually awaited on stage during dress rehearsal for a revision. But when *The Royal Vagabond* opened at the George M. Cohan Theatre in New York on February 17, 1919, it was an instant success. All of the sure-fire Cohan material was there in sharpened form except for the American flag, and that was compensated for by one of the play's themes, a democracy is better than a kingdom almost any old day.

There were no adverse opinions of the play. In the words of one critic speaking for them all, "the show is little better than the best musical comedy that has been produced in New York in years." One of the show's best songs, Cohan's lilting "In a Kingdom of Our Own," became a national favorite and is still heard. Indeed most of *The Royal Vagabond* defies time. It is a play not unfit for revival, pleasing as it does the sensibilities of those who love the sentimental and the ridiculous in goodly order and proportion.

From the euphoria of crafting *The Royal Vagabond* at the zenith of his professional influence to the one trauma of his life was the most precipitous emotional journey Cohan ever took. It was to leave its mark.

Sir Henry Irving has justly observed that the theatre must flourish as a business if it is to survive as an art. The theatre has probably been healthiest when its artists more or less managed their own affairs as Euripides, Shakespeare, Molière and Company attest. When middle-men and money-changers dominate, art inevitably subserves the commercial. This was principally the situation as the American theatre grew vigorously during the nineteenth century until World War I when there were approximately forty theatres operating successfully in New York. Theatre owners and producers were making money at an unprecedented rate. Unfortunately, a good proportion of their income was obtained at the expense of artists indispensable to the theatre—the acting profession.

Because actors, like all artists, tend to concentrate more on their work than its tangible awards, they have usually been easy prey for those in show business more concerned with business than show. In the American theatre of 1919, working conditions for actors were abominable: there was rarely a limit to the hours of rehearsal, actors were frequently not paid for the rehearsals, contracts could be broken at will (the producer's will), and instant dismissal of an actor without cause was also a managerial option. Frequently, actors who had worked hard and long in preparation for a production were casually dismissed after a successful opening night because they were no longer needed once the good press notices were garnered, and less expensive actors could be substituted. Or an actor after such a successful opening could have his salary reduced under threat of such a replacement. Actors furnished their own wardrobe. In 1919, the source of these inequities was the greed of most Broadway producers. Of their number, the Shuberts and Klaw and Erlanger were archetypal.

No one knew better than Cohan of the callous attitude toward actors exemplified in the working practices of these producers. No one deplored the practices more, no one demonstrated in action the rejection of such practices more than Cohan. Cohan actors were always well paid, both for rehearsals and performance, and Cohan's word, like his father's, was an unbreakable bond. But Cohan, great performer that he was, had not worked hundreds of tank towns in the grimy sweat of vaudeville and road shows to insure his own enlightened management just to abjure it, as he instantly assumed the striking actors of 1919 were asking him to do. He had become a manager by working twice as hard as any actor he knew, and he was willing to be double-damned if he were forced into giving up a jot of his hard-earned prerogatives. That the actors were not asking him to give up anything was not apparent to him. They were trying to tell him what he *had* to do, and that he could not brook.

The summer of 1919 began auspiciously enough. After the hectic work on *The Royal Vagabond* and an intense but satisfactory few weeks Cohanizing Rita Weiman's play, *The Acquittal*, in Atlantic City, Cohan was mightily but happily fatigued. There was always a special if strenuous joy in the reworking of a poor play into a playable entity. He put *The Acquittal* into storage for future presentation, and by August, he was ready for a good rest. His wife, unable to leave the children, insisted that he take a vacation. Toward that end she suggested Steve Reardon as the perfect companion for relaxation, knowing that Reardon had a talent for bullying her husband into rest. The two men decided to take a prolonged motor trip—first to Providence (Cohan's feud with his home town was over), thence to Chicago (Reardon always called it "Double Newark") to see friends, then to California without a single business detour. Cohan had been gone only a day when a strike hit the New York theatres the evening of August 7. He returned at once.

Actors had been attempting to organize in the American theatre for years. An English actors union, the Water Rats (Rats: "star" spelled backwards; "water," their holiday excursions were spent on the Thames) had an American membership called the White Rats which at one time was affiliated with the A.F.L. but the Rats failed because of E. F. Albee's bitter opposition. In time, a new group, Actors Equity Association, inherited the White Rats' A.F.L. charter. Most actors were sympathetic to Equity's aims which basically centered around the need to correct working conditions. It was Equity which called the strike on August 7, and half the shows on Broadway went dark that night, with more to come.

The summer of 1919 was a record-breaker for the box office. The professional theatre was big business that year, ranking fourth in the nation's industries, and the losses to producers when the shows closed were tremendous. They deeply resented the walk-out. In the early days of the strike their organization, the Producing Managers' Association, hid its anger in confident statements to the press that the actors would tire shortly and go back to work. What the producers did not realize was that the actors were thoroughly determined to stand united after decades of ill treatment. They used for their rallying call a parody of "Over There" which particularly galled Cohan:

> Over fair, over fair,
> We have been, we have been over fair.
> But now things are humming
> And the time is coming

When with Labor we'll be chumming
Everywhere.
So beware, have a care,
Just be on the fair, on the square, everywhere.
For we are striking, yes, we are striking,
And we won't come back till the managers are fair.

Even actors who had been well treated by management rallied to the actors' cause. Ethel Barrymore, seconded by her brothers John and Lionel, sent Equity a message: WHILE MY ENTIRE THEATRICAL CAREER HAS BEEN ASSOCIATED WITH BUT ONE MANAGEMENT [Charles Frohman] FROM WHICH I HAVE RECEIVED ONLY FAIRNESS AND CONSIDERATION, I FEEL THAT THE TRADITIONS OF MY FAMILY AND MY PERSONAL PREDILECTIONS ALLY ME LOGICALLY AND IRREMEDIABLY WITH THE MEMBERS OF MY PROFESSION IN THE ACTORS EQUITY ASSOCIATION. Stars like Eddie Cantor, Lillian Russell, Al Jolson, Marie Dressler, Frank Bacon, and Ed Wynn shared her feelings.

Not all stars did. Some leading players in an answer to Equity hastily formed the Actors Fidelity League, an organization clearly sympathetic to the producers. Many top stars were inevitably linked to producers in strong friendship. Mutual obligations were involved. None of the Fidelity League members, it need hardly be said, were experiencing the hardships of the rank-and-file actor. Prominent in the Fidos, as Equity members scornfully referred to the group, were such players as Willie Collier, Louis Mann, E. H. Sothern, David Warfield, Ina Claire, Janet Beecher, Fay Bainter, Otis Skinner, Mrs. Fiske, Holbrook Blinn, Charles Coburn, Alan Dinehart, and Laura Hope Crews. Equity members were stimulated to coin a few memorably bitter wisecracks about leading Fidos, the best probably the one which stated that an empty taxi drew up in front of the Friars and Louis Mann got out.

The Fidos did not think of themselves as renegades. The majority sincerely believed that as stars they were above unionism. They had worked hard to reach a certain career plateau where in eminence they could remain aloof from the problems of the workaday actor. If there was selfishness in this attitude there was also something of an American dream—work hard, get the big money, scale the heights where trouble can't touch. This Horatio Alger syndrome Cohan was not ashamed to share. Moreover, Cohan in 1919 was basically management. He had not thought of himself as essentially a performer since his youth.

When the strike began, *The Royal Vagabond* remained open for a time despite a depleted cast. Cohan and even Sam Forrest, his stage director, hastily took over roles, but when the musicians and the stagehands walked out, the show was closed. This was doubly irritating to Cohan because he had reason to resent the stagehands' union. Five years before when *Seven Keys to Baldpate* was moved from the Astor Theatre at 45th Street and Broadway to the Gaiety Theatre at 46th Street and Broadway, the stagehands' union insisted that the move made the production a road show, thereby requiring three additional stagehands. To the end of his days, Cohan remembered that.

There were other wounds for him. In Chicago, a Cohan-made star, the urbane Grant Mitchell, led the road company of *A Prince There Was* out on strike, an especial blow to Cohan. But the deepest affliction Cohan suffered in the strike was the fear it caused his family.

"What a lot of people did not know at the time," Mary Cohan says, "is that my dad had to hire armed guards at our house in Great Neck to protect us. His car was frequently followed and once we were terrified when shots were actually fired at our house." Cohan could take anything in the way of recrimination but a cowardly attack on his family sealed his opposition to Equity. An instinctively stubborn man, his resentment of the strikers became implacable.

As August continued, the Producing Managers' Association began to waver. More and more theatres were closing at a rate of loss management found most uncomfortable. Sixty shows in rehearsal for the fall season were canceled. On the other side, Equity began to build its strike fund with successful all-star vaudeville presentations and, in general, public sympathy was with the actors. Cohan vowed that if Equity won, he would quit the theatrical business and run an elevator, to which his friend, Eddie Cantor, retorted, "Somebody'd better tell Mr. Cohan that to run an elevator he'd *have* to join a union." Cohan ultimately reconciled with Cantor because he knew Cantor's comment was understandable in the circumstances. What Cohan could not understand was the hedging attitude of his fellow managers.

When, in the second week of the strike, the producers began to talk among themselves of giving the actors their way, Cohan resigned from their association. The Fidos immediately asked him to accept their presidency, and he agreed. Proof that Cohan at heart realized the justice of Equity's claim is manifest in the contract which he prepared and offered on behalf of the Fidos to the producers. It contained satisfaction for every grievance Equity had stated. What the new Fidos contract lacked, however, was teeth. Enforcement of claims arbitration was so vaguely specified as to be worthless, and when the new contract was made public, Equity duly pointed out the inadequacy.

Cohan became obsessed with the idea that the Fidos should speak for actors everywhere. At one of the first Fido meetings, he offered the strike treasury $100,000 but this was rejected because it would seem to be money from management, as indeed it was. Cohan kept demanding that the money be taken and the Fidos reluctantly kept rejecting it. At one Fidos meeting, Cohan grew adamant. "I insist that you take it," he told the assembled actors, "and if you don't, I will give it to the Actors Fund, and I will give another hundred thousand, and then another, and another, and another, and another, and another, until we put the theatre where it ought to be. That's the kind of little guy I am!" Wild applause followed, and the money was given to the Actors Fund, the principal theatre charity.

Max Eastman, then a writer for the liberal magazine, *The Liberator,* attended that meeting and marveled for his readers at Cohan's fervent speech. "You can not help doubting whether Cohan is really as silly and egotistical as that looked," Eastman wrote. "And it will be to the benefit of our moralizing to assume he is not. The one sincere thing about him is his indignation. He is stung and hurt and angry and a little painfully bewildered to find himself in so unpopular a position. It is because he really had idealism and a kind of philosophy of life. It was the philosophy of generosity and good friendship and benevolence. And that philosophy and that mode of life—likable as it may be—always breaks down completely when it comes to a conflict between economic classes. Friendships are disrupted, gratitudes are forgotten, generosity is rejected—everything gives way to the formation of a clear line of conflict between the workers who produce the goods and the capitalists who take the profits. And George Cohan will have to readjust his whole philosophy of life completely—so completely that he can realize that actors who owe him gratitude for individual assistance, are right in fighting against him . . ."

Cohan never changed his philosophy very much in the years to come although there is much in Eastman's sensible assessment with which Cohan sympathized inherently. But not at the time. Passions ran high and Cohan, because of his great visibility, became the target of numerous barbs. William Harrigan, actor son of Edward Harrigan, the man Cohan so admired and in some part modeled his career on, sent Cohan a wire: BOTH OUR DEAD FATHERS WERE GREAT MEN. MINE IS SLEEPING PEACEFULLY IN HIS GRAVE. I'LL BET YOUR FATHER HAS TURNED OVER IN HIS BECAUSE OF YOUR TREATMENT OF ACTORS.

There was, however, one small but penetrating voice on Broadway which spoke up for Cohan, an objective voice. Johnny O'Connor, a leading reporter for *Variety,* was sickened by the indiscriminate attacks on a man he regarded as the theatre's principal benefactor. O'Connor felt so strongly on the matter that he personally paid for a full page in

Variety, and in the slangy style that characterized his reports on the Broadway scene, attacked Cohan's detractors. In an open letter to the acting profession, O'Connor said:

> George M. Cohan, until this strike broke, was on a pedestal theatrically. The old-timers loved him. They should. The newcomers admired him because the old-timers educated him. Cohan couldn't be wrong. Cohan was a square guy . . . Three weeks ago if someone put Cohan on the pan to the average showman, he either went away with a good bawling out or a busted face.

After numerous instances of Cohan's unfailing generosity to all members of the theatrical profession, O'Connor came to date:

> But—the strike came along. Cohan, now off the stage, retired as an actor, was a manager. The very fellows whom he had helped, the very fellows who called him "Georgie" and bragged about knowing him when he was a chump kid, the very fellows who at one or another time had only Cohan between them and the morning pork chops, started to yell "scab" at the top of their voices.

After defending Cohan's right to appear in *The Royal Vagabond*, O'Connor discussed at length the virulence of the attacks on Cohan as epitomized in the intemperate Harrigan telegram. To O'Connor, it did not make sense:

> Why pick Cohan? The only one of the mob on the other side of the fence who ever really did something for the actor. Plant the panning where it belongs. Tell the whole world what you think of managers . . . but remember George M. Cohan was always a square guy, is a square guy now, and all the panning you birds slip along won't change a square guy's makeup . . . In my opinion, George M. Cohan has more manhood and guts

to the square inch than the entire area of all those he is sticking with and all those who are panning him contain . . . For a curtain speech: BE SQUARE WITH A SQUARE GUY. KEEP BATTLING, BUT BE SQUARE WITH A SQUARE GUY.

One of the thorns in Cohan's flesh which stuck deeply was the abuse hurled at him by a few prominent members of the Lambs and the Friars. He resigned from both clubs forthwith. There was an uproar of protest over his treatment by levelheaded members of both clubs. Tremendously distraught at his resignation, a majority of the Friars' membership gathered and marched in a body from their clubhouse to the Cohan and Harris Theatre with a plea for Cohan to reconsider his decision. Cohan was not only a great contributor to Friars activities but also served as their chief officer, the Abbot. As the men gathered on stage, William A. Brady, the producer, eloquently asked Cohan to return. Deeply moved, Cohan replied, "This is a wonderful compliment, what you fellows are doing, but I want you to know that I am with my associates, the fellows who helped me get to the position that I've got today." Individual Friars, most of them long-time friends, pleaded with Cohan but he remained firm. The men walked sorrowfully back to the clubhouse.

Cohan never gave in to Equity, but his fellow managers fought only until their pocketbooks well and truly hurt. When the giant Hippodrome, home of super-spectacle shows, closed because its 412 stagehands walked out, the managers conceded. They signed an agreement with Actors Equity Association recognizing the union as the sole representative and bargaining agent for the acting profession. Equity's grievances were fully recognized and on September 6 the four-week strike ended. The theatre was the ultimate victor. The actors had gained, management had benefited despite itself, and there was general hope that all bitterness had ended.

Cohan swore he would never become an Equity member. Nor did he. As the years went on, he would joke that he was the only scab on Broadway. For the rest of his life, although every actor in each of his productions was an Equity member, Cohan performed without the standard contract. When he worked for producers other than himself, he signed a memorandum stating the amount of salary plus the time commitment, and that sufficed for legal obligations. Nor did Equity ever insist—as it could have—that Cohan sign their contract.

In later years, Cohan felt a sense of loss. Indeed what he had lost was considerable. "Were it not for this backsliding," says Abel Green, "Cohan today would still be the patron saint of all actors because he was the most versatile man on the American stage . . . a 'right' guy, a fast man with a buck." Years after the strike, John Meehan who was also Cohan's general stage director for a time found his boss one night with his guard down. "Johnny," Cohan said, "about that strike—if one actor, just *one,* had ever called me up and said, 'Georgie, we're going to pull that show of yours at the Cohan but we don't mean you,' it would have made one hell of a lot of difference."

Arvid Paulson who had acted for Cohan over a wide span of years, like many actors who knew Cohan well, asserts emphatically that Cohan acted not out of perverse pride but on a matter of principle. "There was no vanity there," says Paulson. "His conscience told him what to do. He was just not the kind of man to act in any other way." Shortly before his death, Cohan, sitting with his crony, Gene Buck, over a convivial glass grew unnaturally silent for a minute. "You know, Gene," he said, "there comes a time in a man's life when every circumstance of his training and his background make him absolutely go a certain way. That's the way it was with me and Equity. I'm sorry it happened, but I couldn't *help* it happening."

Equity, it would seem reasonable to hope, might also feel a diminution of bitterness over the years since 1919, and indeed there was one significant indication that the old wounds were on their way to being healed.

On November 9, 1930, at a testimonial dinner for Cohan given by civic leaders of New York City at the Lotos Club, toastmaster Nicholas Murray Butler, President of Columbia University, introduced from the dais a man who had made a special request to speak. This was Francis Wilson, then in his late seventies, a former comic opera star and playright, founder and first president of Actors Equity Association.

The greatly-loved old trouper got to his feet. "It is impossible for me to tell you–," he hesitated a moment and went on, "how very grateful I am for this opportunity indeed–before the curtain rings down for the last time–to say that I yield to no man in my appreciation of George M. Cohan as an actor and a dramatist." Applause swept the room. "As a *man*," Wilson continued, "I cannot speak so authoritatively, because as you see, I have been the one who was denied the privilege of intimacy, so to speak. But I must say this: any man who can go on year after year, as George M. Cohan does, producing success after success for the entertainment, refreshment and edification of mankind; any man who, as Cohan can do, exhibits the capacity for the revelation of character whereby his fellow human creatures may better understand their lives, deserves the love and thanks of man and woman. And I hope I may ask you, without being refused, to rise to salute Mr. George M. Cohan as a public benefactor."

The banqueters arose, applauding vigorously, and the guest of honor, eyes glistening with tears, stood up and fervently took his courtly old opponent's hands in both his own. A knife had been lifted from Cohan's heart.

The knife would probably have been reinserted had Cohan lived to note that the example of Equity's chief founder in putting aside the past has not been taken up by some Equity officials in recent years.

Paul Dullzell, Equity's executive secretary in 1943, told Ward Morehouse that year that any Equity comments on

Cohan "could not be complimentary. Therefore, they are better left unsaid."

In 1958, a $50,000 fund campaign was begun by many prominent people in the American theatre to commemorate Cohan by placing his statue in Times Square. Max Gordon, the producer, approached Equity for a donation, feeling that perhaps the old feelings had diminished. Equity's executive secretary, Angus Duncan, sent $240 to the fund with a friendly letter stating, "There is no doubt that he was a dominant figure in our theatre . . . and so, the Council concluded that indeed the bitterness of the past should be forgotten—that a token contribution should be made in an amount equal to the cost of a life's membership in Actors Equity Association."

Oscar Hammerstein II, spearhead of the movement for the Cohan statue, returned the check to Equity with an angry note: *I remember the old situation very well indeed, and I do not dispute your right to continue a resentment so deep. I must, however, refuse to cooperate in pinpricking George's ghost.*

The next day, Ralph Bellamy, then president of Equity, said to the press that the offer was misinterpreted, that the money was not given ". . . in any facetious tone at all. It was offered in the best possible grace. My feeling," said Bellamy, "was that it all happened so long ago that if George Cohan were alive today, I'm sure it would have been forgotten and we would have been friends."

It would be pleasant to end the history of Cohan and Equity on this gracious note but in late 1970—fifty-one years after the strike—Frederick O'Neal, current president of Actors Equity Association, sent to the American Guild of Variety Artists a letter protesting A.G.V.A.'s decision to name its annual honorary awards "Georgies" in honor of George M. Cohan.*

* In a letter to me dated December 3, 1971, Harold H. Berkin, director of public relations for Actors Equity Association, says that ". . . any ill-feeling still held towards George M. Cohan is only on the part of a few individuals and not an official Equity attitude."

11. INTO THE TAVERN

The Equity defeat was etched in him deeper than Cohan realized, but he made a genuine effort to fall back into his previous life patterns. With a little urging from his mother, he rejoined the Lambs and the Friars. His immediate quarrel with individual actors was forthwith resolved. The man he made a star, Grant Mitchell, who walked out with the Cohan company in Chicago, was brought back into the fold at once. Even the man who sent him the stinging telegram, William Harrigan, was hired a few months later to appear in the Cohanized melodrama, *The Acquittal.* Cohan's argument had never been with actors individually. His argument at base was with the entire idea of unionism, and it was this which was to sunder the professional bond between Cohan and Harris.

If two men ever knew, loved, and understood each other, they were George M. Cohan and Sam H. Harris. Their personalities were almost identical. They had precisely the same sense of humor and were both genial, personable showmen of great integrity. In their professional relationship, their partnership was cemented by mutual need. Harris, the man with the keen fiscal sense, principally handled business matters. He began their partnership as Cohan's personal manager but in time the division of work was even: Cohan created the plays and staged them, Harris produced them. Their only disagreement, a growing one, and largely an unspoken one, was over the concept of organized labor. Cohan was instinctively a rugged individualist, and he had assimilated Jerry Cohan's almost romantic concept that show business belonged solely to the artist. Jerry, as the years went by, yearned more and more for the past, for a far simpler, and in his view more idealistic era of the theatre. One of Jerry's poems his son heard so much that he committed it to memory. Into these few lines Jerry poured most of his scorn of the increasing complexities and commercialization of the theatre:

For the Carpenter, now, not the Actor, is King!
And the Painter and Costumer, just the "real thing"
With their moving ensembles and scenic displays,
And electric effects that confuse and amaze!
For the mind, for the intellect, nothing remains,
Save a glittering, sensual show, without brains.
Not so in the past, when the Drama was "Art!"
When the actor and auditor stood heart to heart.
When salaries were meagre, but no booking fee!
When we rented—not shared—there's but one course for me,
Join a ten-twent-and thirt show of repertoire plays,
'Tis the closest we get to the "Bully old days."

For Jerry, the strolling player must go his way unfettered by the strictures of big business even if, as happened with his son, he *became* big business.

Sam Harris took a more sophisticated and pragmatic view of the expanding theatre. He knew the burgeoning growth of modern life would force labor increasingly to structure itself into self-protective brotherhoods and that it would be folly to defy this trend. When the Equity strike flared, Harris, although president of the Producing Managers' Association, felt an instinctive sympathy for Equity which few of his fellows shared. Some months after the strike, he and Cohan had a frank half-hour conversation in which Harris told his partner that the labor union was henceforth an inescapable part of the Broadway operation, and living with it was mandatory. Cohan disagreed, and the cliché "They agreed to disagree" was made operative. They were deeply saddened at the decision to dissolve partnership but they knew each other well enough to realize that such a basic difference in opinion was bound to have unfortunate results in the future. Broadway was shocked at the Cohan and Harris announcement of separation. The partners considered it inappropriate to reveal the impelling reason for dissolution, and they agreed never to disclose it publicly. Many ridiculous rumors spread at once: Cohan and Harris had quarreled personally, their wives had quarreled, the Cohan-Harris business affairs were awry.

Cohan, in the one absolutely predictable pattern of his life, again announced his retirement from the theatre. This was inevitable prelude to his once more firmly entrenching himself in it a few weeks later. As in all his farewells to the theatre, he meant it very much at the moment; as in all his returns to the theatre, he acted as if he had never been away, as indeed he had not. He thought for a time that he would produce plays in London where Equity could not reach him, but his decision to remain on Broadway was principally triggered by reading a script, a dreadful script, which was to blossom into his finest work for the theatre.

Brock Pemberton in 1920 was acting as play-reader for Arthur Hopkins, and in the process of his duties Pemberton came across a script called *The Choice of a Super-Man*, by Cora Dick Gantt, a lady unknown to the theatre. Miss Gantt at the time she submitted the play to the Hopkins office was a forty-two-year-old stenographer for the Y.M.C.A. She had given the play to Hopkins because he was then considered the most advanced producer on the Broadway scene, and *The Choice of a Super-Man* was clearly not a run-of-the-mill play. What it actually was, Pemberton found hard to say, a sentiment shared by Hopkins who declined it but with puzzled respect.

Pemberton, knowing that Cohan had a taste for the unusual and enjoyed reading every kind of script, sent him the play. Cohan read it and was baffled. He put it aside, read it a week later, increasingly puzzled. He put it aside once again and as his bafflement grew, so grew his interest. He was particularly interested in the leading character, a mysterious individual known through most of the play as the Vagabond. Enigma was the stuff on which Cohan's soul fed, and as he thought about the Vagabond, he thought inevitably of his best effort in the theatre to date, *Seven Keys to Baldpate*, with its lardings of mystery. The plays were quite unalike but they were one in that they shared an atmosphere of unknown forces symbolized by a raging storm beating against an inn harboring an interesting roster of characters.

Finally, Cohan could no longer bear the burden of considering *The Choice of a Super-Man* as a potential property. "Brock," he said in a telephone call to Pemberton, "I keep thinking about that play all the time. It is the god-*damnedest* play I've ever read in my life. I don't know what the hell it means, but I simply can't get it out of my mind. Please tell Miss Gantt that I'm willing to buy it, lock, stock and barrel, and at a very fair price. But it must be clearly understood that once the play is mine, I am to have full authority to do with the script what I please."

Pemberton talked with Miss Gantt who was somewhat overwhelmed by the idea that Cohan wanted to buy the property but she was puzzled and slightly defensive about the idea of altering it. Notwithstanding, she took very little time to decide that she would sell if the price was right. The price was eminently right—$40,000, for the work of an untried author, at a time when the dollar was very sound indeed. Cohan took *The Choice of a Super-Man* and again put it away, again to ponder it.

Shortly after the Equity strike, George Jean Nathan, intrigued by the burlesque strains of *The Royal Vagabond*, asked Cohan to write a one-act burlesque on any topic he liked as a piece for *Smart Set,* the magazine which Nathan and H. L. Mencken were nurturing to success. Cohan had not written in the single-act form for years but he had always enjoyed the crafting of sketches and one-act plays. The charge to write a burlesque was needed comic relief from Cohan's travail of soul. The Equity confrontation had burdened him unduly and he turned to this job of writing with gratitude. The result was a classic one-act travesty on all crime plays everywhere, *The Farrell Case.* The play was first produced at a Lambs Gambol in 1919, then printed in *Smart Set,* October 1920.

The Farrell Case may well have a peer among one-act farces; it is not likely to have a superior. Seven pages long, it has thirteen specific climaxes, each indicated by the master cliché of emotion in all crime plays, "Good God!" The climax is always the culmination of a violent melodramatic turn set in a realistic framework which is dissolved in the final stage direction. *The Farrell Case* utilizes in very short order these crime drama commonplaces: stealthy entrance through a window; taking a loaded revolver from a desk and examining it grimly to make sure it is loaded; a telephone conversation in muffled tones; the placing of a jewel case in a safe; a breathless girl entering with a packet of mysterious letters—one of which is missing; the girl's revelation that the vital letter is missing, thereby causing a man drinking a glass of water to drop it on the floor in astonished horror; a stolen necklace; a query as to the whereabouts of a man who promptly enters unheard and unseen to say dramatically, "Right here!", a man who locks the door and refuses to hand over the key; a gun which does not fire and the cool comment of the one at whom it was aimed that he had removed the bullets shortly before; the nervous handyman with the comic brogue who admits that he has seen the murder but had not plucked up the courage to reveal it until now; the nervous handyman with the comic brogue who turns out to be a suave detective in disguise; the suave detective who is murdered for gain by a renegade cop; the daughter of the suave detective who swears she will avenge his death; the tempestuous wind, rain, lightning, and thunder which rage outside as the girl swears revenge—at which point *The Farrell Case* can best speak for itself in conclusion:

MISS FARRELL: [The suave detective's daughter.] (*Above the storm.*) I will leave no stone unturned to find the man who killed my father!

2ND POLICEMAN: (*At the window.*) Good God, what a storm!

MISS FARRELL: You shall be avenged, dear father—you shall be avenged!

1ST POLICEMAN: (*Hits the Farrell girl over the head with a club. She falls over the body of her father.*)

2ND POLICEMAN: (*Rushes at him.*) Good God, man, what have you done? Do you realize that you've killed the girl?

1ST POLICEMAN: (*Hits the 2nd Policeman over the head with the club and the latter falls over the body of the girl. There is a knock at the door.*) Come in.

(*An Old Man enters. The 1st Policeman shoots him dead and the Old Man falls near the door where he enters.*)

OLD MAN: Good God!

1ST POLICEMAN: (*Rushes to 'phone.*) Get me Police headquarters. —Hello! —Hello! Police Headquarters? —Send a man to the office of Berkley, Berkley and Berkley right away. Hurry! (*He pulls out a pistol and shoots himself in the temple.*) Good God! (*He dies at desk.*)

(*Madigan* [the suave detective] *shows signs of life and wriggles himself to a sitting position. Sees the dead men and stares in amazement.*)

MADIGAN: (*As he sees the dead men.*) Good God! (*He struggles to his feet, falls back again, but gets strength enough to drag himself over to phonograph which is upstage. He touches the spring and starts it playing a brass-band march, one of Sousa's. He faints after starting the machine. There is a sudden crash and the window is broken from the outside. A Policeman enters, gun in hand.*)

POLICEMAN: (*Looks around at dead bodies.*) Good God! (*Horses' hoofs and police patrol effect are heard offstage. Another Policeman enters from door upstage. The two officers stand and stare at each other, then both tear off their coats and start a rough-and-tumble fight. The orchestra picks up a gallop for a "Hurry." The two officers roll over and around the stage and finally work into an acrobatic act. Both are turning handsprings when Uncle Sam appears in doorway waving the English flag as*)

THE CURTAIN FALLS.

This excerpt is perhaps the clearest segment of the ten-minute play in which ten homicides, five of them off stage, occur. One cannot follow the plot, and that is of course the plot, the whole point of the pastiche. It is uproarious fun when played with the utmost gravity.

After he sent *The Farrell Case* on to George Jean Nathan, Cohan felt the first sense of relaxation since his busy days on *The Royal Vagabond* and *The Acquittal*. And it was with *The Farrell Case* fresh in mind that he began to contemplate Cohanization of *The Choice of a Super-Man*. In view of the turgidity of the material in the Gantt play, an apter description of Cohan's reworking would be hyper-Cohanization. *The Choice of a Super-Man*, in its quiet way, merits in full Cohan's description as the god-damnedest play he or perhaps anyone ever read.

Its plot essentially is the following:

Act I, Scene 1. A winter evening at a tavern on a highway

leading to a modern [1919] city. A number of people come in from time to time to escape the snowstorm which is blocking the roads and stalling cars. Old Wilyum the proprietor, Davy, seventeen, his son, and Mary, the young slavey of all work, welcome these strangers:

The Vagabond, cynic and self-styled fugitive from his own thoughts. A man of mystery.
Violet, a painted woman and harlot.
Eve Dedhart, forty, vain and haughty.
Julia Dedhart, nineteen, her lovely daughter.
Drylust, a middle-aged man.

After we meet the working personnel of the tavern, the Vagabond enters. Outside, he has just knocked to the ground a woman who has offered herself to him—"and for money," the Vagabond snarls. Violet, the shameless one, enters and opines that "It's a strange world, with all the odds against the women, and no chance for independence." The Vagabond, despite his abounding disgust with Violet and all women, tells Old Wilyum he will pay Violet's way. Drylust, fat, foolish and forty, enters with stylish Eve Dedhart and her charming daughter, Julia. Julia must marry Drylust for his money, and she despises her mother for forcing her into this engagement. The Vagabond identifies himself candidly as a wealthy, cowardly cynic who likes to play God. Indeed, God, he asseverates, *is* money because money is all powerful. The Vagabond bets Drylust $5000 that he will never wed Julia, tomorrow or ever. Tomorrow has been specified as the happy day. The wager is accepted. Eve Dedhart encounters the Vagabond alone and recognizes him as her great love of twenty years before. She spurned him then, and now they are coldly antagonistic. As to who or what he is now, the Vagabond says, "Once, long ago, I lost something that was precious. For a time I did not know that it was lost; and now I go about the world seeking it. That is my history."

Act I, Scene 2. Later that night. The stage is empty. From the rooms above is heard a voice crying for help, but it is silenced—as if by choking. (This is all that happens, making it perhaps the shortest scene in the history of drama.)

Act II. 4 A.M. next morning. To the accompaniment of the insistent snarl of the snowstorm and frightened screams, it is revealed that Drylust has been murdered in the night. Left alone, the Vagabond and Eve accuse each other of the murder. The Vagabond finally says that he will pay Eve anything she likes if they both agree to cease their mutual accusations. Mary, the lovely young slavey, states a major theme of the play. She has, she states winsomely, been at the tavern for some time and here she has seen all types of men and they are alike in this: they only want women who are either "beautiful or bold"—not women of substance. An old doctor summoned as emergency coroner is bribed by the Vagabond with $100,000 to declare the murder a suicide. Old Wilyum is bought off for only $10,000 to say absolutely nothing. This is not a hardship for a man of Old Wilyum's capacities. As the Vagabond proceeds to bribe everyone in sight to silence, Violet sneeringly observes that the circle of life is closing in on the women present: "Wherever we turn, we are confronted with the power of the male; it is his point of view, his morality, that dominate the world . . ." But the Vagabond's money is not enough to buy off little Mary who rejects the plea of all assembled to conform and say nothing of what she has seen and heard. (What she and the others have seen and heard is never revealed by the author, a serious dramaturgical flaw.) Mary is sent out into the snow by Old Wilyum, angered by her intransigence. The Vagabond rages at Mary but she goes out, unsullied. Conscience-stricken, Old Wilyum sends Davy after the girl to protect her.

Act III, 11 P.M. that night. The storm outside has diminished. The wind has quietened, and the snow now falls sedately. The Vagabond tries to appropriate Julia, sans marriage, but she scorns his male philosophy that her only stock in life's trade is her sexual worth. News is brought that plucky Mary has died fighting her way through the snow. Davy is heartbroken. The Vagabond condemns Eve for killing the passion of love in him which in turn let loose the force of murder—for, yes, he admits, he killed Drylust to punish his presumption. The policeman investigating Drylust's death is lurking nearby and overhears the Vagabond's confession. He rushes in to arrest the Vagabond but stands back in awed deference the moment he sees him. The Vagabond cannot possibly be the murderer, the policeman says to all, because the Vagabond is none other than Stephen Allen, the richest man in the world. Everyone, including Eve, is properly agog. The policeman, on hearing that Mary is dead and learning of the circumstances of her demise, declares that she must have been Drylust's murderer,* and so the case is closed. Mary surely did it, says the policeman: otherwise why did she run away? And, he continues, it would be clearly impossible for the richest man in the world to do such a thing.

The Vagabond and Violet decide to marry: she on the grounds that hereafter her knowledge of his crime will insure his good treatment of her, he on the grounds that his worst expectations of Violet could not exceed her actual vices. They leave, together with a fawning Eve. Just before she departs, Julia tells an uncomprehending Davy that the tide is too strong for them both. Davy and Old Wilyum are left to bicker over money, and as the snows desist, one of the tavern's regular patrons, a workman, who has heard of Davy's treatment of Mary, solemnly assures the boy that "there is something wrong."

CURTAIN

* In later years, Miss Gantt removed the quasi-allegorical element from the play by renaming the Dedhart family "Gerard" and Drylust "Marston." She also retitled the play *Our Betters* to sharpen its anti-masculine thrust. Under either title, the play was never produced.

As ridiculous as all this is, there is one underlay to *The Choice of a Super-Man* which is sadly authentic, a theme documentable now in this day of Women's Lib. Miss Gantt was speaking out of the frustrations of a woman living in an almost totally dominant male world, and this splendidly bad melodrama, for all its many incredibilities in situation and character, possesses something its synopsis cannot reveal—an intense, mordant dramatic power which at times almost belies the play's absurdities. Its pervasive theme of woman's slavery in our society was hardly new even in 1919, the year before women got the vote in this country. What is new and singular in the play is its leading character. Cohan's love of mystery was strongly piqued by this enigmatic, oddly compelling vagabond who roamed the world seeking his lost self.

In July 1920 Cohan began to write *The Tavern*, his reworking of *The Choice of a Super-Man*. He thought first of making it a travesty in the manner of *The Farrell Case* but he was also tempted to approach the material in a style totally new to him, a style best characterized as poetic whimsy. He set the play in the early nineteenth century, making the Vagabond a warm-hearted François Villon, who speaks of his life mission as "greeting the first flower of spring and finding where the rivers begin." At a tavern he encounters Violet, now transmuted into a romantic outcast. Drylust is altered into the governor of the state (carefully unspecified), a crusty man who once loved Violet in her youth. Julia becomes Virginia, the governor's daughter, affianced to Tom, the cold lieutenant-governor, whose political influence has put the governor where he is. The spine of the play was the focus of Violet's and Virginia's romantic interest in the Vagabond. The play was vibrantly melodramatic but yet gently humorous and suffused with whimsical romanticism. The Vagabond, for all his lighthearted, mysterious charm, was a serious character.

Cohan put this version of *The Tavern* into rehearsal at Atlantic City early in August 1920. For the leading role he forgot the experience of ten years before and selected Arnold Daly, a bit past his romantic zenith and grown somewhat stout, but still a superb actor. Daly's aberrant conduct during the Cohan and Harris production of *The Penalty* was forgiven handily.

As the rehearsals progressed, Cohan became increasingly dissatisfied with what he had written. It had small substance. The Cohan Vagabond had little character to project; he was essentially a cipher and his humor was too wispy. This Vagabond had no reason for existence other than to be vaguely, pleasantly, rather boringly mysterious. It was not enough. Moreover, Daly's waistline gave Cohan pause. It did seem a bit much.

In beginning a rewrite, Cohan thought of *The Farrell Case,* and it proved to be the keynote in refashioning *The Tavern.* If the Vagabond was to be mysterious, Cohan would make him the farthest reach of all men of mystery; if the play was to be melodrama, it must be the ne plus ultra of its kind. Cohan scrapped his entire script and, holding the actors in abeyance, began to write furiously.

12. THE TAVERN

Cohan put the new version of *The Tavern* into work after he had finished the first few pages, the cast plunging into frenzied rehearsals, receiving the script in installments. Arnold Daly was not happy with this piecemeal growth, but he recognized the fact of emergency. What the largely veteran cast found as they began work on the new version of *The Tavern* was a play unlike anything any of them had ever before encountered.

Characterizing a farce in written report is rather like describing a football game in hieroglyphs. The essential life and movement are sadly missing. But to the extent that words can convey the bustling activity of the final version of *The Tavern,* perhaps the following summary will serve.

The Tavern begins with three concurrent stage directions: *Thunder-crash, Pistol shot,* and *Howling wind.* These sounds complement the dialogue and action of the play throughout. Indeed the storm outside is perfect counterpoint for a play crafted to celebrate robust melodrama. Like the soft snow falling gently during the moody introspections of *The Choice of a Super-Man*'s third act, the driving rain, the thunderclaps and stark lightning flashes in *The Tavern* perform every bit as much as do the characters walking the stage. As in the old days of melodrama—the word originally meant "play with musical accompaniment" —the storm is the musical accompaniment, the equivalent of "Hurry music," "Stealth music," or "Climactic crescendo." The most frequently used stage direction in *The Tavern* is "*Crash*," employed every time the outside door is opened and frequently when it is not. These crashes serve as the exclamation points of dramatic punctuation, unrelenting yet never overdone.

The play is set in Zaccheus Freeman's rustic tavern, probably in the early nineteenth century. It is midnight. The stage is empty. Thunder crashes, a pistol shot, and the howling wind are heard. After eight seconds (a Cohan specification: he knew precisely how long an empty stage would "hold" with only sound effects), the large door upstage opens (*Crash*), and Zach, the innkeeper's son, enters with a load of firewood. He staggers to the fireplace where he deposits it. He calls for Sally, the little slavey of all work, and she enters to comfort him in his paroxysm of fear. (Zach and Sally are Davy and Mary transmuted from *The Choice of a Super-Man.*) Zach has seen the shadow of someone hiding in the woodshed and he is not sanguine about either this mysterious presence or the stormy night. "They do say that nights such as these bring courage to the blackest hearts," he assures Sally fervently. She suggests calling Freeman, the innkeeper, for help. Zach scorns this, determined to take the shotgun and search the shadows, when Freeman [essentially Old Wilyum from *The Choice of a Super-Man*] enters from above, and is told of the mysterious shadow. Freeman, a bluff, almost brutal figure, defies fear and takes his shotgun out into the night (*Crash*) to seek out the mystery of the woodshed.

Sally and Zach, obviously much in love, cling together as pistol shots ring out from the vicinity of the woodshed. On the stairs appears Willum,* the hired man, an energetic, un-

* The name but not the character obviously derived from Old Wilyum. In late 1920, Cohan's press agent released a story (subsequently believed by many, including Gilbert Seldes in his *New Yorker* profile on Cohan)

comprehending and obsessively curious dullard, who for the first time anywhere utters a question which was to enter the American idiom, "What's all the shootin' for?" Willum, aflame with unrequited love for Sally, is infuriated to see the lovers alone, and he threatens to tell Freeman that hanky-panky has flowered. Freeman (*Crash*) comes in out of the storm, his search unavailing. Willum tattles and Freeman orders him and Sally to retire. An argument over Sally erupts between father and son, the former scorning any female who comes undowered. Zach resists and is ordered to his room. (*Crash and thunder.*) There is heard an imperious knock at the door, and (*Crash*) in steps the Vagabond, a man of indeterminate age but clearly not a youth, high booted, and (as Cohan describes him) wearing "white shirt open at the throat, corduroy trousers, dark vest, long patched coat, large dark brown hat, long dark green cape, staff."

VAGABOND: Greetings, my friends. 'Tis a glorious storm, is it not? By God, gentlemen, it was worth being born to have lived on a night like this.

FREEMAN: Throw up your hands.

VAGABOND: What?

FREEMAN: Throw up your hands.

VAGABOND: What a childish idea.

FREEMAN: Throw up your hands, or I'll shoot.

VAGABOND: Shoot and be hanged. If you shoot, you'll kill; if you kill, you'll hang. That's the penalty, I believe, and so, my dear sir, if you have the insane desire to rid yourself of the responsibilities of this life, by a spectacular climb to the gallows, why not shoot someone worth while? It's *who* you murder that counts. That is—if you'd have the world celebrate the date of your execution. (*He turns up and leisurely surveys the room.*)

---

that *The Tavern* bore little if any resemblance to *The Choice of a Super-Man.* As in Willum's name, the derivations in *The Tavern* are minor but they are many. Enough, one would guess, to justify an M.A. thesis on the subject.

FREEMAN: (*After a pause.*) Who are you?

VAGABOND: (*Turns to Freeman with a laugh.*) Ha, ha, that's just it! Who *am* I? Who *was* he and why did the madman kill him? Those questions would be on everybody's lips. It would be a waste of time and ammunition. (*He takes a gun from his pocket and throws it in armchair. Freeman raises his gun.*) Don't be alarmed, it's the only weapon I ever carried—the only one. You may search me if you think I'm cheating.

FREEMAN: (*After a pause.*) What is it you want?

VAGABOND: A smile and a kind word, that is all I ask of any man.

FREEMAN: What sort of a man *are* you?

VAGABOND: A fugitive.

FREEMAN: A fugitive—from the law?

VAGABOND: No—from my own thoughts.

FREEMAN: Where are you bound for?

VAGABOND: I've arrived.

FREEMAN: Where do you think you are?

VAGABOND: Ah, 'tis well I know where I am. I'm at the beginning—and end of the earth.

FREEMAN: The beginning and end of the *earth?*

VAGABOND: The beginning and end of the earth. Wherever I am it's just that, for I never return to any spot until I've circled the globe, and so you see, my starting point is really my destination. (*Indicates with circling motion of stick.*) Do you follow me?

FREEMAN: Are you crazy?

VAGABOND: Yes, as crazy as you think I am—and as sane as you think you are.

FREEMAN: I don't understand you at all.

VAGABOND: I never met the man who did. But don't be alarmed. I'm harmless, quite harmless—I'm harmless as the little orphan girl that you threatened to turn from your door at dawn.

FREEMAN: What do you mean?

The Vagabond reveals that he has been outside, listening with delight to Zach's "manly protests . . . against the suggestion that he trade his name for lands and cattle." Freeman accuses the Vagabond of returning his warning shot in the shed but the Vagabond denies it, having indeed thwarted an attempt on the landlord's life by wresting a gun from the hands of a woman who even now lies fainting and prostrate in the shed. The Vagabond asks that she be given brandy, and Freeman (*Crash*) runs out into the night to see for himself.

Zach is left to guard the Vagabond with a shotgun but when wide-eyed Sally enters, the Vagabond asks that she hold him with the gun while Zach hurries off to get the brandy. This is cautiously done, and (*Crash*) Freeman enters bearing the apparently lifeless body of the woman. Brandy is brought and administered to her by the Vagabond, and they are both severely cross-examined by Freeman. She confirms the Vagabond's story: she fired at Freeman because she thought him a ghost in her dream. She is deeply fatigued by her long journey on foot to see the governor, and she still has fifty-two miles to go. Freeman scoffs at her story, more so when she admits that she has no appointment with the governor. She is going, she says, to demand a hearing. The Vagabond tries to defend her gallantly from the sneering doubts of Freeman. She faints and Freeman orders Zach to carry her to a bedroom. The Vagabond is in an ecstasy as Violet (for that is her fittingly chaste name) is carried upstairs. He exults:

VAGABOND: At last, at last, my dream's come true. All my life I've longed to be a hero. First I save the landlord's life and now I see the deserted maiden placed upon her downy couch where she may dream her dreams of vengeance sweet. By gad, what a night. It's a story book night for me. (*Crash*) What a storm! What a damn fool any man is to be indoors on a night like this. (*Crash*) Lead on, my boy. Oh, what a night! What a storm! Lead on, my boy! (*Zach carries Violet upstairs and the Vagabond follows them off.*)

Willum is ordered to go to the sheriff's house and bring him back at once. Willum persistently and impertinently inquires of Freeman, "What sort of a night is this, anyway? Thunder, lightning, shootin', screamin'—" and Freeman damns him, ordering him to go. (*Crash*)

WILLUM: (*Goes to window.*) No man can ride through a storm like this.

FREEMAN: You can and must.

WILLUM: If you don't care for my life, think of the horse.

FREEMAN: (*Pushing him out.*) To hell with the horse. Go, I say! (*Crash*)

The Vagabond and Zach come downstairs after making Violet comfortable, and the Vagabond charms the acerbic Freeman, much against his will, into providing him with a supper. Freeman is under the impression that the Vagabond is going to reveal his life story in exchange for the supper and when the Vagabond says it will be another man's story, Freeman calls him a blackguard. The Vagabond calls Freeman a liar, causing the landlord to point his pistol at him and demand a retraction. With steely disdain, the Vagabond says he is damned if he will.

FREEMAN: Take that back or I'll kill you.

VAGABOND: You're a liar, you won't. You haven't the nerve of a child. I dare you to shoot.

FREEMAN: (*Taken aback.*) You're a brave man, whoever you are.

VAGABOND: Well, not necessarily brave, for I happened to know that the gun was empty, you see. I saw to that when I disarmed myself a while ago.

(*Freeman laughs.*) I was sure it would amuse you. Damned silly, my pretended bravado, but I loved the drama of the thing.

The Vagabond asks Freeman to bring on the supper and roaring entertainment will be the landlord's reward—amazing card tricks, or perhaps the Vagabond's own ballad:

As big as a cow, as tame as a calf,
She settles the problems of life with a laugh.

The Vagabond sings this nonsense with outrageous self-assurance, stirring Freeman to hilarity. A forceful knock on the door is heard. Freeman unbars the door and (*Crash*) in steps Governor Lamson, Mrs. Lamson, Virginia, their lovely daughter, and Tom Allen, her haughty fiancé. Freeman is delighted, astonished, servile, and aggressively hospitable when he learns that this is indeed the governor of the state. The four newcomers have evidently been through a disturbing experience in addition to the perilous storm. The Vagabond treats them with unobsequious deference and he shows Virginia a gallantry she finds captivating, and Tom does not. The Vagabond dexterously draws out a secret the new arrivals have been trying to hide—they have just been held up on the nearby pike. Freeman shows his distinguished guests to their chambers as the Vagabond bids them an effusive and flowery good night. Virginia, going upstairs, asks the disdainful Tom, "Isn't he the quaintest man you ever met?"

Zach comes in (*Crash*) with the travelers' luggage and the Vagabond assures him that Sally will yet be his, and admonishing the young man to be quiet, the Vagabond falls asleep instantly in his chair. Freeman comes downstairs and tells Zach to wait on the road for Willum, and order him to hide the sheriff in the barn. The sheriff must not be brought into the tavern before the governor leaves in the morning.

Zach goes out (*Crash*) into the night and Freeman awakes the Vagabond to tell him there is a place for him to sleep.

> VAGABOND: Oh, am I to sleep? Well, I had no idea of sleeping—! Tired, weary, exhausted, driven from the roads by the downpour of the rain and the sting of the hail. Drenched to the skin and trembling with fear and cold. [*An intense speech he had given much earlier to describe Violet's sad condition.*] However, I had no idea of sleeping but—but—if you insist. (*Sings.*)
>
> As big as a cow and as tame as a calf,
> She settles the problems of life with a laugh.

This splendid *non sequitur*, lustily sung, causes Freeman to admonish the Vagabond to silence because the governor is at rest.

> VAGABOND: Oh, is he asleep already? (*Crash*) Ha, ha! Well, if he was, he isn't.
>
> FREEMAN: Hush, hush, hush.
>
> (*When the Vagabond reaches the stair landing: Crash. Vagabond looks toward Heaven, puts finger to lips and raises them toward ceiling three times, exits slowly upstairs. Crashes continue until curtain is down.*)

And the first act is concluded.

Act Two begins with an empty stage again, lightning, thunder crashes. It is two hours later. Virginia sneaks downstairs and cuddles up dreamily before the fire. Seconds later, the Vagabond comes down and surprises her. In quick humorous banter, Virginia learns that he likes her but ". . . that does not mean so much—for I do not like women as a rule." Virginia says again that he is the quaintest man she ever met. In reply to her request for it, the Vagabond thinks it unimportant that he possess a name because, as he observes, a name will not transform him into what he is not. He admits to being an enigma, and questions her closely about Tom whom the Vagabond suspects of being a villain. Virginia assures him amusedly that Tom is far from that. This news crushes the Vagabond because, as he insists, ". . . there's got to be a villain—so why not he?"

The Vagabond is also shocked to discover that Virginia chose Tom herself. The Vagabond cannot believe it: after all, her parents seem so satisfied with her fiancé. Unhappy because he now has no opportunity to fight Tom and release her from an undesirable match, the Vagabond ruefully and gallantly kisses her hand. At which moment Tom appears on the stair and barks out an incredulous "Virginia!" The Vagabond spins gleefully to the audience and shouts, "Ah, *ha!* The damned thing may not be a farce, after all!"

Tom and Virginia quarrel over Tom's possessiveness. "Bravo, my lass. I applaud your grit," says the Vagabond. (*Crash*) "Ah, ha!" he shouts, "even the elements enter into the spirit of the scene." Virginia's mother takes her away upstairs and the Vagabond faces Tom, greatly pleased at what promises to be a stirring dramatic confrontation. Surprisingly, Tom shows no rancor, apologizes for Virginia's flirtatiousness, thereby further depressing the Vagabond. Tragically, he says, "And is this all there is to be to the big *moment?* I hoped it would lead up to a strong dramatic climax. Ye Gods, is there no *drama* left in the world? (*Looking plaintively at the audience.*) Am I to meet with this disappointment the balance of my life?"

Suddenly Violet rushes downstairs, eyes ablaze, thrusting her keeper, Sally, aside. Violet advances to Tom and accuses him of being a black-hearted wretch. In supreme delight, the Vagabond assures the audience that it was worth being born to be thrilled like this. Violet continues her imprecations, telling Tom that "I'll have my revenge if I have to hound you to the end of my days." "By *gad,*" says the Vagabond approvingly, "I never heard the line read better. Beautifully rendered, dramatically correct. Go on, my lass, let's hear some more." Tom rushes to the Vagabond and warns him that if he is Violet's accomplice, he is dealing with a desperate man.

VAGABOND: Repeat those words again.

TOM: You're dealing with a desperate man.

VAGABOND: (*Hurt.*) Nothing like it, my boy. Do you expect me to rise to the situation when words are uttered in such a cold, colorless, mechanical way? Impossible. (*Tom stares at him in amazement.*) Come, put more fire, more vigor, more strength behind it all so that I may meet and combat the attack. Now, then, once more—the "desperate man" line.

TOM: Are you trying to poke fun at me? (*Raises his fist.*) If you are, by God, I'll—

VAGABOND: (*Delighted.*) That's it! Splendid! Now for my reply. (*Crosses to Tom who backs away.*) Take care, you kid-glove ruffian, or I'll thrash you within an inch of your life. (*Draws out the word "inch"—"in-n-n-n-nn-nn-nch." Taps Tom on the chest.*) See—that *means* something. Now go on with the play!

Tom is stunned at all this but before he can gather his thoughts Violet tells him scornfully that she is on her way to the capitol, to tell her story to the governor. The governor, at this moment, enters on the stair, and asks sternly *what* story she is going to tell the governor. The Vagabond, in a transport of excitement, says to the audience, "By *gad*, what a *smashing* situation!"

The governor identifies himself, and Violet faints. "Damn the luck!" says the Vagabond confidentially to the audience. "'Twould have been a great scene but for that!" Tom, convinced he is among lunatics, runs out the front door (*Crash*), greatly thrilling the Vagabond. Sally enters screaming, followed by Virginia and her mother. The Vagabond tells Virginia that she is rid now of the man she would have married of her own free will. He exults:

VAGABOND: Ah, what a night! What a delightfully dramatic night! And how fortunate that I should have happened here on a night like this. There had to be a hero. 'Twould have been a dull, old tavern without a hero tonight. (*Crash*) What a storm! What a storm! How I envy the man who is out in a storm like this. Clever dog, that villain, to have even thought of the idea. What a night! What a glorious storm!

The Vagabond helps Freeman take Violet upstairs, and on return the governor questions him closely, asking him the inevitable "Who are you?" The Vagabond's reply, one of the longest speeches Cohan ever wrote in a play, is Cohan's fundamental life view:

VAGABOND: Question number one: the inevitable "Who are you?" The answer is, I don't know who I am and if I did, I'd be the most miserable man on earth, for my greatest happiness lies in the fact that I occupy a most unique position—that of not having been cast for a part in the great world drama of life. (*Slight pause.*) I am a lonely, single-handed spectator sitting back looking on and laughing at the monkey-shines of the great all-star company of several billions of men and women who are unknowingly playing the piece for *me*. I am the audience, but a good audience, withal, for I laugh! I am the audience, and if I may say so, a highly intellectual audience, for in all the changing scenes of this ever-beginning, never-ending plotless plot, I recognize the spiritual hand of a great director, a master director, who has so skillfully staged this tightly woven, disconnected, tightly knitted spectacle of tragic nonsense, and so I am amused, and I laugh, and I applaud. (*Vagabond applauds.*) And if I'm any critic, it's a bully good show, and I hope some day to meet the Author, and compliment him upon his marvelous entertainment. Alas, I have no one with whom I may discuss the merits of the play, for all the rest are on the stage. I'm sitting out in front, alone, all alone. (*Turns to governor.*) Do you follow me, your Excellency?

GOVERNOR: Sounds like the ravings of a madman. I don't understand you at all.

VAGABOND: Of course, you don't. I'd have been horribly disappointed if you had.

GOVERNOR: Disappointed?

VAGABOND: Yes, disappointed that a man brilliant enough to have understood me should have wasted his time on an ordinary political career.

The governor, understandably, becomes more confused by the Vagabond as the interrogation continues, but it is Freeman's guess that both the Vagabond and Violet are members of the gang that held up the governor's party.

Willum (*Crash*) enters and says the sheriff has not been home all night—"and now that I've seen his wife, I wouldn't be surprised if he never went home," Willum says. He protests that sending him out this night was cruelty to animals: "The horse will never forgive you for sending her on a trip like that . . . What kind of a night is this anyway?" Violet screams from above, attempting to leap from her window. Freeman and the governor race upstairs to her. Zach guards the Vagabond, and the sheriff and his men (*Crash*) enter, carrying the fainting Tom. Tom is dropped in an armchair near the fireplace. The sheriff quickly learns of the doings in the tavern, including the governor's presence. The sheriff orders his men out to guard the tavern, telling them to shoot anyone who escapes.

As Tom slowly revives, Violet's voice is heard upstairs fervently describing how, as a schoolgirl, she was wooed, won, and ruined by the son of a millionaire. The Vagabond, thrilled at this heart-rending story, points an accusing finger at Tom who rises groggily. "And turned me into the streets," shrieks Violet, "to become what I am today. I'll pay him back. I'll pay him back! I'll hound him to his grave!" Tom, terror-stricken by these incredibilities, runs yelling out into the storm (*Crash*), and the Vagabond shouts exultingly, "Ah, ha! He's gone *again!*" "Who?" asks the sheriff. "The villain!" cries the Vagabond in delight.

The sheriff rushes out, and four pistol shots are heard. Freeman comes downstairs to learn that the sheriff has just left. Two more pistol shots are heard, and Willum rushes down in apprehension. The women appear on the stairs landing, and six more shots are heard.

WILLUM: What's all the shootin' for?

VAGABOND: (*To the audience.*) Sh-h! A big melodramatic moment: the ticking of the clock. (*Four strokes on metronome are heard.*) The dropping of a pin. (*He takes a pin from the lapel of his coat and drops it. Heavy thud offstage.*) 'Tis indeed a spell-binding situation!

The police (*Crash*) enter, carrying Tom exactly as before, and dump him down by the fire exactly as before. "I didn't want to have to shoot that feller again," says the sheriff, "but he just won't stop running away." The sheriff goes upstairs to look for a room secure enough to hold Tom, and Willum follows him plaintively asking, "What the hell kind of a night is this anyway?"

The governor's wife excitedly tells her husband that she is sure she recognizes the sheriff's voice: it is the man who held up their coach hours before. By a ruse, the governor on the sheriff's return, confirms his guilt. The sheriff confesses, and tries to explain his dereliction of duty.

SHERIFF: (*Utterly cowed.*) I'm not thinking of myself. I'm thinking of the wife and twelve children.

GOVERNOR: (*To Vagabond.*) He's thinking of his wife.

VAGABOND: Twelve children. Ye gods, did he *ever* think of his wife?

The sheriff is led off, and the incredulous Willum comes in to plead, "For the love of God, will somebody tell me what's going on in the tavern tonight?" Violet is heard screaming, and comes down to plead on the sheriff's behalf. He is, she assures all, the one man who has stood by her throughout her terrible grief and struggle. She cannot believe the governor's assertion that the sheriff is a crook. She pleads for his freedom—"for the sake of our child—the little child." "For the sake of the *child?*" says the governor incredulously. "Ah, ha! Thirteen!" says the Vagabond. "Poor, unlucky infant."

It is all too much for Willum who comes forward to ask whether everyone is conspiring to drive him crazy. "What kind of a night *is* this anyway?" he demands insistently.

"That voice!" Violet says icily, turning to Willum. "I understand it all now. *You're* the instigator of this outrage, are you? At last we meet face to face, you black-hearted snake!" She accuses the stunned Willum of abetting her downfall, of turning her into the streets, of being responsible for the fact that she stands in the market-place today. *But,* she shouts, "I'm going to make him suffer . . . degrade and destroy him. There's nothing I want but revenge! Revenge! Revenge!"

"For God's sake, let me out of here!" howls Willum, rushing (*Crash*) out into the storm. "Ah, ha!" shouts the Vagabond. "*He's gone!*" Six shots are heard outside. Upstairs Tom can be heard breaking down the door of his room, and he runs down the stairs to be confronted once more by a ravening Violet who again calls him a black-hearted wretch.

At this moment, at the exact moment where relief from

furious action is needed, a solemn, measured knock is heard at the door. "Open the door in the name of the law!" is the demand, and Freeman opens it to reveal a somber-faced man, a stranger to all, named Stevens. Stevens asks why the men outside killed the man who just left the tavern. Freeman cannot believe that Willum is dead.

STEVENS: Dead as a doornail.

VAGABOND: Dead as a doornail. Lucky devil, died as he lived.

The governor assures Stevens that the murderers will hang for this, but Stevens says no, he shot and killed them himself in self-defense. The governor, perturbed, asks Stevens who he is, but he is waved aside. Going to Violet, Stevens touches her on the arm and greets her softly by name. Violet turns, calls Stevens a dirty dog, a beast, a devil—and promptly faints in his arms. Violet, Stevens explains, is an escaped lunatic. She imagines that every man she meets is the cause of her downfall—a most interesting case. She heard the governor was to pass the institution (which Stevens heads) on his way to the capitol, and she decided to put her case before him.

STEVENS: She's the first patient to have escaped from the Institution for a long time.

GOVERNOR: You're lucky to have found her.

STEVENS: I should say we were—very lucky. They do get away sometimes, and they stay away, too. There's one patient been gone from up there over three years. They haven't found him yet. He got away shortly before I went to work there.

GOVERNOR: Gone three years, you say.

STEVENS: Yes. Harmless sort of fool. The boys up there tell me he was all right except on the subject of the drama.

FREEMAN: The drama?

GOVERNOR: (*Slight pause.*) The drama?

(*Vagabond, after a pause, rises, then goes slowly up for his hat, cloak and staff and starts for door. Freeman, barring the way, shakes his head "no." Vagabond turns appealingly to the governor, his hand outstretched, mutely asking for his intercession.*)

GOVERNOR: (*Pause.*) All right, landlord; he's a good lad, it seems.

VAGABOND: Thank you for those words, sir. (*To them all.*) I thank you all for a few hours of delicious, delightful nonsense. (*Turns to Tom.*) My humble apologies, my aristocratic friend. 'Twas my mistake to cast you for a villain. (*To Virginia.*) Marry him, Miss Virginia; he deserves it—for he's the quaintest man I ever met. (*Turns to Freeman.*) A word of advice, friend Freeman. Don't tear the young lovers apart from a fond embrace for fear of what might happen to a broken-hearted girl. (*Indicates Violet.*) Behold the sweet maiden of the woodshed. (*To Freeman.*) Promise me that you will not insist that your son shall trade his name for lands and cattle. Your hand. (*Freeman takes extended hand.*) Well done, sir! (*Turns to Sally and Zach on stairs.*) Sally—Zach—my blessing. (*Turns and bows to governor.*) Once more to you, sir. Goodbye and good luck to you always —(*bows to Mrs. Lamson*)—and to your most helpful wife—(*bows to Virginia*)—and your extremely charming daughter. (*He comes down center, throws his cloak over one shoulder with a grandiloquent sweep, turns, facing the door, his back to audience. Raises staff.*) Now then, Mr. Landlord, if you please. (*Freeman throws open the door. There is a TERRIFIC CRASH OF THUNDER as the door is opened.*) (*As he goes up:*) Ah, what a night! What a glorious storm! What a blessing to be free on a night like this! (*Dancing around and singing:*) Goodbye, my lass—goodbye, my lass!

(*Continual crashes until the Vagabond is well off stage. Freeman closes the door and leans against it as though tired.*)

STEVENS: (*Pause.*) Who is he?

FREEMAN: Huh?

STEVENS: That man—who is he?

FREEMAN: (*After a pause.*) Oh—just one of my lodgers.

SLOW CURTAIN

This is the play that Arnold Daly rehearsed by installments mid-August 1920, in a sweltering Atlantic City. He enjoyed the new characterization given the Vagabond. Instead of a vaguely romantic figure, the Vagabond now had bite and an abiding sense of humor, and the intratheatrical references Daly found particularly felicitous. In rehearsing and learning the lines almost sheet by sheet as they left Cohan's pencil, Daly looked forward eagerly to the inevitable grand climax of all this frantic bustle. When, however, he received the final scene and found that his dashing Vagabond was a madman, Daly was considerably deflated. It was not what he had been expecting.

The Tavern opened in Atlantic City and was enthusiastically received, relieving Daly's anxieties about the play's ending which he thought rather risky. Daly needed a success badly. Prior to *The Tavern,* he had spent two years in England, and he now wanted to re-establish American bases. Moreover, he was the victim of a growing dipsomania, and Cohan was paying him the largest salary he had ever received or was ever to receive, $1500 a week. The good reviews for the show in Atlantic City cheered Daly and he began to enjoy playing *The Tavern.* Like many behind the scenes, he was puzzled by Cohan's failure to claim authorship. He was billing the play as "The Cora Dick Gantt play," never explicitly stating that *The Tavern* was "by" Miss Gantt, a very fine distinction which understandably escaped most critics. Cohan did not intend to claim authorship until he could really be proud of the results, reserving for himself the right to revise further. As it happened, there was no need.

Atlantic City's leading critic, Will Casseboom, was greatly moved. He wrote, "When on the wings of rumor came the whisper that Arnold Daly was to make his reappearance on the American stage, there walked the wraiths of *Candida* and *Man and Superman,* and one speculated upon what manner of play it was that might challenge the mettle of such an actor. Speculation was set at rest last night at the Apollo Theatre when *The Tavern* made its appearance, but wonder grew as the thing unfolded bold-facedly, deliberately, fascinatingly, mordantly satirical, with the lash of Shaw and the geniality of Barrie. And a woman, a writer comparatively obscure in the theatre, was responsible for it . . . a panoramic satire of life . . . It is through the Vagabond's eyes that we see with almost excruciating clarity, the absurd and tragically futile processes which Sanity calls Life . . . Everything happens without rhyme or reason. What a splendid arraignment of life." Cohan grinned when he read the review and said to Daly, "I had no idea that's what I did. I guess I'm minor league Shaw now, Arnold."

John Meehan in staging *The Tavern* under Cohan's supervision directed the play so that its absurdities were manifest but not thrustingly obvious. The audience did not notice immediately that the characters were all costumed in different periods. Recognition came by degrees and made the fun all the richer. The Vagabond wore a 1790 wig, an 1840 cloak and coat, an 1812 hat and eighteenth-century boots. Mrs. Lamson was vaguely Civil War, and Virginia was attired as a modishly colorful Italian peasant girl. The sheriff and his men wore garments suggesting the Wild West. The *Variety* reviewer sent to Atlantic City, as a pro, recognized the costume plot's suitability to the play's spoofing framework and was delighted with it. He was especially taken with Virginia who enters without luggage, garbed as a sporty peasant in Act I, and comes downstairs in Act II in a modern tea gown costing hundreds of dollars.

Meehan made sure that the sound of the thunder came from thunder sheets that were clearly thunder sheets. Characters coming in and out of the rain were always obviously dry. That the play was a travesty, that it was meant not to be taken seriously, was apparent to all *The Tavern*'s out-of-town critics and audiences.

Not so, strangely, in New York. The critical reception from the metropolitan dailies was mostly hostile. There were certain irritations for the critics on opening night. The play began forty minutes late and the first act was played at a fairly slow tempo by the company because it was waiting for the many interruptions of laughter characteristic of out-of-town performances. The New York audience on opening night, September 27, 1920, with few exceptions took the first act most seriously. During the second act, laughter from a small coterie in the audience which had enjoyed the play loudly from the beginning finally ignited the rest of the audience but it was too late.

The majority of the critics were puzzled. They called the play "ponderous," "heavy," "dull." The prevailing opinion was that the joke, the spoofing, was too long delayed. The critic of the theatrical trade paper, the *Clipper*, spoke for many when he said, "Without question, it is amusing and clever, but it takes far too much time to get going." Alexander Woollcott said the sum total was ". . . quite disappointing—grievously so to those who had gone to the theatre in the simple faith that they were about to witness another *Seven Keys to Baldpate*. With that masterpiece, *The Tavern* does not deserve to be mentioned in the same breath . . . The first act does jog along as ordinary but faintly interesting melodrama. Later, as the evening wears on, the scoffing note enters . . . and the vein of nonsense running deep under the play bursts forth in a riot of fooling that is vastly entertaining." Woollcott also spoke of Daly's ponderous playing and of his being "injudiciously dressed."

Heywood Broun was also not amused by the first three-fourths of the play. Like most of the critics, he knew, despite the Gantt billing, that the play was almost all Cohan and, like Woollcott, Broun was expecting another *Seven Keys to Baldpate*. Broun was also considerably off-put by Daly's appearance as a romantic lead. "It is bad enough," he said, "that character after character must inquire 'Who is this young man?' when it is quite evident that it is not a young man, but a middle-aged actor in a blond wig, and even worse that Mr. Daly should be asked to sing snatches of song and to dance. With each thump, it seemed as if another nail was being driven into the coffin of a romantic character . . . We are perfectly aware of the fact that Arnold Daly is an exceptionally fine actor, but he must run ten times around the park each morning for many a day before he can again become a romantic figure in a costume play." Another influential critic, Alan Dale, complained that the play ". . . went so far as to burlesque itself," which is a bit like saying that tomato sauce is awfully full of tomatoes.

After the daily critics had their say, the little coterie in the opening night audience which howled at the play from its first lines had the opportunity to speak up. The coterie was tiny—just three young people, Robert E. Sherwood, Dorothy Parker, and Robert Benchley, then magazine critics. On opening night these three bucketed about in their seats, laughing immoderately and earning the haughty scorn of all around them.

A few days after the opening, in the drama column of *Life* which Benchley had inherited from Cohan's old enemy, James Metcalfe, *The Tavern* was given a review that few playwrights experience even in their most optimistic day-dreams.

"There can no longer be any doubt that George M. Cohan is the greatest man in the world," was the Benchley lead-off. "Anyone who can write *The Tavern* and produce it as *The Tavern* is produced places himself automatically in the class with the gods who sit on Olympus and emit Jovian (or is it Shavian?) laughter at the tiny tots below on earth. In fact, George M. Cohan's laughter is much more intelligent than that of any god I ever heard of . . ." Benchley pointed out that the process of disintegration from straight romanticism to travesty in *The Tavern* was so gradual that unsuspecting members of the audience were likely to take it seriously and think that, for instance, when Zach opens the door and, looking out into the howling wind-machine, says, "Father, no man could ride out on a night like this," or "When I marry, 'twill be for love," it is being said for the first time. Benchley even preferred the first act to the second because ". . . every line and situation in it can be either serious or burlesque, according to the individual powers of discernment of the listener. In the second act, even the most naïve of the newspaper writers felt the force of the burlesque and commented on it indulgently."

Benchley found almost incredible the criticisms that Daly was too old for the role and was too strangely costumed: "The only gesture on hearing these comments is to raise clenched fists to the sky, and the only reply is to shriek through the teeth. Of *course* Arnold Daly would not be young enough for the part if it were a serious part, but for the part of a mature madman who thinks he is François Villon, there is probably no one in the world (one has to be extravagant in speaking of *The Tavern;* it is an extravagant event)—there is no one in the world who could have brought the delightful and subtle burlesque romanticism into the play that Arnold Daly brings. Of *course* he was injudiciously dressed. No two characters in the play were of exactly the same period . . ."

Benchley pointed out that Cohan was entitled to be discouraged at *The Tavern*'s critical reception, and that the playwright might well have to return to his soft-shoe dancing which everyone could probably understand. Benchley was particularly enthralled with the performance of Spencer

Charters as Willum.* It is, said Benchley, one of the funniest parts ever written, accurately voicing "the query of the be-jazzed audience in his reiterated demand to be told 'What kind of a night is this anyway?'" Benchley burnt his critical bridges behind him by declaring flatly that *The Tavern* was to date "the biggest night in [my] theatregoing career, for it marked the birth of something *new* on the stage, a gorgeous insanity from which it is to be hoped the drama as an institution will never recover. And if George M. Cohan will run for President, this department will be dedicated to his service."

Dorothy Parker in *Ainslee's Magazine*, December 1920, was equally fervid in her declaration of love. She admitted that it was uncomfortable to be at variance with the regular critics, yet what is one to do but protest over the treatment accorded the best entertainment of the season? "There is nothing left," she said, "but to mutter sullenly that one may not know anything about art, but one knows what is perfectly great . . . an evening to look back on for the remainder of a lifetime. One, or at least, this one, which is what is usually meant by the person employing the word —has long dreamed non-Freudian dreams of a burlesque, built of a situation and speeches from all the particularly hair-raising productions that have gone before; Mr. Cohan has built his burlesque of these and has done immeasurably more by adding those masterly touches which no other living playwright could add . . ."

Mrs. Parker went on to describe the superb burlesquing of the character types, dramaturgical devices, sound effects and costumes, but concluded that her words were not up to the job of exegesis. "No, there is no use in trying to report it," she said, "the typewriter's touch is too heavy. All one can do is to throw awe of the newspapers recklessly

* Spencer Charters went on to Hollywood where he played a long line of bespectacled justices of the peace. He can be seen in the film, *Yankee Doodle Dandy*, as the stage manager in Walter Huston's solo dance scene at a theatre, just prior to George M. Cohan's birth.

aside, and proclaim that here is an entertainment sent from heaven, via Mr. Cohan. See it for yourself. See the whole company . . . show how to take a joke. And if *The Tavern* is not running by the time this comes out, write to your congressman and demand its immediate revival." George Jean Nathan loudly seconded Benchley and Mrs. Parker, calling *The Tavern* great stuff and defining it as "burlesque artfully tucked between the sheets of melodrama."

Cohan advertised these appraisals sufficiently to rally support for *The Tavern* at the box office.* It ran on Broadway for almost two seasons, with Cohan ultimately taking over the role which he had written instinctively for himself. Years later he described Daly's severance from the play.

"He came to me," said Cohan, "and said, 'George, when do we have a change of bill?' 'What do you mean—a change of bill?' I countered. 'This show will run a year longer.' 'Not with me in it,' said Daly. 'I'm through now.' 'Don't be silly,' I argued, 'if it's a raise you're looking for, we're friends—spout it out.' 'I'm fed up with the part,' said Daly. 'I'm going to do Ibsen and Shaw at Wednesday matinees at the Comedy Theatre.'

"And he did. Poor old Arnold—just before he was burned to death [1927], he telephoned me for $500. I knew he was drinking, so I sent him $250. The messenger hardly had time to reach him with the money when the telephone rang. It was Daly.

"'Thanks for the cash, George,' he said. 'But you forgot something.' 'What was that?' I asked. 'The I.O.U. for the other 250,' he said."

The Tavern was Cohan's favorite play. He played it on Broadway and on the road and later revived it for both New York and an extensive national tour in 1930. Lowell

* Cora Dick Gantt was surprised at *The Tavern*'s popularity. She always preferred her own play although, perhaps instinctively, she turned in later years to the writing of comedy. In light of the ultimate revelation about Cohan's Vagabond, it is sadly ironic that Miss Gantt died in a New York mental hospital in 1958 at eighty-one, after fourteen years' confinement.

Sherman and John Meehan each headed professional companies of the play on tour in the early twenties, and there have been many revivals since in stock, summer stock, and university and community theatres.

The play's most notable recent revival was by the Association of Producing Artists under Ellis Rabb's direction off-Broadway in 1962. Walter Kerr, like most of the critics, was struck by the play's unique vitality. "You know something?" he asked in the New York *Herald Tribune*, "*The Tavern* is not only a better play than I suspected it was, it is probably a better play than George M. Cohan suspected it was. Mr. Cohan was most likely only kidding when he took hold of a shotgun melodrama that had been thoughtlessly written by a Miss Cora Dick Gantt and then twisted its frostbitten ears until it yelled 'Uncle' and 'Murder!' and 'What's all the shootin' for?' . . . But there is something more in it—the sigh of a theatre man who has never been quite real, not even to himself. 'What does it matter who I am, as long as I amuse you?' asks George Grizzard in the Cohan role, with just a trace of uncertainty, and a faint taste of Pirandello, in his cocky smirk. 'Oh, I just love the drama of the thing,' he adds by way of explaining why he has taken the trouble to compound an inprobability that was already staggering in its firelit surprises and tumble-down-the-stairs terrors."

This is deeply perceptive criticism. Kerr goes direct to the underlay in *The Tavern*, amorphous though it is, which touches on Cohan's personality. Here, truly, is a man whose only world is the theatre because he has known no other, and although he wishes no other, the world beyond is there, faintly looming, almost threatening. Cohan would just as soon not think of that world and what he might have been in it. Cohan did not think of himself specifically as the Vagabond in the rushed days of the play's composition but when the need for a "philosophical" comment by the character seemed in order, Cohan had to refer for source to his down deep convictions both as a man and as a man of the theatre. These convictions are the nub of the Vagabond's long speech to the governor answering the question, "Who are you?" In the speech, Cohan cheerfully admits that he is not a part of the comedy that is life; he is very much outside it, fully enjoying its many hilarities, and with absolutely no desire to participate in them.

Kerr sees the speech as "a small, disturbing note of unromantic common sense which threatens to turn the plot reasonable for one moment." This "doubt within the delirium" Kerr does not want to make too much of (". . . it might frighten somebody . . ."), but it suggests to him "that there is also something here that is, or once was, strangely and specifically American: a confident, resilient, tall-story innocence come face to face with a world gone melodramatically mad." This innocence in confrontation with an increasingly complex world was, in precise fact, George M. Cohan's intellectual history from 1920 to his death.

The Tavern is not a masterpiece; its sheer brilliance structurally makes it a masterwork. It is intratheatrical device brought to apotheosis, and consequently it has special appeal to those behind and before the footlights who believe in entertainment at the essential theatrical experience. Its precisely crafted comic tensions hold from first to last curtain, and when well played—which means played seriously—there is no better American farce. It was written in three days.

13. THE TREADMILL YEARS

One afternoon in the early twenties, as Cohan was looking through the New York papers, it struck him that he had not seen his name in some time. This was not a spasm of vanity. Publicity is heart's blood to any showman and no one knew that better than Cohan. It was Cohan who first said to a newspaperman (who wanted some information about *Broadway Jones* in 1912), "I don't care what you say about me, as long as you say *something* about me, and as long as you spell my name right." That remark, in numerous variations, has been credited through the years to many men, but it was Cohan who said it and it was Cohan who meant it. On the particular afternoon when he was searching for his name in the newspapers, the sentence he uttered a decade before returned to confront him.

"Eddie," he said to his long-time press agent and general factotum, Eddie Dunn, "I haven't seen my name in the papers for a hell of a long time." "To tell you the truth, George," said Dunn, "you really haven't done very much in a hell of a long time." "Well, rumor me, rumor me," said Cohan.

This episode was symptomatic of Cohan's altered position in the theatre after 1920. He no longer had the keen business instinct of Sam Harris at his beck, and although Cohan did some memorable things in the twenties and thirties, it was Harris who ultimately went far ahead as a producer.

Cohan's first production after the split with Harris was *Genius and the Crowd* by John T. McIntyre and Francis Hill, a turgid comedy about a great violinist who is so bedeviled by women adorers that he plans to give up his career and withdraw into solitude with his secretary. She is a ravishing creature and he adores her, but does not realize this until his best friend clears the violinist's vision by inducing jealousy, whereupon the genius gets the girl and goes back triumphantly to his career. That such trivia should seriously occupy Cohan was an index to his growing uncertainty as to what would please the theatregoing public. Postwar America was a new world, and Cohan was never to be fully at ease in it. *Genius and the Crowd* had a stirring opening night in that Cohan (not the authors) was cheered by the audience, and he gave a charming curtain speech which ended with a little dance. The play was taken off after three weeks, which was more of a run than it merited. The general Broadway opinion was that Cohan without Harris was lost.

With Augustin MacHugh's *The Meanest Man in the World,* Cohan returned to producing the kind of play that nourished him. Its plot he loved because it was a plot he practically invented. A shy, soft-hearted young lawyer comes to believe himself a failure and is advised by his best pal that in order to be a success one must become a paragon of meanness. Determined to become the meanest man in the world, the young lawyer goes to a small town to collect a long-overdue debt, and discovers the debtor is a beautiful young girl caught in the financial toils of the town skinflint. The lawyer disavows his meanness, frees the girl, turns the town (in a key line of the dialogue) from a bum town into a boom town, and marries the girl. This was something more like a script Cohan could work on with pleasure. The MacHugh script, as Cohan admitted to a reporter at the time, had been soundly Cohanized. He usually kept details of his play doctoring to himself but at times and always with the playwright's approval, he would admit that he had Cohanized a show. This happened most often when he wanted to give a production an added boost at box-office pre-sale, as in the present instance. The reporter Cohan talked to about the show persisted in asking just what Cohanization entailed. Unable to answer without extensive illustration, Cohan uttered some generalities about seeing that the story was true to life and true to the rules of good entertainment. But one bit of news Cohan offered was that not a single play presented by Cohan and Harris in their seventeen-year partnership had remained untouched by the Cohan pencil. He refused to document the extent of his additions to the material.

Cohan always preferred to begin creating a show with his own material but when he found other sources for good entertainment, he knew how to use them. This could be almost complete alteration as with *The Choice of a Super-Man* or partial reworking as with *The Meanest Man in the World* or *The House That Jack Built,* a musical with book by Otto Harbach and Frank Mandel and music by Lou Hirsch that came to him in 1920. It was quite respectable artistically as most musicals of the time went but its authors knew that production treatment by Cohan would enhance the property. He did not alter the ostentatiously simple story very much: a young man loses his money, goes out west to regain his fortune, and strikes oil. The Cohanization consisted of a title change, to *Mary* (a title Cohan had been wanting to use for years), and intense reworkings of the dance numbers from conventional to the frantically eccentric. Cohan also demonstrated his gift for ingenious placement of actors onstage. The chorus, for instance, did not cluster casually around a principal singer as they did in most Broadway musical comedies; in *Mary* they were made to form an arrangement that was natural yet visually arresting. Choruses of the time were not accustomed to this careful attention. Above all, the cast was told to move onstage fast, move offstage fast, never to slow down.* In *Mary*, as in all his musical shows, the actors learned speed, not then a prime requisite for musical comedy pace. *Mary* played for many successful weeks in Philadelphia and Boston, and some of its songs filtered back to New York where they became great favorites with leading café orchestras long before the New York opening.

When *Mary* came to the Knickerbocker Theatre in New York on October 18, 1920, the critics were enthusiastic. It looked as if Cohan was not going to need Sam Harris after all. Robert Benchley said in *Life:* "It is quite obvious Mr. Cohan's strict directions for a musical comedy success are: 'Keep moving. It doesn't make much difference what you do, as long as you keep moving.' And they are pretty good directions, too. The thing has a plot involving . . . oil wells. But there is so much music and so much dancing that it really doesn't make much difference what the story is about. All you need to know is that it is a story that you can go home and tell without first having to send the children out of the room on an errand for Daddy . . . The fact that the song-hit of the piece, Mr. Hirsch's, 'The Love Nest,' had already become the national anthem before it reached New York does not seem to have dulled its appeal to any great extent. It simply means that the woman behind you is able to hum it the first time it is played by the orchestra, growing bolder with each encore, until she is with difficulty restrained from standing up in her seat and taking a curtain call for herself. It simply means without 'The Love Nest' accompaniment, you are thrown back for a loss of two weeks, all the time trying to sing the tune without its incredibly awful lyric. A good way to accomplish this is to keep re-

* Years after, George Jean Nathan, in speaking of George Abbott's reputation as the inventor of rapid directorial timing, said, "It was, many forget, the late George M. Cohan who first brought this quick-step species of direction into our theatre and who, long before Abbott, brought it to perfection. One of Cohan's very earliest productions, it should be remembered, was called *Running for Office*, and in it there was so much of the running that the office itself didn't show up until the last minute.

peating the words, 'Just a love nest, cozy and warm' over and over in place of the rest of the words which were written for it."

By mid-October 1920, Cohan had three solid hits, *The Tavern, The Meanest Man in the World,* and *Mary,* running on Broadway, and they ran well into the following year. It was just the time for him to produce a failure if the Broadway law of averages was to hold up. This inexorable law is that no man can produce hits without let-up, and Cohan verified it by succumbing to a weakness of his, a play tinged with mystery and featuring a compelling protagonist. *Nemesis,* unfortunately, was by the very well-known playwright, Augustus Thomas, who had expressed distress at Cohan's plot structure for *Seven Keys to Baldpate.* With that bright in his memory, Cohan never so much as dreamed of altering the Thomas play. This was a mistake. *Nemesis* traces the plotting of an old man, a wealthy and strong-willed cuckold, to revenge himself on his beautiful young wife and her lover. He kills his wife, and after securing clay impressions of the lover's finger tips, has them molded into rubber duplicates which are then stamped all over the furniture. The lover is convicted of the girl's murder and sent to the death house. The old man in the concluding scene stands outside the gates at Sing Sing at the moment of execution mumbling to himself on the glories of circumstantial evidence. If ever a script cried out for Cohanic satire, it was *Nemesis,* but it remained untouched, and played to quick failure.

It was enough to drive a man back into sure-fire formulas. The Harbach-Mandel-Hirsch team which produced the elementals for *Mary* came up with a not dissimilar effort Cohan refashioned into *The O'Brien Girl.* A poor stenographer splurging a small windfall at a fashionable resort meets a rich young man who finally convinces his haughty parents that the O'Brien girl is a gem without price. This was a plot old even in 1921 but the show's vitality impressed Broadway and *The O'Brien Girl* did excellent business.

17. Josie and George in *The Yankee Prince,* Knickerbocker Theatre, 1908.

18. George in typical dressing room stance; he disliked sitting down. He began to gray early, a hereditary not an environmental circumstance.

19. Jerry, George, and Tom Lewis in *The Little Millionaire*, Cohan Theatre, 1911.

20. Willie Collier and George in *Hello, Broadway!*, Astor Theatre, 1914.

21. Family birthday party, Great Neck, c. 1914. From bottom: Agnes holding baby George. To her left is Walter J. Moore, a family friend; behind him is Agnes' sister Alice, wife of Sam Harris, who is holding Mary on his lap. To his left is Helen; to his right is George M. Cohan; Agnes' sister Mrs. Dorothy Holland and Agnes' brother Raymond Nolan.

22. Some of the Friars in the Friar's Frolic, May 1916: Standing left to right—Andrew Mack, Neil O'Brien, James J. Corbett, Harry Kelly, Felix Adler, Harlan Dixon, George Daugherty, Vaughan Comfort, Johnny King, Tom Dingle, Eddie Garvey, Julius Tannen, George Sidney, Tommy Gray, Bert Levy; Seated left to right—Max Figman, Laddie Cliff, Will Rogers, Sam Harris, Jerry J. Cohan, Louis Mann, Fred Niblo, George M. Cohan, Lew Dockstader, Frank Tinney.

THE QUAINTEST MAN YOU EVER MET

Telegraph "The laughter swept into a huge round ball of screaming hilarity."

Commercial "The Tavern is one of the big hits of the season."

Mail—"Cast, acting and play excellent."

Times "The vein of nonsense is vastly entertaining."

Sun-Herald "The play attained an undeniable hilarity."

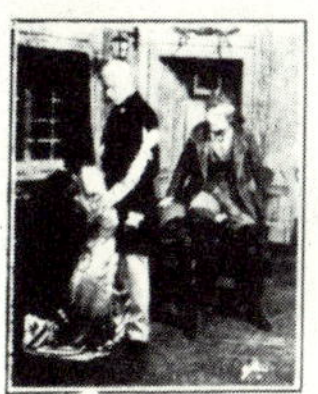

World "A mirth provoking entertainment. Cohanesque surprise finish."

Journal of Commerce and Commercial "Well worth seeing. The acting is excellent."

WHAT KIND OF A NIGHT, IS IT ANYWAY?

23. Center photo: Violet (Elsie Rizer) points an accusing finger at the Vagabond (Arnold Daly) as the Governor (Morgan Wallace) and Willum (Spencer Charters) look on aghast. *The Tavern*, Hudson Theatre, 1920.

24. Cohan as the Vagabond, *The Tavern*, Hudson Theatre,

25. Cohan as "Hap" Farrell, *The Song and Dance Man*, Hudson Theatre, 1923.

26. The subway scene in *The Merry Malones*, Erlanger's Theatre, 1927. Ruby Keeler is one of the girls but which one is anyone's guess.

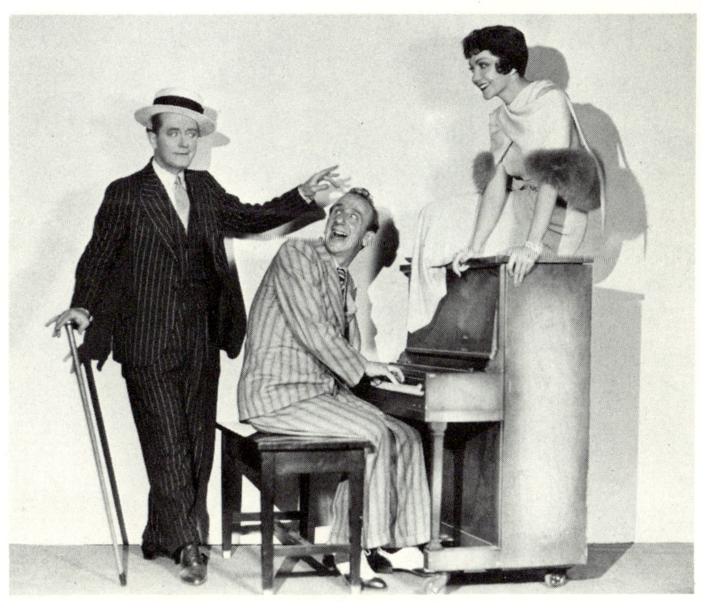

27. Cohan displays his showman's wares to Jimmy Durante and Claudette Colbert. A still from *The Phantom President*, a Paramount Picture, 1932.

28. The superb Edward Steichen rendering of the George M. Cohan-Eugene O'Neill coalescence for *Ah, Wilderness!* Taken for *Vanity Fair*, 1933.

29. Cohan as Magee the novelist faces a truculent "Boss" Cargan (Walter Hampden) in The Players' revival of *Seven Keys to Baldpate*, National Theatre, 1935.

30. Cohan, Daniel Frohman and Noël Coward in the 1930s.

31. Franklin D. Roosevelt presenting Cohan with a special Medal of Honor authorized by Congress for writing "Over There" and "It's a Grand Old Flag," 1940. (*Culver.*)

32. Cohan's last appearance. As the Vagabond in *The Return of the Vagabond*, National Theatre, 1940. In white dress at foot of the stairs is Celeste Holm. *(Lucas and Monroe Photo.)*

Cohan began to suspect that musical plays about pert young Irish girls had a considerable future when he interrupted himself theatrically to practice a pleasant if unfruitful act of nepotism. His daughter, Georgette, had expressed an interest in the theatre and to prove her worth had gone to London where she played Peter Pan. Well received there, she wanted to try Broadway, and Cohan was willing to abet her plan. He wrote a farce for her, *Madeleine and the Movies*, which had about as much substance as its title. Its scene is the apartment of Garrison Paige, screen idol, who is attempting to give succor to a pretty young stranger, Madeleine Madigan (again the Cohan jingle). Madeleine has burst into Paige's apartment terrified that her puritanical father and brother will do an injury to the actor. She has idolized Paige, and her closely guarded hoard of his photographs have been discovered by her family, convincing them of Paige's nefarious designs on their girl. The attempts of the two men to confront Paige, together with the comings and goings of miscellaneous film people (from Fort Lee, New Jersey) is the backbone of the play if anything so slight can be said to have anything so substantial. The good lines are few and they trade on Cohan's well-known affection for Jews, as: Paige when calling the studio at Fort Lee, asks: "Is Goldberg there?—No? Then give me Finkelstein.—No? Oh, well, give me Lesinsky.—No? (*Resignedly.*) Oh, all right, give me O'Hollaran." When the farcical complications of *Madeleine and the Movies* convolute at play's end into a Gordian knot, Cohan blithely cuts it with a cheat ending. It has all been a dream, the dream of Paige's butler who has been reading a script which details the action just seen.

It is, as Alexander Woollcott properly called it, a very little play, "something of an eighth key to Baldpate, or perhaps a play Cohan concocted out of some things he happened to find in the icebox when he was in a hurry." James Rennie played the film star but gladly stepped down after a few weeks when Cohan asked if he might play the role to force-feed a run. The play lasted almost three months and Georgette Cohan, in the undemanding role of Madeleine, showed genuine charm and ability as a light comedienne. It is hard to say what her future might have been had not marriage taken her from the theatre.

The *Madeleine* company rejoiced in the presence of Ruth Donnelly playing one of the wise-cracking roles she was to create so memorably in scores of Warner Brothers films in the thirties. Miss Donnelly has warm memories of Cohan with whom she also played in *The Meanest Man in the World.* "He was such a great man of the theatre, the great professional," she recalls today. "It was a joy to watch that timing of his. He knew to a half-second just how long to pause in the middle or end of a line to give it that special punch that would bring a big laugh. Offstage, he was charming, unworldly even—and you couldn't possibly guess that he was a man of wealth. He never went to any great social events in New York, and he had just a few friends, men like Steve Reardon. Men's men. Mr. Cohan always thought the real purpose of the theatre was entertainment, and I know if he were alive today and saw the things that are on Broadway and off-Broadway he would be absolutely appalled."

Cohan's tastes for entertainment, as he frequently said, lay principally in the musical play, and pleased as he was at the success of *Mary* and *The O'Brien Girl,* for him they lacked a vital element—they were not written by George M. Cohan. He was aware that by the early twenties the musical comedy had come a little distance from his breathlessly farcical confections of the previous two decades, and he set about trying to find new recipes.

In *Little Nellie Kelly,* one of the best entertainments of the 1922 season, he seemed to come up with a serviceable formula shaped in part on his recent work in the theatre. He wrote a time-worn love story of Nellie, lower-class Irish-American beauty, wooed by both a gold-plated playboy and a wise-cracking lad from the Bronx whose only gold is in his heart. Realizing that the plot was absolute cliché, Cohan kidded it with intratheatrical references. The New York *Times* critic noticed the device and its frequency, and how "Cohan resorts to the method of talking to the audience about his plot just at the time it really has begun to drag, and he promises to speed it up." Woven into the love story is an echo of *The Farrell Case,* a much-guyed mystery story involving Nellie's police captain father and an open-air detective (as distinguished from a *house* detective) who have something to do more or less with a vanished and recovered necklace. The critic of the New York *World* was captivated by the Cohanic mélange but found it hard to define: "This is not revue. Yet it is not conventional musical comedy. It is a little bit of drama, a great deal of comic pertness, a scenic delight and through all runs an almost continual strain of lovely music . . . Its dialogue becomes so serious at times you scent melodrama, and then one of the heavy dramatists burst forth in silly dance steps. There are moments of thrilling mystery and then the police captain looks at his wrist watch and dashes his pink handkerchief after the dignified matron who lost the pearls."

In sum, the phantasmagoria of hokum, and the show was dedicated lovingly and informally to Cohan's parents. It was not noted at the time that the charming leading characters, a sparkling young couple, were named Nellie and Jerry.

Little Nellie Kelly, for all its deficiencies, was a great success because it was great fun, and Cohan began to think of a little more of the same. On the way to his next musical, there were a few interruptions, the successful Cohanization of Vincent Lawrence's comedy, *Two Fellows and a Girl,* which opened on Broadway in the summer of 1923, and the continuation of Cohan's unsuccessful fight against Equity (the Fidos' membership had diminished in three years from 2000 to 150). All during these distractions in 1923, Cohan was quietly itching to get at another musical. In his anxiety to repeat the success of *Little Nellie Kelly,* he repeated rather too much of its formula. *The Rise of Rosie O'Reilly* (now all his titles seemed to jingle) continued what one critic called Cohan's amiable process of glorifying the Irish-American girl, but the process had become predictable and reminiscent. Arthur Hornblow shared most critics' affection for the show but he said that all Cohan shows now seemed to resemble each other: "Rosie O'Reilly looks like all her little sisters who have gone on before."

Rosie, who runs a flower stand under the Brooklyn Bridge, meets a young millionaire who marries her despite parental disapproval. So flagrantly tired a plot needed a great deal of help and Cohan gave what he could muster in the way of running reference to the plot's inadequacy. Jimmy, the play's raisonneur and well-cut in the mold of Cohan himself, speaks to the audience in the direct spirit of the Vagabond. When a character is summoned by telephone, Jimmy confides out front, "A handy little thing to have around when you're trying to get a character off the stage. Teasing tricksters, these play-builders."

The role of the cheeky millionaire who wins Rosie was played by Jack McGowan, who was to become a Broadway playwright and in recent years has been a leading screen writer. McGowan, today still trim and in good voice in his early seventies, was a Cohan protégé. "I first met George in 1914," McGowan remembers, "when I went to read for a leading part in one of his shows. Howard Gail of the Cohan-Harris organization had seen me act and he brought me to meet Cohan. 'No,' said Cohan to Gail about me, 'he's a baby. He won't do.' Then turning to me, Cohan said, 'Don't get me wrong, kid. I like babies but not on the stage to follow me in a part I wrote for myself. Is that clear?' 'No, sir,' I said. 'What?' 'I'm nineteen,' I said. Cohan replied, 'I'm thirty-six.' 'You don't look it,' I said. I sounded quite argumentative, but he laughed and said, 'You want to fight,' 'No, sir,' I said.

'Forget it, kid,' said Cohan, 'I like spunk but don't ring up when the overture is playing. Your timing's off. Come and see me when you're full grown.'"

McGowan did. In 1920, Louis Hirsch and Otto Harbach asked McGowan to disprove Cohan's contention that "The Love Nest" was too complicated to sing because it had an octave spread between the first and second notes. "George knew damned well it was singable," says McGowan, "but he enjoyed being convinced." McGowan sang it for him and Cohan liked the feisty kid who had now grown to young leading man stature. He cast McGowan for the juvenile lead in *Mary*.

"George would never fully direct his shows," McGowan says. "Sam Forrest or Julian Mitchell or Johnny Meehan would block them out and then George would take over, sometimes as late as two days before the opening, to give it his special touch.* He was very fond of saying to an actor, 'Now don't copy me but this is the way to do it,' and then if you didn't do it the way he did it, he'd say, 'I just *showed* you the way to do it!" McGowan roars with laughter at the memory. "But that's the kind of guy he was. He was quite a guy—a real guy. I remember that he called the entire company together once when I was playing the lead in *The Rise of Rosie O'Reilly*. I had been drinking before a performance. Because I was drunk and got mixed up, the actors opposite me had to jump the whole opening scene. George got word of it, of course, and after he had called the entire cast of the show on stage, he said, 'This is directed at Jack McGowan.' He looked at me and he said, 'I understand

* Selena Royle, one of Hollywood's loveliest character women, says of Cohan: "He was the only one I ever knew who directed a show with his feet. As a director, he would sit in the front row of the theatre, put his feet up on the orchestra rail and indicate by moving the left or right foot just where the actor should move. He always spoke the directions too, of course. Another funny thing. After giving an order or change in direction, he would say 'Gay-head, gay-head,' which meant 'Go ahead, go ahead.' We never knew why he used that particular pronunciation. He was an unusual man and he was a delightful man."

you've been drunk several times during the run. I'm going to London for a month, and when I come back—if I find that you've been drinking, you'll never work for me again.' Then he thanked the cast for coming, and he walked out. Well, Emma Haig who played one of the leading roles in the show came to me and said, 'Jack, he likes you so much but he won't put up with this. Come on. We'll keep busy—play golf, ride horses, keep active.'

"So George came back [McGowan continues] and he talked to me. He said, 'I hear you've been a pretty good boy.' 'You bet I have!' I blurted out. 'Well, don't brag about it,' George said, 'Emma Haig gets the credit for it.' And you know what Cohan did then? He took me out that very night after the show and got me drunk! That's the kind of great little guy *he* was."

Cohan was never much given to thinking about the kind of guy he was. Even in long, detailed interviews over the years, he was markedly reticent about his personal views. Granted that the early years of this century were not notable for candid journalism, Cohan was in any case not a man to expend opinion or venture confidences on anything other than his professional self. The same reticence marked his personal friendships. Indeed he had little to confide personally. A classic example of one whose life was his work, he rarely spoke of anything but the theatre because he was not interested in anything else.

Nevertheless, there was anticipation in many quarters that Cohan might reveal his secret self when Harper & Brothers announced in 1924 that they were publishing Cohan's autobiography, *Twenty Years on Broadway,* subtitled *And the Years It Took to Get There.* The titles should have been reversed. Of its 264 large-type pages, the first 200 take Cohan only up to *Little Johnny Jones.* The book makes clear that Cohan reveled only in memories of his earliest years. This was the theatre that interested, fascinated him. His autobiography does not mention his marriages, his children or anything that might give a clue to his inner person and one learns nothing of his personal tastes. *Twenty Years on Broadway* is little more than an extended feature article. It had one side effect. The writing of it put him in the mood for reminiscence and from this flowed his next play.

The Song and Dance Man is George M. Cohan's autobiography pulled inside out. Written simultaneously with much of his autobiography, the play is a projection of himself as he might have been. One day when Cohan was walking to his office, a vaudevillian his own age approached him for a loan and recalled the week when they had both worked the same bill as song and dance men. "I can't tell you how proud I am, Georgie," the old-timer said, "that you always keep referring to yourself as a song and dance man. I guess you aren't ashamed of it." "Ashamed of it, hell," said Cohan, "I'm proud of it kid, damned proud of it."

He demonstrated the intensity of that pride in *The Song and Dance Man*. He set his creativity to work on an interesting premise: what would have happened to George M. Cohan had he wound up like the vaudevillian who made the touch. Where would Cohan have gone if he had degenerated, in one of the play's key phrases, into a "hick trouper"? The answer seems to be that he would have remained in the theatre at any cost save the cost of deep friendship for a pal, but that inevitably he would somehow return to the footlights.

"Hap" Farrell of the team of "Farrell and Carroll—Songs, Dances and Funny Sayings" has been a hick trouper for seventeen years, a pronounced failure. At Carroll's death (exacerbated by the hardships of their life), Hap comes to New York where his own situation deteriorates. At a theatrical boardinghouse he finds Leola Lane, an actress who had been kind to his partner in his last days. Hap gives all his earnings to the poverty-stricken girl and is consequently forced to hold up a wealthy illustrator who easily overcomes the hunger-weakened vaudevillian. Hap tells his long, unhappy history so movingly to the illustrator and his friend, a theatrical producer, that they stake him to a chance in some other field than the theatre. Leola becomes a great success on Broadway, thanks to the producer, and Hap vanishes from sight after promising his two benefactors to repay their investment in him one day. He does so, in a few years, and with interest. Hap ultimately returns to his New York friends and reveals that he has given up his very well-paying job in the mining industry for the uncertainty and near-poverty of life as a third-rate song and dance man, for that is what he now realizes he was always and will be always. But for Hap, it is still heaven: ". . . My freedom . . . into the open. Back to my own."

Leola is by now engaged to the wealthy illustrator and has given up the theatre in consequence. But Hap (and Cohan) plead with her, "Don't you ever leave the theatre—there's no happiness for people of the theatre outside of the theatre—take it from me." Hap assures her that if giving up the theatre was torture for him, how much worse would it be for her, a success. Leola is convinced, and faces an uncertain but exciting future with Hap.

This hackneyed melodrama, with hardly a memorable line in it, proved to be an absolutely enthralling theatrical experience. For the first time in his life, Cohan controlled his audience's emotions with his sheer virtuosity as an actor, without music, or dance, or humor. This was a Cohan Broadway had never seen before—a quiet, reserved, serious performer able to ring changes, many changes, of pathos in a banal role. When the production was on the road, Hap was originally played by the versatile comedian, Lynne Overman, who just missed extracting full values from the deeply sentimental passages. Cohan, realizing both a personal opportunity and the need to buttress a weak show, took over the role prior to its Broadway opening at the Hudson Theatre on New Year's Eve, 1923. Additionally what he was bringing to Broadway was an implicit tribute to Jerry Cohan, an honoring of the indomitable troupers who year after luckless year continue in show business because their love of it precludes their ever dreaming of anything else. Jerry

Cohan, lacking the son he had, would have been a Hap Farrell, remaining all his life in the tank town circuits. And happily, as the nickname attests.

Alexander Woollcott for the New York *Herald* said that *The Song and Dance Man* sounded as if Cohan "had written it on the back of an envelope while he was waiting for the barber," but like all the critics, Woollcott was surprised "to find how deft, how artful, how quiet, how winning and how gently pathetic a comedian is George M. Cohan." Heywood Broun of the *World* said that the play confirmed his long-held suspicions that "producing and playwriting were diversions and digressions in the career of George M. Cohan, actor . . . Perhaps the most illuminating thing which can be said for Cohan's performance is that he by no means merely plays himself. He is cast as a bad actor and he does it so beautifully that you believe him."

In the final chapter of his autobiography where he discusses the general reaction to his appearance in *The Song and Dance Man,* Cohan says, "And now comes the big laugh of the story, the real punch to the tale. The actors admitted that I was a *good actor*. Gosh darn it! Why did they keep me waiting so long? Well, anyway, at last I'd come into my own. My dreams had all come true. My highest ambition satisfied at last. Hurrah! I'm a good actor!"

Despite this genial sarcasm, Cohan's pride in the theatre's "discovery" of him as an actor was strong. He was, indeed, and to the very end of his days remained a song and dance man, but the thought that he was also a respectable "straight" actor gave him much pleasure. This was one of the reasons why he turned in the mid-twenties to the writing of non-musical drama. Additionally, Cohan was becoming aware, apprehensively aware, that a new world was building. It was a world much different from the one he loved the most, the world of Rector's, Weber and Fields, Lillian Russell, Nat Goodwin, Ned Harrigan, and the Four Cohans . . . 1925 was a time when the word "sophistication" in the sense of "worldy wise" began to appear increasingly in talk and print as a cachet of distinction. Cohan knew that he had to keep up. His musicals had always been *au courant* in respect to American slang and argot along Broadway, but what Cohan saw as the second decade of the century progressed was a deep national change. He knew Broadway was changing with it, and it was a change in more than language. "In the raucous twenties," says Brooks Atkinson, "nothing turned out to have been as simple and sublime as Americans had assumed. The truth was less uplifting than the realities. Since the truth rejected traditionalists, it liberated young people who were sick of cant. 'Bunk' was the freshest word in the vocabulary."

But "bunk" was a word Cohan found hard to use. (He did, in fact, use it only once, in his last play, in the 1940s.) Cohan had virtually been a pioneer of slang in his plays but the newer words had an uncomfortable biting edge to them which he did not favor. Still, he tried. He kept up to the extent of referring liberally to "booze" and "bootleggers" in *The Rise of Rosie O'Reilly*. *The Song and Dance Man* contains phrases like "I get you," and "ukulele fiends" and "isn't this immense?" But these were only appurtenances and protective covering. Cohan was set immovably in 1910 although he tried hard not to show it. The success of *The Song and Dance Man* seemed to offer him a new creative pattern, that of non-musical melodramas and comedies in modern guise which could be sustained despite their weaknesses by the strength of his acting or the skill of his staging. For the rest of the decade and well into the next, he wrote and staged plays adhering to this pattern.

American Born (1925), *The Home Towners* (1926), *The Baby Cyclone* (1927), *Whispering Friends* (1928), *Gambling* (1929), *Friendship* (1931), and *Confidential Service* (1932) are typical of these plays, so alike in attitude and form that one can only wonder at Cohan's uncharacteristic doggedness in persisting at such uniformity for so long and with such scant rewards artistically. He was never afraid of formula but it was not like him to prolong it when it failed to work. A capsule view of the plays in this category indicates their slightness:

THEME	TYPICAL CRITICAL COMMENT
American Born	
COMEDY. An American inherits an English estate which he visits in hope of selling.	"A play that would not last a week out if Cohan did not play it himself." (Alexander Woollcott). "I enjoyed it though I felt a little mortified for having done so." (Percy Hammond).
The Home Towners	
FARCE-COMEDY. A middle-aged Hoosier comes to New York for an old friend's marriage to a young girl, and tries to break up the romance because he considers the girl a gold-digger. He is proved wrong.	". . . some of the largest and longest cuds of meditative jocosity Mr. Cohan has ever allowed to be chewed on the parade grounds of his humor." (Gilbert Gabriel). "Ungainly, ill-shaped and barren . . . [yet] . . . Mr. Cohan writes in a familiar and congenial idiom, with all the versatility of a circus showman." (Brooks Atkinson).
The Baby Cyclone	
FARCE. "Cyclone," a Pekinese spoiled rotten by his mistress, is sold impulsively by the henpecked husband who comes to regret his action.	"Cohan, the old wizard, made something out of nothing . . ." (Richard Watts). "A not very subtle plot . . . you would not believe could possibly fill any stage from 8:45 to 11:00. But Mr. Cohan is a master of padding." (*Theatre Magazine*).

THEME	TYPICAL CRITICAL COMMENT
Whispering Friends	
FARCE. A couple just back from their honeymoon are suspected by two close friends of marrying only for mutual convenience. The friends are proved wrong.	"An extremely turgid play, inflated by its own dialogue . . . more than a bit confusing . . . the talk has little of Cohan's crispness or flavor . . ." (N. Y. *Times*).
Gambling	
DRAMA. A gambler attempts to track down the murderer of his adopted daughter after the police fail. The girl's boy friend confesses.	"Like the play [Cohan's] acting is transparently tricky but, for all of that, warm and endearing." (Brooks Atkinson). "One of the palest of Cohan plays . . . Cohan plays winningly, admirably . . ." (Arthur Pollock).
Friendship	
DRAMA. A widower has supported a night-club hostess for three years during which she has improved herself culturally. She believes he does not love her but after a brief engagement to a younger man, she and the widower find each other.	"Frequently tedious . . . generally untidy drama . . . but Cohan is a joy to watch." (John Mason Brown). "The First Actor glows in a play that needs glowing." (Percy Hammond).
Confidential Service	
DRAMA. On her commission, a private detective investigates for a lady her husband's private life and discovers his adultery with her best friend. The detective resolves all complications.	"Mr. Cohan makes a most genial detective in a most obvious little domestic drama." (Chicago *Tribune*).

These plays, perfunctory in concept and form, give the strong impression of a playwright trying desperately to be modern. Cocktails are amply and gratuitously in evidence, and there is bright, forced chatter lacking even the glitter of genuine tinsel. Worse, the dramaturgical construction of these Cohan pieces from 1925 to 1932 is makeshift. There are too many convenient telephone calls, too many people eavesdropping, too many characters fortuitously able to come into the scope of action when needed.

What these plays did have which made them enjoyable to many audiences both in New York and on the road was either the constantly growing beauty of Cohan's acting or the Cohan ability to invest the plays with such theatrical dynamics as to make them seem worthwhile.

Percy Hammond, the critic Brooks Atkinson has described as knowing more about the theatre than any of his colleagues, was disturbed by the anomaly of Cohan appearing in claptrap, especially claptrap of his own making. In 1931 after Cohan's appearance in *Friendship*, Hammond made a forthright request in the New York *Herald Tribune:* "I am one of those who have never asked a favor from Mr. Cohan, and I hesitate now to do so. I do not expect him to grant it, for it is a boon much too extravagant. Yet as a reluctant ambassador of several indigent playgoers it is obligatory for me to make a request. This is that he abandon such flimsy frame-ups as his late drama, *Friendship*, and justify his position as America's First Actor by appearing in a real play. I believe that while advancing as an actor, Mr. Cohan marks time as a dramatist, and that he does not realize that the gravies of yesterday should be changed to the sauces of today."

Cohan realized this only too well, but there was little he could do about it in view of his essential commitment to a 1910 point of view. The only other alternative was to appear in the plays of other people, and this he was not yet quite prepared to do. "Mr. Cohan's own old-fashioned entertainments, though they strive eagerly to be new-fangled," wrote Hammond, "are not the stuff by which a fine actor can perpetuate his otherwise substantial glories." Cohan was gradually becoming accustomed to being called a fine actor, and from the early 1920s, for the first time in his life, he had been pondering the imponderables of fine acting and what it should be. During a trip to France he saw Lucien Guitry act the role of Pasteur, and the event marked his own acting thenceforth. "I couldn't imagine any actor better than Nat Goodwin," Cohan said, "but here he was. The same ease and command of presence Nat had, but something else. A deeper reserve. Guitry never opened up but you always knew he had plenty to open up with if he so wanted. I don't understand a word of French but I knew everything Guitry was saying because he was saying it with his eyes and his posture and the way he listened to his fellow actors."

This description could be applied to Cohan more and more during the twenties, and to at least one actor Cohan helped to stardom. In 1926, Cohan was directing a play he had just Cohanized, Margaret Vernon's *Yellow*, and in a small but vital role he cast a young man not long from Milwaukee, Spencer Tracy. Katharine Hepburn tells the details: "It was a story I heard Spence tell often. At the time of that show, he was very worried because of medical problems with his son, and of course he was very determined to make good for Mr. Cohan whom he idolized. Rehearsals were going badly and seemed to be getting worse. Cohan was giving all the actors except Spence a very hard time, but Spence wasn't fooled. He *knew* Cohan was watching him in such a way that it was only a matter of time before he was fired. In any case, Spence had a very big speech at the end of one scene, and at one particularly disastrous rehearsal he had to give it when he was most upset and worried. Still, he struggled through to the end of the speech, thinking to himself 'Why doesn't Cohan come right out and fire me? Why does he have to torture me like this?' After Spence finished his speech, there was an awful silence out front. Then Cohan came slowly down the aisle, looked Spence straight in the eyes and said, 'Mr. Tracy, you are the best actor I have ever seen.'" That was the day Spencer Tracy decided to remain an actor.

Tracy's acting derived essentially from Cohan. As Garson Kanin has pointed out, it was Cohan's "influence on Spencer's style that helped Spencer to evolve that remarkable relaxation, that seeming ease." Those who have never seen Cohan act can see it live again in Spencer Tracy's quietness, his powerful reserve. Indeed, Cohan found much of his younger self in Tracy—the self-confidence, the brashness on occasion, the Irish charm. So pleased was Cohan with Tracy's work in *Yellow* that he decided to write his next play for both Tracy and Grant Mitchell, another Cohan favorite. The result was *The Baby Cyclone,* a piece of fluff made memorable only by its acting and staging. Cardinal to the success of the acting in the play was a piece of advice from Cohan to Tracy. Larry Swindell in his biography of Tracy says that after one session which Tracy thought went rather well, Cohan pulled him aside and said, "Spencer, you have to act *less.*" It was a lesson long remembered and one that helped Tracy attain his eminence as the greatest American film actor.

The 1920s were basically treadmill years for Cohan. He watched others in his bailiwick of entertainment go forward. He saw the progress and steady growth of the musical play under such bright talents as Vincent Youmans, Richard Rodgers and Lorenz Hart, Jerome Kern and Oscar Hammerstein II, Cole Porter, and George Gershwin; in comedy, George S. Kaufman, Marc Connelly, Sidney Howard, Philip Barry, S. N. Behrman, and Robert E. Sherwood were writing plays which reflected accurately the growing sophistication of New York life. Cohan's only growth was in his acting, and while it took on deeper nuances of integrity, his playwriting was repetitive, and by the end of the decade it seemed he had even ceased to think of writing musicals. In 1927, he wrote *The Merry Malones,* much his same mixture as before, overflowing as Richard Watts said, "with all of the materials that have made the Cohan name eminent—the flags, the sentiment, the hokum, the persistent kidding of the plot, the Irish-American family humor, all managed with the most skilled of showmanship."

Cohan had by now almost made a fetish of denigrating his own musical plots before his audience or the critics could rise to do the job for him. In *The Merry Malones,* the juvenile goes to the footlights to sing:

"Ev'ry little play has got a plot
So a little plot this play has got,
Though it doesn't mean an awful lot
But still it's story. CHORUS: It's story.
It may be rot, it may be not,
But *that's* the plot!"

Burns Mantle amusingly sums up this plot: "Joe Westcott, of the rich Westcotts, loves Molly Malone of the Bronx so much that he is willing to give up a hundred million dollars and be a soda clerk just to sing duets with her." Cohan does not fail to include a comic mystery element and a gag-dropping detective. Yet for all its inconsequence, *The Merry Malones* has charm, several delightful songs, and much lively dancing. In a theatre which today finds great entertainment in a revival of *No, No, Nanette,* there should surely be a place for *The Merry Malones* and its robust humor.

There were a few flashes of humor during its rehearsal which might well have been left in the show. In helping the director stage the production, Cohan encountered one actor who was having memory difficulties. "Mr. Cohan," said the actor spiritedly, "I know these lines. I know them *backward.*" "And, son," came the reply, "that's just how you're saying them." Still flubbing minutes later, the actor came down to the footlights and said to Cohan almost indignantly, "Look, I knew these lines in bed last night." "Props!" ordered Cohan. "One bed!"

Cohan's last musical production was *Billie* (1928). A musicalization of his old play, *Broadway Jones,* it was pleasantly received but some of the critics were almost defensive about its old-fashioned quality. Arthur Pollock of the Brooklyn *Eagle* said that one may know "how quaint and of yesteryear it is when I tell you that the chorus men act manly." Although it is not quite contemporary musical comedy, Pollock thought, it was nice to have around even if sometimes it got to be pretty thoroughly old-fashioned. Pollock was struck by the innocence of Jackson Jones, the hero: ". . . a boy very eager about living. Mr. Cohan evidently goes to the theatre very little these days. The author must have got him out of his own head."

Which, of course, is where he came from. Jackson Jones was Cohan of two decades before, unchanged. For Cohan the world was still, or still should be, 1910. The critic of the Boston *Evening Transcript* wondered that Cohan would "have no traffic with jazz, though he syncopates plentifully and is as fond as ever of the short rhymed line set to a crisp rhythm. The sophisticates may deride, the Europeanized mock. Nobody expects them to see *Billie*." The Boston critic stood up defiantly, a shade too defiantly, for Cohan musical comedy. He called it "an American institution, peculiar to this land which up and down it long cherished—the Cohanic musical play. Times change, fashions alter; but year in and year out, it keeps its public. A little more middle-aged, a bit more disposed to settle stoutly in its seats."

What the critics probably knew and were not saying, certainly what Cohan knew and said to only a few close friends, was that the Cohanic musical play had no chance to remain in a world whose innocence and optimisms it no longer mirrored.

14. NEXT TO CLOSING

Getting off the treadmill was not easy for Cohan. The past seemed to be receding at an ever-increasing rate; his old playwriting formulas were out of fashion and his new ones seemed to be too. His last real link with the past broke with the death of his mother in 1928 and he took the loss hard, displaying a bravery he did not feel. He felt rootless and nowhere more so than in his profession. In these circumstances, he did the only thing he knew which might work for him, revival of past successes.

He reopened both *The Tavern* and *The Song and Dance Man* for a brief Broadway run in May–June 1930 prior to a long tour of both plays in repertory. It was an eminently successful tour, and he was deeply touched by the opinion of Chicago's dean of critics, Ashton Stevens, who said of Cohan in *The Tavern:* "But over and around all this Cohan clowning was something else. Maybe it was what one calls 'romance,' what another calls 'glamour,' what yet another terms 'spell.' Name it as you will, that was there, too—that quality which you feel only in the Chaplins, the Chaliapins, the Gardens, the Lillies, the Fiskes, the Cohans. It is very difficult to describe because it is the quality of greatness."

After his tour and the short-lived production of his poorly received *Friendship* (in which his daughter, Helen, had a small role), Cohan was at ends loose enough to consider Hollywood. He had said frequently that he was not at all interested in films after his desultory experience with them in the silent days. He had even expressed his keen disappointment to Spencer Tracy over his young protégé's giving up the theatre for the artistically less rewarding world of motion pictures. But in 1932, Cohan was tempted when Paramount Pictures approached him for a role in *The Phantom President*, a film which under the present situation of Cohan's idleness was not easy to turn down.

Jesse M. Lasky, one of the few movie moguls Cohan respected, finally talked him into appearing in the film which was to center around an intelligent but dull presidential candidate, and his double, a charismatic medicine show man, who was picked to do the campaigning for his alter ego. Cohan thought the story had possibilities in that 1932 was a presidential election year, and he concluded a gentleman's agreement with Lasky that he would be involved in working on the script as well. He went to Hollywood with some degree of enthusiasm and was ready to begin work the day after arrival. He was told to wait. His arrival coincided with the eruption of a major power struggle among Paramount executives, and Cohan's friends in the studio lost. The emergent powers regarded the Cohan contract as something they would have to suffer through. Whatever their pangs, Cohan suffered more.

In an interview with A. J. Liebling several months later, answering a question as to whether he left his footprints at Grauman's Chinese Theatre, Cohan said, "I did not. I was so busy the first seven weeks trying to find out what it was all about and the last two weeks making the picture I was supposed to be making the first seven weeks that I didn't have any time to act like an important guy." What Cohan might well have said was that he was an important guy who had received rather marked short shrift. Gilbert Seldes details the treatment Cohan received at Paramount: "His motorcar was stopped at the studio gates—only those belonging to 'stars' were admitted; Cohan laughed that off. But when he was asked to write a scene into the script and then was rebuked for daring to offer a penciled manuscript to a nineteen-year-old supervisor, and given to understand that he was merely in competition with half a dozen writers in the studio, Cohan's professional pride was outraged. His contract expired before the picture was finished; he could have left things that way, but he said to the producers, 'I'm solvent, you're not,' and remained another two weeks." At the end of his tour of duty, Cohan said that if he had his choice between Hollywood and Atlanta, he would take Leavenworth.

Teet Carle, publicist for *The Phantom President*, recalled for *Screen Actor*, house organ for the Screen Actors Guild, another indignity heaped on Cohan in the name of publicity. At Paramount's request, Cohan had written a song called "The Country Needs a Man," thematic to the film, and Carle sought opportunities for Cohan to sing it on promotional junkets. Carle asked the Los Angeles Breakfast Club, a hearty Rotary-Kiwanis type organization, if they would like to hear Cohan sing the song. They would, if Cohan agreed to honorary initiation. Carle told Cohan that it could hardly be much of an ordeal, and he assented. Carle describes what happened: "The initiation consisted of this leading figure in theatrical history sitting blindfolded on a wooden horse and taking an oath while a chortling baldie held Cohan's palm pressed upon a platter of sunny-side-up eggs and greasy ham. In the front row sat I," says Carle, "eyes closed and paraphrasing a Robert W. Service triteness: 'God forgive my publicity sins . . . the other kind don't matter.' Yet somehow Cohan could forgive. There were many afternoons when I and the others who adored the man would sit with him on a curbing in front of his studio dressing room and talk for hours. For, to the undying discredit of inefficiency or purposeful belittling, many were the days when Cohan was made up for work at 9 A.M. and waited until mid-afternoon (or even day's finish) before being called onto the stage."

The Phantom President is a mildly diverting picture. Claudette Colbert as the love interest is properly beautiful and Jimmy Durante as Cohan's sidekick in the film is enchantingly no one but himself. Cohan is suitably gelid as the presidential candidate and suitably lively as the medicine show man. His dancing is delightful but too brief, and he sings pleasantly and unmemorably. *The Phantom President* is not a film for the ages.

Cohan returned to New York to get the bad taste of Hollywood out of his mouth, resolving to do it with comedy. He wanted to create a comedy with an interesting contrivance, something genuinely innovative. Frequently with Cohan, the propelling mechanism in steering him toward a theme and a mode of expression was a little thing, sometimes nothing more than an overheard scrap of conversation. He loved Central Park. He walked daily around the reservoir there and on these vigorous outings would usually wear out men half his age with his pace. At times he stopped to feed the pigeons, and one day while so doing he heard a lady remark to a companion, "I don't know if it's him or not. Is he the kind of man who feeds pigeons in the park?"

Cohan smiled, went home directly and took out his yellow legal pad and pencil, his invariable writing paraphernalia. With just a few later revisions in rehearsal, the play *Pigeons and People* was completed in five days. Its theme is that it has no theme, and its appropriate subtitle is "A Comic State of Mind in Continuous Action." Cohan was quite serious in his project to write a very funny play about absolutely nothing and for the most part he succeeded. *Pigeons and People* is second only to *Seven Keys to Baldpate* and *The Tavern* in the body of Cohan's plays for comedic value. It is full-length, written to be performed without intermission, and like many good Cohan plays, centers around a mystery.

Into his expensive apartment comes Heath, a tall, handsome man in his thirties, bringing with him Parker, the character played by Cohan, a man accurately described by the author as "a medium-sized, whimsical man of indeterminate age." The two men have just come from Central Park where Heath, after many days of observing Parker feeding the pigeons, engaged him in conversation. Stimulated by Heath's friendly curiosity, Parker tells his life story (which the audience never hears), a story apparently centered around the tragic disappointments from which he is running away, or seems to be running away. With Parker, one is never sure.

Heath, in any case, regards himself as Parker's likely savior. He considers Parker's story the most tragic one he has ever heard—no, on reflection, the most *comically* tragic story he has ever heard—and if he, Heath, can help Parker get back where he belongs, "it'll be one of the few really decent things I've ever done in my life."

Parker is grateful but really must go. Heath is adamant in his charitable mood and virtually forces Parker to stay. Parker thanks him but repeats that he must be going. After all, says Parker, "I may be an impostor, a crook."

HEATH: (*Smiles.*) No, no. You're no crook.

PARKER: Well, I may be for all you know. I told you that Parker was a phoney name. I wouldn't admit what part of the country I came from. Remember that stuff about burying the identity with the past? I told you all that, didn't I?

HEATH: (*Very much interested now.*) Yes.

PARKER: Well, there you are, you see. You couldn't even check up on me, even if you wanted to. I'm going to ask you a question. Did you really believe that story I told you in the park?

HEATH: Yes, Parker, I really did.

PARKER: Well, I'll tell you something. If I'd been in your place, I wouldn't have believed it. Never in a thousand years, no sir.

HEATH: Well, I think I'm a fairly good judge of human nature, Parker.

PARKER: You think you are, eh?

HEATH: I do. And I'm satisfied you're not a faker. And what you've just said is proof conclusive that you're not a crook.

PARKER: How do you mean?

HEATH: Well, no crook who was clever enough to invent a story such as you told in the park, and succeeded in making a man believe it, would then turn deliberately around and warn that man to be on his guard in case that story turned out to be a lie. (*Chuckles.*) No sir—no crook would do that.

PARKER: Now you see, that's where you're dead wrong, because a clever crook might do just that.

HEATH: For what reason?

PARKER: Well, to get the fellow figuring just as you're figuring it out now. That no crook would do such a thing. See what I mean?

HEATH: No, I don't.

PARKER: Oh, yes you do. You see it—you see it. (*Smiles.*) And I've got you thinking now, too. Now 'fess up, haven't I?

HEATH: Well, naturally, what you're saying is more or less confusing.

Which is the whole idea. This scene is the pattern for all ensuing action; it is the process for all Parker's confrontations with the other characters in the play: Heath's housekeeper, his detective friend, a doctor, a cop, a nurse, the house boy, and two pretty girls. Singly or in groups they all encounter Parker and he baffles them. Baffles them, but intriguingly, almost endearingly.

Just at the moment any character establishes a basic attitude of belief toward Parker—that he is a criminal, or the ex-lightweight boxing champion of the world, or one of the foremost detectives in America, or a world traveler (except to Japan) or a middle-aged Romeo—Parker carefully, almost logically destroys that belief even though he is the one who has implanted that belief. *Pigeons and People* is something of a comic echo of Pirandello's identity plays ("Every man is many people.") but there is no real derivation because Cohan never read Pirandello and would have been exasperated if he had. Pirandello, for all his mocking raillery, had in short supply the thing Cohan prized most in drama—fun.

By the end of the play, the destruction-of-belief device begins to wear a little thin, but only a little. So diverting is Parker, such (in John Mason Brown's words) "a born trouble-maker, a verbal trickster of incredible power, a sane lunatic in what he believes to be an insane world" that his hold on the audience is unrelenting.

At the end of *Pigeons and People*, Parker grows serious. After a spectrum of moods ranging from expansive geniality to moments when he breaks into disturbingly real crocodile tears, he quietens. Addressing all the characters in the play prior to his departure, Parker says:

> . . . I can't get along with people. That's why I hang out with pigeons. I don't know how in God's name you put up with each other—on the square, I don't. Why, it's a madhouse, a monkey cage. You can't live in it and be yourself. Not if you have any convictions, or strength of character . . . (*Looks at the detective.*) Now look. There's the Police Department. Organized to keep the peace. Where do they keep it? Where is it? Isn't that good? (*Laughs, indicates the doctor.*) And the big doctor—the great reliever of pain—the great diagnostician. Diagnose my case, will you, Doc? Not a chance, is there? You bet there isn't. The old Doc doesn't know right now whether I ought to be put in a straitjacket or sent to the United States Senate . . . Sermonizing. And what's the sermon? (*Pointing above.*) Is it what He preached, or is it diplomacy? (*Laughs.*) Why put up with it? I'm cured . . .

Parker assures them he is going back to the park, and does not want to be disturbed. Everyone is stunned because for almost two hours he has been leaving or threatening to leave, and now astoundingly he is leaving. Parker looks at them and asks if he is not going to get the usual goodbye. There is a fervent chorus of goodbyes.

> PARKER: (*Laughs heartily.*) There's another damn fool habit, you know, that hello and goodbye. (*Mimics.*) Hello, goodbye—hello, goodbye. (*Laughs again.*) Who is he? What's he got? How'd he get it? What day is it? What's the date? How's the weather? Stocks are down. Down with the rich. Pity the poor. God save the king. (*As he exits.*) Merry Christmas. Happy New Year. It's a fake. The whole thing's a fake. (*He is heard laughing until the outer door slams.*)

The detective tails Parker and shortly after telephones Heath to tell him Parker finally admitted his identity. He clearly is "somebody" but before the audience can be told, the curtain falls.

Parker is inherently the Vagabond, whimsical, ingratiating, dramatic, delighting in the many moods which seize all the characters in the play, but Parker is a Vagabond brought almost perforce into the modern world, a world in which he clearly does not belong. This displaced Vagabond is Cohan, unalterably the humorist, but also a man shrinking from a world rapidly losing its innocence. For Cohan, pigeons are really nicer than most people in this strange day and age.

The play opened at the Sam H. Harris Theatre, on New York's 42nd Street, January 16, 1933. Most of the critics enjoyed *Pigeons and People* as a splendid theatrical experience. Trying to describe the play, Gilbert Gabriel said, was "like trying to make mashed potatoes out of rosebuds," and most critics did not try. "It's like no other play that you can think of," said John Mason Brown. "For nearly two intermissionless hours it goes its way . . . standing on its head and making you feel as if you must be standing on yours. But such is the ingenuity of its nonsense, and so amazingly contrived is it as a prank, that not until the last fifteen minutes or so have been reached, are you aware of the passage of time . . . A very good if utterly crazy evening." Brooks Atkinson while unimpressed with the Cohan philosophizing at play's end, called Cohan "the most beloved of the performers on Broadway and the most uncanny as a theatrical prestidigitator."

Pigeons and People had all the attributes of success save one. The public did not come. Cohan closed it after two months of scant but appreciative houses. For at least the tenth time in his life, he announced his retirement from the theatre, and by now a few people were tending to believe him. A pal asked him a few weeks after the end of *Pigeons and People*, if Cohan honestly didn't have a hankering to play again. "I just closed a hankering," said Cohan.

He sensed that the American theatre was becoming an institution in which he might not now have a strong role. If the critics were right and his plays were either stunts or warmed-up melodramas, it may well *be* that his last retirement should be his last. At this psychologically apposite moment, Theresa Helburn of the Theatre Guild, who had been talking to Cohan for some months about acting for them, sent him the manuscript of Eugene O'Neill's new play, *Ah, Wilderness!* Cohan and O'Neill on the face of it seemed the unlikeliest of combinations. The optimistic yea-sayer and the dour explorer of tragic consciousness were not brothers under the skin except for the one thing *Ah, Wilderness!* celebrated: a pervasive sense of nostalgia. This comedy of recollection, as O'Neill termed it, was native American to the core, affirmative of the "old" values—and its action occurs on the Fourth of July.

Cohan found the role of Nat Miller, the rural newspaper editor and understanding father, foursquare to his affections and talents. The play's central episode—the winning and tactful governance of an adolescent boy by his humorously wise old father—was literally a page out of Cohan's own life. Consequently he shaped the role of Nat Miller into the person of Jerry Cohan, the warmly stern gentleman of the old school. As happy as he seemed about the role (and the billing: his was the first name the Theatre Guild ever put up in electric lights at the top of its marquee), there was some apprehension among Cohan's friends as to whether or not he would be amenable to direction from people other than his own staff. The entire experience was new for Cohan: a director he did not know, actors he had not cast, and above all, the speaking of lines he had not written. Some cast members expected temperament flareups in rehearsal.

The rehearsals were models of order. Cohan the Pro was in absolute function. Gene Lockhart, together with the rest of the cast, was astonished that the First Actor of the American theatre listened to the director, Philip Moeller, with full, obedient attention. It was not in the tradition of leading actors. Cohan not only took the instructions for his movements and stage business without demur but when scenes not involving him had to be extensively reworked, he waited with inexhaustible patience, sitting on an old pile of canvas at the rear of the stage.

When *Ah, Wilderness!* opened October 2, 1933, there was some critical disagreement over the worth of O'Neill's excursion into mittel-American nostalgia but there was not a murmur of dissent about Cohan. Alexander Woollcott, retired from active newspaper reviewing, sent Cohan a telegram: THIS IS A BURST OF APPLAUSE FROM AN AGED PLAYGOER WHO WAS DEEPLY MOVED BY YOUR BEAUTIFUL PERFORMANCE TONIGHT. Brooks Atkinson called it the "ripest, finest performance" of Cohan's career, and made the telling point that *Ah, Wilderness!* "has dipped deeper into Mr. Cohan's gifts and personal character than any of the antics he has written for himself. Ironic as it may sound, it has taken Eugene O'Neill to show us how fine an actor George M. Cohan is."

J. D. Salinger saw Cohan in *Ah, Wilderness!* "He was perfection in it," says Salinger. "He'd apparently put his mind to it, as well as everything else he had, and out came the first unstagey acting I think I ever saw on the stage. A real mind working. He was wonderfully clever and talented, too, of course, but he also had a mind, no less than somebody like Paul Scofield has one. Impossible to forget him in that."

An actor in the original cast of *Ah, Wilderness!* who does not wish to be identified believes that Cohan resented Atkinson's remark that it took Eugene O'Neill to give Broadway Cohan at his finest. Whether he resented it or not, and there is some evidence he did, it was true because *Ah, Wilderness!* was the best play Cohan had yet appeared in. Cohan's disappointment that he had not written the vehicle for his best New York performance to date was mostly swallowed up in the great personal success. The same original cast member had other memories of Cohan: "He was, whatever else he was, a real pro. That word meant something to him. I didn't care for him personally because outside of Gene Lockhart, he just ignored the male members of the cast. He wasn't rude to us, just indifferent. To the women, he was most courteous. He sent them flowers at Christmas, I recall. The reason Cohan liked Lockhart, of course, was because they were a couple of old pros together. Cohan also treated our stage manager with great respect because this was a man who knew his business, who knew to an inch where every actor onstage should be. Cohan admired that kind of professionalism greatly. As to Cohan the man—I somehow felt that his life, his real life, was up there on the stage, and that all the good things in him and for him lived only on the stage. By the same token, I think that all the bad things that happened to him were the things offstage."

Cohan was, of course, free from his usual managerial

tensions and responsibilities during the run of the play. He could even relax to the point of reserving almost every Saturday night for his pal, Gene Lockhart. The two men would go out for some sedate conviviality, giving each other (in a pet Cohan phrase) some good drinking lessons. Cohan held nightly open house in his dressing room after the performance, and old friends came back to congratulate him with a vigor they had failed to show in his more recent appearances. A film producer, Harold B. Franklin, was a visitor and invited Cohan to make a film, any film, and under Cohan's terms. It was decided that the 1929 play, *Gambling*, might have a certain topicality in view of the newspaper space then being given to Nick the Greek and his cohorts.

During a vacation break for *Ah, Wilderness!* the film was shot in four weeks at studios in Astoria, Long Island. Wynne Gibson who played in *Gambling* recalls it with little pleasure. "In terms of worth, the film was very unimportant, and disastrous for me. I had no chance to get to know Mr. Cohan, to learn if I would like him or dislike him. I was in awe of him; he had been a star for ages and ages. The female parts were nil. They were played by Dorothy Burgess and me, and about the only contact we had with Mr. Cohan or the closest he ever got to being friendly was a joke he made. Dorothy and I during the first day's shooting were standing in a doorway, and he said, 'Ah! They had to send to Hollywood for two stars to hold up the door frame.'" The film critics who saw *Gambling*, and they were not many, correctly assessed it as a photographed stage play rather than a film. It received scant distribution and was heard of no more. All prints seem to have disappeared.

In the late fall of 1934, during the national tour of *Ah, Wilderness!*, Cohan received permission to make a sentimental gesture to the town he most associated with his boyhood. He took the cast to the Town Hall of North Brookfield, Massachusetts, and on its rickety stage, without make-up, scenery, costumes, or props, presented the play for his old friends and neighbors. It was a shiningly beautiful performance and the simplicity of its presentation, much in the spirit of Thornton Wilder's *Our Town*, affected those who saw it deeply. On the tour, Cohan's acting took on certain extensions not present in the Broadway production. He began to add little touches and bits of business which, together with a growing tendency to pause reflectively in reaction to lines spoken to him, stretched the play's original playing time by half an hour.

Theresa Helburn asked him tactfully if the play had not become too long. For New York, yes, said Cohan—but not for the heartland. These were the Americans actually being represented on stage, he said, and they were not the kind to be in a hurry. He was right. The audiences were much taken with Cohan's restful quiet pace and delivery; he seemed their own, one bred from their own stock, a Norman Rockwell illustration come to life. Cohan was not afraid to project the naturalness of his interpretation by unusual stage positions, at times looking directly at the audience, at other times turning his back to them protractedly.

"Cohan was the only actor I have ever seen," says Pat O'Brien, "who could act with his back. Just from the way he held himself and cocked his head, you could tell everything he was thinking even though he wasn't saying a word or showing his face to the audience."

After the closing of *Ah, Wilderness!* in February 1935, the Players Club in New York asked Cohan if he would honor them by appearing in a limited-run revival of *Seven Keys to Baldpate*. He did so, exuberantly, in May 1935. It was a special joy to appear in one of his favorite plays whose comic excitements pleased audiences just as well in 1935 as they did in 1913. One night not long after the revival closed, Cohan was taken to the theatre by an old friend to see a new play, *Remember the Day*, by Philo Highley and Philip Dunning, a pleasant, sentimental comedy about a boy who falls in love with his teacher and then is heartbroken when he learns she is in love with the school's athletic coach. The boy's parents help him to forget by sending him away at his insistence to boarding school, and before he goes, the teacher helps the boy to find himself. Hardly a world-shaker of a play, but Cohan fell deeply in love with it and returned to see it again and again. Since the play had no role for him, his interest was objective. Like *Ah, Wilderness!*, it is a memory play, set at the turn of the century, and its well-wrought sentiment took Cohan back to his childhood, the childhood he might have had. To Cohan the play was a beacon in a darkening world, and he urged the public to see *Remember the Day*. In a few paragraphs he wrote gratis for the authors' advertising purposes, he said:

> Philo Highley and Philip Dunning have contributed to the American stage something more than a good play in their *Remember the Day*. They have taken me and countless others back to those delightful days of our childhood. They have made us think, all of us, what a wonderful and sweet existence this short term on earth really is. Nothing of the wild and frustrated scene as currently enacted in America in this play. Nothing of the exaggerations of a hapless world; nothing to make one wish that the curtain had fallen, and that life was far too long and much too weary.
>
> Night after night, in the National Theatre, I watched the pleasant performances of the talented troupe of players and I listened to honest childhood expressions, truthful thoughts and straight-from-the-shoulder drama. I believed every word of the play; I lived every word of it. It was my play. Sometimes I thought, as I watched the lights dim and the curtain rise, that the Messrs. Highley and Dunning had written their masterpiece only for me—a song and dance man. And I was grateful. When anybody does something grand for a song and dance man, I am grateful.
>
> Thrilled with emotion, and thinking of my own child-

> hood, I went directly home after seeing the play—the first time I had lost interest in night life and in a cold community. For hours I sat at my window looking out at the lights on the Avenue, at the dizzy damsels and at the hysterical heathens one sees after midnight on a Manhattan street. My mind was on the play—the real thing. A play! And not a synthetic, make-believe reality. As I gazed upon the frenzied crowd below my window, I felt like shouting: "Sober up, all of you, and rush down to see *Remember the Day*. It's what all of you need." Instead, I wrote a telegram to Mr. Dunning: "It is the best play I have seen in ten years. It is a play that every man, woman and child should see."

The time specification pointedly excludes *Ah, Wilderness!* as Cohan's favorite play of time just past. *Remember the Day* is, in fact, a thoroughly charming play and the kind of play Cohan was to see less and less in Broadway listings as the thirties progressed. His espousal of it emphasized his growing disaffection with the new themes of American drama. Cohan told Ward Morehouse about a time he met his friend, Bert Lytell, on a reservoir walk in Central Park. Lytell, then president of Actors Equity and very much a part of the Broadway scene, told Cohan that the best play he had been to in years was Elmer Rice's *Street Scene*. "I told Bert I'd heard lots about it," Cohan said to Morehouse, "but I asked him one question. I said, 'Yes, Bert, but is it pleasant?' He didn't seem to understand me. I guess people don't understand me any more, and I don't understand them. It's got so that an evening's entertainment just won't do. Give an audience an evening of what they call realism and you've got a hit. It's getting to be too much for me, kid."

But Cohan persevered. In March 1936, he produced *Dear Old Darling*, "an oddly amusing, freakish evening of showshop suspense . . . a typical Cohan mystery," Brooks Atkinson called it. It merited its subtitle, "A Comic Experience," because of Cohan's performance, but as a play unadorned with Cohan's acting it is one of the treadmill variety he had turned out in the twenties. Cohan's role is that of an engaging man in his fifties, profitably retired from business, relentlessly pursued by a twenty-year-old beauty who turns out to be a con woman. Her blackmail scheme is thwarted and she is removed into proper custody, but before she is taken away one receives the distinct impression that the girl really likes the dear old darling. There is a cheery and quite artless vanity in Cohan's self-identification with this situation and the play's title.

To compensate for the plot's slightness, Cohan pulled out all the performing stops, showing that he could scuttle his quiet reserve as an actor when needed. John Anderson of the New York *Evening Journal* said that *Dear Old Darling* "may be a rattletrap piece of stage machinery, but Mr. Cohan makes it seem pretty fascinating. That ridiculous skip, the bent-knee-action walk, the wink, the leer, the down-at-the-mouth voice, the face turning against the movement of the eyes and all the assorted tricks that have endeared him to us all as permanent trademarks of a favorite, are all here to be analyzed, or belittled if you please, but never explained except in terms of an actor's living and comic greatness." Or stated more baldly, Cohan mugged endearingly a very great deal, even at one point breaking into a soft-shoe routine. "If this column had its way, which seems unlikely," said Brooks Atkinson, "Mr. Cohan would abandon some of his mugging and some of his soft-shoe dancing at the close of a scene. When he is too insistent upon being roguish he is a little embarrassing. But perhaps a subtle, temperate fellow would not be George M. Cohan, the prince of Broadway, which would be our loss in the end."

The Cohan posturings, if not the play, delighted all the critics and a very small percentage of the public. Cohan took the play off after two weeks.* The play's closing disturbed him but as usually happened in his life when solace or compensation for a blow was needed, comfort was not long in coming. This time it arrived from the unlikeliest of sources, the United States Congress. Private Law 727 of the 74th Congress on June 29, 1936, awarded a gold Medal of Honor for Cohan's meritorious service in World War I. The service was specified as the writing of "Over There" and "It's a Grand Old Flag." This was the first time in its history that Congress had given a medal for the writing of songs, and it was a signal recognition of music's power of inspiration in time of war. This Medal (which now hangs in the front hall of the Lambs Club), to correct a general misconception about it, is not *the* Congressional Medal of Honor which is awarded only for personal valor but *a* Congressional Medal of Honor given for specified services. After its award, Cohan's medal was available to him anytime he cared to go down to Washington and receive it personally from President Franklin D. Roosevelt. Cohan, although he did not announce it, did not care to go down —not just yet. A lifelong Democrat and one of Al Smith's closest friends, Cohan in the early days of FDR's first term had written an enthusiastic lyric about the President, "What a Man!", to the tune of "Over There." In it, he praised the President for getting the country moving again, but by 1936 Cohan thought the country had moved too far, particularly along the line of unionism. "In 1939," Walter Kerr recalls, "I had dinner with Cohan at the Plaza one night when John L. Lewis was at another table, and Cohan made no attempt to conceal his loathing of the man and what he stood for."

Cohan held a kind of court in the Plaza's Oak Room in his later years, and a great variety of friends would sit

* Marian Shockley Collyer who played the ingenue in *Dear Old Darling* remembers that part of the fun in acting the show was that at each performance one scene was deliberately played ad-lib. Cohan and whoever was on stage with him "would just make it up as we went along," Mrs. Collyer reports.

with him at a *Stammtisch* of good talk. He was by instinct a check-grabber and lavish tipper, not out of a big-shot complex, having no need to prove himself one, but because he loved to entertain in every sense of the word. Socially he was the most genial of men, when the company was few. He enjoyed liquor—bourbon, Scotch, martinis, champagne—but never overindulged and had a horror of those who did. He smoked cigarettes but preferred mild cigars. He loved ice cream and had a partiality for fish, especially bass. A sense of order always marked his person, as was seen in his suits, well-tailored, conservative cut and shade, usually dark blue. He liked dark, solid-color ties and white shirts but disliked formal wear. The only luxury items of dress he favored were custom-made shoes to accommodate his small feet. Early in his career he tended to wear Cuban heels on stage to increase his height but in later years he never bothered. Conversation at his table inevitably centered around the theatre or baseball but occasionally he discussed the world of books. He knew Thackeray, loved Mark Twain and had read most of Dickens whose salty character types he cherished. In his last years, Cohan took particular pleasure in telling anecdotes about the many fascinating show people the Four Cohans had encountered on their long cross-country tours. Sam Harris enjoyed stimulating this memory flow with proddings like, "Tell them about the time you joined the Vesta Tilley show, George," and Cohan obligingly held the table engrossed for hours with his anecdotes.

It was in the mid-thirties that Sam Harris came back into Cohan's life. Cohan's producing career had been a series of ups and downs after the dissolution of Cohan and Harris. The Harris record was much brighter. By 1935, he had already produced such great successes as *Once in a Lifetime, Dinner at Eight,* and *Of Thee I Sing;* and in the future lay *Stage Door, You Can't Take It With You* and *The Man Who Came to Dinner*. Over the years after their business separation, Harris had not seen Cohan as much as he wanted to. Their family connection had been broken with the death of Harris's wife, Agnes Cohan's sister, and Harris in any case was about the busiest producer on Broadway. Cohan and Harris relaxed from their respective careers one memorable evening in 1934 when they appeared as a pair of song and dance men during the course of the Jewish Theatrical Guild's dinner in their honor. For the floor show, Cohan and Harris, wearing raked derbies and carrying canes, got up to dance and sing a song Cohan had composed for the occasion:

"We've always been good old pals,
Dear old pals,
Ever since 1903.
Down in Herald Square
We had our offices there,
That's where we used to be.
Hand in hand
Throughout the land,
We put on many a show.
We've been a couple of good old pals
Since thirty-one years ago."

They went into a hilarious soft-shoe routine climaxed by simultaneous clicking of their heels in the air. During the speeches following, Cohan said that at long last he was willing to reveal why he and his pal Sam had split up years before. The audience grew serious. "It was simple," said Cohan. "The real story is—I wanted to run the office, and Sam wanted to be an actor." The audience relaxed into laughter.

After this occasion, Cohan and Harris began to see more of each other. One night in July 1936, they got together over one of their favorite tipples, bourbon, soda and lemon twist, to do little more than celebrate their similar taste in drinks. After a few of them, and only partially because of them, the two men admitted to each other that the breaking of their partnership had been a mistake. The thought came impulsively that although it was too late to renew permanent partnership, it would be a warm mutual gesture to co-produce Cohan's next play. The difficulty was there was no next Cohan play in sight.

In going through a pile of scripts at his office shortly after, Cohan came across *Yesterday's Lilacs,* by Parker Fennelly, the actor later to win radio immortality as Titus Moody on Fred Allen's "Allen's Alley." It is instructive to see how *Yesterday's Lilacs,* a perfectly good play, was metamorphosed into a less than good play, Cohan's *Fulton of Oak Falls.* In the original, Ed Fulton, a hen-pecked bank clerk, in his anxiety to get away from a nagging wife and a selfish daughter, revisits a small country hotel where twenty years before he had had an affair with an enchanting girl, Muriel, also a guest there. It was the first such experience for them both. Ed wanted to marry Muriel but conformed instead to what was expected of him by his family and married the girl who now plagues him. In returning to the hotel after all these years, Ed encounters another charming girl, a maturer version of Muriel, and they become lovers. Not expecting to find her father there, Ed's selfish daughter appears at the hotel to spend a few days with her boy friend. Shocked, Ed orders them to separate and returns home himself. The daughter has proof that Ed's friendship with the girl at the hotel is more than casual, and she intends to inform on him unless he gives her a new car. Ed, finally seeing his family for what it is, casts them off and goes back to the girl at the hotel.

Cohan's alteration of this story into *Fulton of Oak Falls* is principally one of moral stance. Ed Fulton (played by Cohan) does return to the hotel where his first romance had bloomed but that early romance in the Cohan version is old lace and lavender with absolutely no physical consummation. The new girl Ed meets at the hotel is very attractive and he is easily attracted to her, but their connection is also chaste. Ed's daughter turns up at the hotel for a clandestine weekend but she is really decent at heart, and

Ed returns to the bosom of his family permanently, self-sacrificially, to see that she is properly married to her young man. The Cohan version of the story is one he would have written in 1910. *Yesterday's Lilacs,* despite the intrusion of coincidence at a pivotal point, has a core of reality; *Fulton of Oak Falls* is warm-hearted soap opera and just as memorable.

Fulton of Oak Falls opened at the Morosco Theatre in New York, February 10, 1937, with floral horseshoes cramming the lobby and with numerous theatre people present to celebrate the reunion of Cohan and Harris. "Broadway is sentimental about a small list of personalities," said *Variety.* "George M. Cohan is definitely on that list. And Sam Harris, too." But once again the critics were put in the awkward position of praising Cohan and condemning his play. Richard Lockridge of the *Sun* summed it up: "Like all of Mr. Cohan's recent appearances this one puts a reviewer slightly up against it. Mr. Cohan is, as always, friendly and disarming and unaffectedly expert in his art; his play is, as his plays have so frequently been in recent years, disturbingly antiquated in its unrestrained sentimentality, and its whole point of view is that of another day."

This was the critical consensus. Cohan once again had opted for the mores of yesteryear and had written what Brooks Atkinson perceptively called a "distaff *Ah, Wilderness!* brought up to date." It is also a modern play determinedly back-dated.

Kathryn Givney who played in *Fulton of Oak Falls* retains from that engagement a memory of Cohan the old-fashioned gentleman. "He was such a kindly man," she says. "During our try-out stand in Baltimore when it was cold and rainy, Mr. Cohan contracted a severe cold as did others including me. His valet had ordered a taxi which arrived prior to my calling one. Mr. Cohan—this unusual man, and mind you, he had no understudy—stood in the cold rain *demanding* that I take his cab. How many stars would do that?"

Another, sadder memory of Cohan during the brief run of *Fulton of Oak Falls* comes from Marian Shockley Collyer who had played the young golddigger in *Dear Old Darling.* She came backstage one night after a showing of *Fulton of Oak Falls* to reminisce a bit and say hello. Cohan waited until everyone had left the dressing room, put his arms around her and began to sob, repeating "They don't want me any more, they don't want me any more." "I must have been there fifteen minutes comforting him," says Mrs. Collyer. "My heart just ached for him, he was so miserable."

Fulton of Oak Falls lasted only thirty-seven performances in New York. Unhappy though he was, Cohan's innate resiliency asserted itself soon enough. He told his closest friends that the sentimental, folksy type of play whether he loved it or not, was a liability at the box office, and there was little sense in doing them hereafter. But there was one kind of play he knew could never die. "As my dear dad used to advise me," Cohan told a pal, "son, always hang on to your dancing shoes."

15. REGARDS TO BROADWAY

In 1937 Sam Harris discussed with Cohan the possibility of his appearing in a musical comedy under the Harris aegis. Cohan had agreed on general principles but said he needed some rest which he anticipated finding on a European trip with his wife. He sailed on the *Ile de France* in April 1937 and under stern orders from Mrs. Cohan devoted himself to sightseeing. He had an idea that *The Tavern* might take the British sense of humor and was actively contemplating a production of it in London when a cablegram arrived from Sam Harris. Harris said that George S. Kaufman and Moss Hart had written a musical comedy expressly for Cohan and were most anxious for him to read it.

When Cohan returned in the early summer of 1937 he was handed the script of *I'd Rather Be Right,* and found to his tremendous surprise and slight disquiet that he was being asked to play the role of Franklin D. Roosevelt. The play was an affectionate lampoon of the New Deal, occasionally quite witty, but lacking in any satirical depth. So enthusiastic was Harris about the script that Cohan wanted to let him down lightly; he did not relish telling his old friend that he failed to share Kaufman and Hart's affection for the President. The excuse Cohan gave for rejecting the script was basically one he had given the

Theatre Guild some months before when they asked him to impersonate Roosevelt in a new play called *If This Be Treason.* Cohan had told the Guild, and now told Harris, that the public would never accept a song and dance man as President of the United States. But Kaufman and Hart were not to be refused. They called on Cohan and in a three-hour session carefully presented an argument that in refusing *I'd Rather Be Right* Cohan was turning down a chance to bring a song and dance man to the highest dignity of the land. *Their* president, the authors argued, was after all not a song and dance man as President but a song and dance man President. It was a distinction Cohan appreciated, and he found it irresistible.

Cohan had two additional reasons to be wary of the show: the writers of the score, Richard Rodgers and Lorenz Hart. Cohan was prejudiced against them because they had written the music for *The Phantom President,* a score Cohan had been told he would write at least in part. Ward Morehouse believed that since Cohan's school of melody was not Rodgers and Hart's it was natural for Cohan to think of them as upstarts in a game he had mastered before they were born. In any case, Cohan had a preliminary session with the composers, sitting glumly through Rodgers's playing of the entire score, failing to react in any way whatever. After an hour and a half of listening, Cohan got up, patted Rodgers on the shoulder, and said, "Well, take care of yourself." He left without another word, and never met them again either during rehearsal or production. Rodgers and Hart were stunned.

During rehearsals Cohan airily referred to them as Gilbert and Sullivan, frequently telling the stage manager, "Tell Gilbert and Sullivan to run over to the hotel and write a better song." This was said facetiously but in any spirit this was gratuitous banter from a man who had accepted the show's leading role without qualifications. The songs in *I'd Rather Be Right* were not Rodgers and Hart's best but there was at least one superb ballad, "Have You Met Miss

Jones?", which has lasted, and other good tunes kept from posterity only by their strong topicality. The book for the show was particularly weak, consisting of little more than cleverly affectionate gags about FDR, his family and leading administration figures.* The show could hardly fail. Its publicity was mountainous, rolling up a tremendous pre-sale. A song and dance man American President was one everyone wanted to see.

Cohan, although very pleased to be playing the leading role in a Broadway musical success, was far from his ease in *I'd Rather Be Right.* Yet he performed his role unflaggingly, and to great critical acclaim. "Mr. Cohan's triumph," said John Anderson; "His greatest performance," said Robert Coleman; "It brings that grand little candidate for supreme musical comedy honors . . . to the peak of a musical comedy career that stretches over thirty-five years," said Burns Mantle. But the hard fact of the matter was that Cohan simply did not enjoy appearing in plays by other writers.

He said as much to Robert E. Sherwood in October 1939, following the long Broadway run and triumphant national tour of *I'd Rather Be Right.* Sherwood, speaking on behalf of his colleagues in the Playwrights' Company, approached Cohan to play a leading role in Sidney Howard's new play, *Madam, Will You Walk?* The role was Dr. Brightlee, a suave and genial incarnation of Lucifer, who helps an intelligent, withdrawn heiress find the world and herself. Howard had cast Leslie Banks in the Brightlee part and rehearsals were to begin in September 1939 when Howard was killed in a tractor accident on his farm. The war prevented Leslie Banks from coming to the United States from London, and his successor in the role, Wilfrid Lawson, returned suddenly to England for war service. It was at this point that Sher-

* In Boston Cohan altered a playful Lorenz Hart lyric about Alfred E. Smith out of deference, he said, to his old friend. After being told tactfully that it must not be repeated, Cohan agreed without visible resentment but it hardly improved his relationship with the composers.

wood approached Cohan who was candid about his reluctance to play in works not his own. Sherwood persisted. He recalled the delight he shared with Dorothy Parker and Robert Benchley at the opening of *The Tavern,* and *The Tavern,* in fact, said Sherwood, was one of the reasons he thought Cohan might find some interest in *Madam, Will You Walk?* Dr. Brightlee, Sherwood said, was a mysteriously intriguing character bearing a resemblance to the Vagabond and to Parker in *Pigeons and People.* This was enough to at least assure Cohan's reading of the script, but upon finishing it, he told Sherwood that both the role and the play were too cerebral for him.

Sherwood was not to be downed. He assured Cohan that no other actor in America could bring to the role the depth and the style he would impart. Cohan, unpersuaded, said he would undertake the role only under the stipulation that he be allowed to withdraw on ten days' notice if needs be. The proviso was accepted, and rehearsals began under Margaret Webster's direction in mid-October 1939. On October 20, after the third day of rehearsal, Cohan sent a letter to Sherwood saying that it would be better for all concerned if he withdrew from the play. "Quite simply, I am miscast," he told Sherwood. Sherwood and Elmer Rice (who had first suggested Cohan for the role) met Cohan over quite a few drinks and talked him into returning despite his grave doubts. "And also, to be quite honest," he said to the two playwrights, "I do not at all feel comfortable playing the devil, however witty he is." Unhelpfully, this was an opinion never communicated to the director.

"'Uncle George' was very benevolent to me—a young director, brought in at the last minute," says Margaret Webster. "He, too, as you know, was a last-minute piece of casting because Wilfrid Lawson left for England when the war broke out. The Playwrights did it without consulting me, and to tell the truth, I was a little aghast. I didn't know whether the subtlety of Sidney's satire would be quite George M. Cohan's dish. Neither, I think, did he. He could really have played the part on his left ear *if* he had had any confidence in himself as an actor—as *not* just being George M. Cohan. But I don't think he had. I never quite got his wave-length. I was, of course, very chary of imposing anything on him, and waited (as I always do with good actors) for indications of what he wanted to do, or give, or be. But I got none.

"He was most amiable; called me 'Maggie' (which no one else in my life has ever done—it's always 'Peggy'); mumbled his lines; made a *great* parade of not being able to pronounce 'Prometheus' and asking me again at every other rehearsal what it was, though I was damned sure he knew perfectly well. And did *nothing*. We couldn't even persuade him to cut loose with his 'own thing' in the scenes which cried out for it—the vaudeville act bits. [Cohan did a buck and wing, briefly.] The Playwrights' (Sherwood and Rice especially) assured me that he would 'come through on the night.' Sara Allgood (an old trouper) and I looked at each other in tacit agreement that things don't happen that way. And they didn't.

"When he finally gave up the part, [concludes Miss Webster] I had been called away by an SOS from Maurice Evans, on tour with *Hamlet*, and I got stuck in St. Louis with tonsillitis. When I got back, he had decided to leave and the company closed, at least for the time being.* I never knew why he did it. Maybe he thought the play would be a flop but I don't think so. I don't think he ever trusted himself in the part, and maybe he felt it was too late in the day to take chances with the end of his career. Or

* After some attempts to get Cedric Hardwicke as a replacement for Cohan, the play closed. S. N. Behrman in his *People in a Diary* (1972) speaks of Cohan's cost to the show: "It was an expensive contract. Cohan explained that it was his habit when he went on the road, to travel with an entourage and that previous managements had not hesitated to pay for it . . . The envoi to the history of *Madam, Will You Walk?* was supplied on his deathbed by George M. Cohan. He had a twinge of conscience for having made us pay so heavily when he signed his contract with us for himself and his entourage. He sent us an explanatory note and a check for fifteen hundred dollars."

maybe he just thought he was plainly bad in it. In my view, he was!"

Madam, Will You Walk? opened in Baltimore on November 13, 1939, and the critics on the whole enjoyed the play and the players while noting the evening's verbosity. The production moved the following week to Washington, D.C., where the critics felt the play, in an ancient phrase, needed work. Although he had completed only two weeks of a ten-week contract with the Playwrights' Company, Cohan agreed with the critics and asked for his release. Sherwood gave it to him. In this entire episode, Cohan's professionalism can clearly be faulted. He did not try hard enough. But to balance the picture, he did not want to do the play from the outset, said so repeatedly and deferred to some heavy persuasion in accepting the role.

In December 1939, Cohan's unhappy experience with the Playwrights' Company was forgotten in the warm nostalgia of his own life revisited. He was most pleased to act as consultant on a play about his life work in the theatre, *Yankee Doodle Boy*, by Walter Kerr and Leo Brady, presented by Catholic University's Harlequin Club in Washington, D.C. Utilizing Cohan's best music over the years, *Yankee Doodle Boy* concentrated on his professional life. The show was career-long, career-deep, and thoroughly charming.

"Basically, *Yankee Doodle Boy* came from my passion for Cohan's songs," says Walter Kerr. "They were then decidedly out of vogue—in that middle period between the original enthusiasm for them and the later nostalgia—but I continued to love them, probably because I grew up among aunts and uncles who played and sang them around the piano every night when the songs and shows were new. I still have some of that sheet music. Anyway, it occurred to me that you could build a biographical musical using a man's songs as a part of the narrative of his life. This had not been done at the time, although of course it became a commonplace in films later. Up to that time, as in a film like

Alexander's Ragtime Band, a story unrelated to the composer was always invented as a thread to string his songs on. So the 'musical biography' concept, at least, was then original. As it happened, one of my colleagues at Catholic University, Dr. Josephine McGarry Callan, had known Cohan personally for some years, and I asked her to write to him for permission to do such a show—on the campus only. Much to our surprise, Cohan quickly gave his permission, and made himself available to us for questioning . . . Though the show was a college show, and primitive by professional standards, Cohan professed to enjoy it thoroughly and I think his enjoyment was genuine. I say this not because of any comments he may have made later, but because of his very lively responses in the auditorium when he saw it."

After helping *Yankee Doodle Boy* to life, Cohan returned to New York and a few personal worries. For some time his wife's health had been declining, and at the end of 1939 he took her to the Cohan country place at Monroe, in Orange County, New York, for a long stay. Cohan was ever the mold of understanding husbands; as a father he tended to be repressive. He did not have a lot to do with the training of his eldest child, Georgette, who came principally under the influence of her dynamic mother, Ethel Levey. Cohan's children by Agnes Nolan—Mary, Helen, and George M., Jr.—had a most agreeable childhood. Their father delighted in entertaining them, chiefly in composing his own variations on Mother Goose rhymes which he sang and danced for them unendingly. Mary Cohan still remembers his version of "Jack and Jill" which he sang for his children every morning in Great Neck as he danced down the stairs to breakfast. But when the children attained adolescence, Cohan began to lose touch with them. As one who had never experienced adolescence because of his precipitate thrust into creative and managerial responsibility at that age, Cohan found this period of life unknown country.

Dan Healy, great vaudevillian and virtually Cohan's only

professional friend who also knew his wife and children well, saw deep into the situation of Cohan as father. "George was a very old-fashioned fellow," said Healy. "One must remember that. His *dad* was a very old-fashioned fellow, and he treated George with a strictness which George duplicated in raising his own children. But times had changed. To George, women were always to be on a pedestal, and what that also meant was that they were never to come into a man's world. For George, the world of the 1920s and the 1930s was a kind of roughhouse. For him life should always be the way it was back in the old days. Away from home was *man's* place; women stayed home and did the things of home. I think that's why he never encouraged Mary in her musical work and then he got a bit conscience-stricken about it, so he helped Helen along in her career."

The Cohan children were not encouraged to enter the theatre although all made at least tentative efforts to do so. Georgette, after her brief run in *Madeleine and the Movies,* left the theatre out of disinterest. Helen made a few films in Hollywood and after a brief spurt as a Wampas Baby Star retired to marriage and a family. George M., Jr., for a time did a stunningly impressive vaudeville act built around his father's songs but he also retired to manage a palatial inn at Goshen, New York. Mary, of all the children the one most vitally interested in a show business career, was also temperamentally the one most like her father. Unusually gifted in music, she had yearned from her earliest years to be a concert pianist. Her teachers, knowing her talent, urged her to go to Europe for a needed rounding of her style, and when she asked her father if he would send her, Cohan said no. On her own decision, Mary gave up the piano, and later, quite suddenly, left the repressions of home for marriage. To her gain, she married George Ronkin, a professional musician, who urged her to channel her remarkable musical abilities into composition. While raising a family, she began to write songs. In 1969 she was hired by David Black and Konrad Matthaei, producers of the Broadway hit, *George*

M!, to do the musical and lyric revisions of her father's music for the production, and in 1970 she wrote a series of songs for *The Tavern*, her favorite of Cohan's plays. The songs were integrated into the text of the play, and they do it the remarkable service of amplifying and precisely counterpointing its rich theatricalism. These songs have a musical nuance Cohan could only have loved had he lived to hear them and they augment *The Tavern* splendidly, giving it even deeper comic resonance. The script is presently seeking a producer.

By the spring of 1940, Cohan found he had enough of country life. In considering his inevitable return to the theatre, he resolved to do it on his own, to reject offers to appear under other management even if it meant enforced retirement. In planning his return, he thought first of a *Tavern* revival. His best sense told him that such a revival would not be likely to fail; his sense of adventure told him that a sequel to *The Tavern* might be a bit more fun. A sequel was the decision, and he took rather more time writing it than he did *The Tavern.* Two weeks was leisurely time for Cohan to write a non-musical play. He wrote plays quickly for a fundamental reason: he enjoyed writing plays quickly. There was the excitement of drama itself in the very fact of beginning a play, as he usually did, with only the vaguest idea of how it would turn out, frequently with a tight deadline date just ahead.

While writing the new play, Cohan realized that he could no longer put off his visit to receive his Congressional Medal of Honor from President Roosevelt. He did not look forward to the journey but it had been four years since the award. At the time of presentation, Roosevelt was at his most charming, and Cohan, who knew a lot about charm, was distinctly uncharmed, although he did not show it. In deference to the President and in genuine gratitude for the medal, Cohan did one of the finest acting jobs of his life and was most convincingly charmed. In any event, he was not disposed to the acceptance of honors publicly given. In

1935, President Clarence A. Barbour of Brown University, Providence, Rhode Island, had offered Cohan an honorary degree from the university to be granted on the usual condition for such degrees that the recipient be present at the conferment. Cohan, after extended thanks in a letter to President Barbour, added, "However, because I have refused heretofore tenders of honorary degrees from other colleges, and having a disposition to withdraw from the gatherings which sought to honor me by presentations of medals or documents (except from those within the theatre to which I have devoted my life's work) I have decided after careful consideration not to accept the proposed degree." This again was the Cohan never at ease away from his own world.

In 1940, he was back in the inmost recesses of his own world. His new play, *The Return of the Vagabond*, again had Cohan in his favorite role. As the mugging, posturing stranger mad about the drama, he was playing himself. In a very real sense, Cohan *was* mad about the drama, and *The Return of the Vagabond* is full, overfull, of intratheatricalities even down to personal reference, as in Zach's surprise at seeing the Vagabond up and about hours after bedtime:

ZACH: I thought you'd retired.
VAGABOND: Retire? I'll never retire. It's been said about me, but I'll never retire.

It is the same old tavern with the same cast of characters save Willum who is replaced on the tavern's staff by Algernon, a spouting, frenetic Italian. Sally and Zach are married, and Zach goes to night school where, unknown to his still censorious father, he studies drama. Zach reads plays to Sally every night in bed and when he is angry with her, he reads her Ibsen.* The governor and his wife have re-

* This, it perhaps needs to be explained, was a gag, and not a reflection of Cohan's attitude toward the father of modern drama. Cohan not only knew Ibsen's work well but admired it. Arvid Paulson says that Cohan was particularly taken with Ibsen's sense of play construction.

turned to the tavern accompanying Virginia and Tom on the first leg of the young couple's honeymoon. This is the wedding night, and a howling storm outside is its fitting atmosphere. In again, during a spectacular thunderclap, steps the Vagabond who has heard of Virginia's marriage and has come to pay his respects. But he has also come for a more urgent reason, he hints darkly, and his promise to reveal the reason ultimately is the play's central device to maintain suspense. It is not much of a device. The principal action in the play is the apprehension of two bank robbers by the Vagabond. This simple statement is as bare as the dramatic texture of the play. Tom Allen is again nervously distraught by both the storm and the Vagabond, and spends much time under rather than in his bed.

Again, from time to time, the Vagabond points out to the audience the various dramatic highlights of the action, but this time they are not high enough. Despite some determined comings and goings by various law-enforcement officials, the excitement the Vagabond predicts for the audience never arrives. After the criminals are apprehended, the rising storm reminds the Vagabond that he must be off into it. He reveals at last why he has returned to the tavern:

GOVERNOR: Are you really leaving in a storm like this?

VAGABOND: A storm like this? (*Laughs as he drops his cape.*) I revel in it. I glory in a storm like this. I'm a fish out of water in fair weather, your Excellency. I virtually live in a storm of ideas. (*Seriously.*) Governor, it's only fair that you should know what brought me here tonight. And so before I go, I wish to make an honest confession. On my last visit here, on my last meeting with you and your family, sir, that night I fell in love. (*Not a movement from the others, excepting Allen who steps forward resentfully; all register their embarrassment.*) It's true. I fell in love with this old tavern. (*All breathe a sigh of relief as the Vagabond looks around the room.*) And I'm still in love with all the happy memories of that wonderful night and all its fantastic happenings. A thousand times I've felt the urge to return here. (*Points to his heart.*) But fear of disappointment, disillusionment, was always here. And it cried out to me, "Don't be a fool, you fool. Keep away." I knew it wouldn't be the same, it couldn't be the same without you, your Excellency, and your most helpful wife, and your extremely charming daughter.

(And, alas, it was not the same.) After giving the governor a printed copy of his "Who are you?" speech, the long philosophical self-identification he declaimed in *The Tavern,** the Vagabond thanks the governor and prepares to go. But he is interrupted.

FREEMAN: (*Going to door and holding it.*) Wait! One word before you go.

VAGABOND: (*Hat on now.*) Speak up, man, what's the word?

FREEMAN: Promise me that you'll come again.

VAGABOND: (*Laughs heartily as cape goes on.*) Thank you very much, but I never accept invitations. I go where I please, I do as I please, I live as I please. And as the late James O'Neill, in his memorable characterization of Monte Cristo used to say, "The world is mine!" So throw open the door, Mr. Landlord, and present me with it! (*Freeman opens the door. Big storm effect. The Vagabond starts to do his dance, singing "Big as a cow," and dances his way out into the storm. Freeman holds the door open, till three claps of thunder are heard, then closes the door and bars it. All turn & look at Governor as he sits on the arm of the chair and reads.*)

GOVERNOR: "Who are you? The answer is I don't know

* Cohan had thousands of copies of the speech printed up for insertion into the theatre programs of *The Return of the Vagabond.*

> who I am and if I did, I'd be the most miserable man on earth, for my greatest happiness lies in the fact that I occupy a most unique position—that of not having been cast for a part in the great world drama of life. For in all the changing scenes of this ever-beginning, never-ending plotless plot, I recognize the spiritual hand of the great Director, the Master Dramatist who has so skillfully staged this tightly-knitted spectacle of tragic nonsense, and so I am amused and I laugh and I applaud."

AND THE CURTAIN FALLS

And reaffirmed in the last speech before exit is Cohan's happily insistent sequestration from the world outside the theatre. The world he wants is the world he has, the fustian world of Monte Cristo, the world of James O'Neill not the world of his brooding son, the world where one escapes into delicious storms which leave one conveniently dry.

In some ways, *The Return of the Vagabond* is a better written play than *The Tavern.* Its humors are quieter and more fey. There is one segment between the Vagabond and Virginia, an interchange of high whimsy in which the Vagabond with happy pointlessness asks her why she doesn't visit Honolulu, which is almost as good as anything out of S. N. Behrman. If *The Return of the Vagabond* was played in tandem with *The Tavern* on alternate nights the whole could be an invigorating theatrical experience. But in writing a sequel to *The Tavern,* Cohan made the elemental mistake of writing it twenty years after. That proved to be the chief undoing of *The Return of the Vagabond* and its first showing in 1940 is likely to be its last. The play is simply not sturdy enough to stand on its own.

The critics were kind. "There is a special critical woodshed for Mr. Cohan in which all the punishing adjectives are upholstered with plush," said John Anderson. Even so, John Mason Brown said that, devoted Cohan fan though he was, this play had driven him into temporary disloyalty. Cohan, said Brown, is "in more of a stagestruck than a dramatic frame of mind . . . The evening is more impersonal history than a play." Celeste Holm who played Virginia in *The Return of the Vagabond* thought Cohan in gathering his cast tended to rely too much on old actor pals than on brighter, younger talents.

"But the play really couldn't hold up for an audience unless they knew *The Tavern*," Miss Holm admits. "Mr. Cohan was, for me, a living acting lesson. His acting had a purity I adored. He knew the right thing instinctively. He had this great ability to *listen* to the other actors—not just hear them and wait for his cue to speak—but to *listen* with total intentness as if he were hearing the lines for the very first time. Also—he had a tremendous and very practical sense of humor. During rehearsal, I recall asking him at one point what my motivation was. Now, this was a newly fashionable phrase among young actors, and the old veterans in the company almost fell down laughing. Mr. Cohan looked at me kindly and said, 'Why not just say "Why?"' Then he went on to say seriously, 'My dear, you'll find out your motivation on opening night before an audience.' And, of course, he was right. That was a very smart lesson I learned, and one I've never forgotten."

The Return of the Vagabond lasted only seven performances. Cohan's last appearance on Broadway was to be his shortest. Just before the curtain was to rise for his last Broadway performance, he stood with Celeste Holm, looking at the closing notice on the call board. "I'll never come to New York again," he said to her. "They don't want me any more." He confided to close friends that he was retiring, finally and for all, ending his career. Ward Morehouse says of Cohan at this time in his life, "George M. Cohan was through. Through, and he knew it. And tired. Tired of a theatre in which he was no longer interested . . ."

Morehouse was echoing Broadway opinion—reasonable, well-conjectured opinion—and it was opinion completely, resoundingly, wrong. What Broadway had no way of knowing was that three weeks after his statement to Miss Holm and his pals that this was the absolute terminus of his many retirements, Cohan got out his pencil and yellow pad and began writing a new play. This, his last work for the theatre, he titled self-descriptively, *The Musical Comedy Man.* Its production and his appearance in it were prevented only by his death.

His writing of *The Musical Comedy Man* was interrupted by a sequence of melancholy events. In July 1941, his deeply loved friend, Sam Harris, died. Cohan was with him a number of times during the last months, and they relived many of the old days in gusty reminiscence. They were serious only once. Cohan said, "Sam, the one question they never stop asking me is, why did you and Harris split up?" "I know, kid, it's the same with me. What do you tell them?" "I tell them to ask Harris." "It's the same with me," said Harris. "I tell them to ask you." Cohan asked gently, "Sam, tell me. Why *did* we ever separate?" Harris smiled. "That's funny," he said. "What's funny, Sam?" "Why, I was just going to ask you the same question."

The loss of his old friend was another reminder that this was a world and a time sadly altered from the days of his youth, the days he could remember in minute detail when he talked of them, as he increasingly did. George Buck of the Catholic Actors' Guild asked Cohan to write an article for the 1941 Anniversary Issue of the Guild's magazine, *The Call Board.* As President of the Guild, Cohan replied:

Dear George Buck:

Just received your letter in which you call upon me to write seven or eight hundred words for the anniversary number. Now let me tell you something, kid. Seven or eight hundred are a whole lot of words—I could tell a number of guys what I think of them in less words than that. And to be truthful, I don't honestly think I know seven or eight hundred words. There aren't that many words in my entire vocabulary. As a matter of fact, in my whole circle of acquaintances I can't think of any one right now, aside from a few English actors and your brother, Gene, who can spill that many words.

As a dancer, I could never do over three steps. As a composer, I could never find use for over four or five notes in my musical numbers. As a violinist, I could never learn to play above the first position. I'm a one-key piano player, and as a playwright, most of my plays have been presented in two acts for the simple reason that I could seldom think of an idea for a third act. I remember hearing Marcus Loew say one night that he left school as soon as he had learned how to count ten—he claimed that any learning beyond that was altogether unnecessary. And mind you—that was before he ever became a big moving picture magnate.

I remember an old-time advance agent named Sam Dessauer telling me years ago (he was working for Gus Hill at the time) that Hill hollered so loud about telegrams being sent to him "collect" by his various advance men, that he called them all together one day and insisted that there wasn't anything in the world that couldn't be fully explained in ten words. Of course, they had to sit up nights figuring how to phrase their messages, but all admitted afterwards that Mr. Hill was absolutely right.

Speaking of words, there are two words necessary to every man's vocabulary—"yes" and "no." The former is used a great deal out in Hollywood, I understand. When some fellow says, "If you happen to see Mr. So and So, I wish you'd put in a good word for me," does he mean that you should look through Webster's dictionary for a good word or does he mean to actually say something nice about him? If he wants a plug, why doesn't he say so? And when some guy says, "You can take my word for it," why doesn't the guy he says it to ask him what word in the English language is his word? He's made the claim, and he should be challenged.

Cohan, as always a conscientious playgoer, had recently found his patience wearing thin with the moral climate of Broadway:

> And, since we're on the subject of words, have you heard some of the current Broadway plays? Oh, man! Them is words, them is! Barroom conversation is like a prayer meeting compared with some of the dialogue in present-day stage productions. And little children are brought to the matinees, too! Shades of Augustin Daly! I've talked to several playwrights and to some of the producing managers about all this unnecessary profanity being slung at the threatre-going public, but it's all a waste of words to get them to eliminate these objectionable words, because they seem to think that the word gets around that there are certain nasty words spoken in a play, the words on the signboard in front of the theatre read "Standing Room Only." Well, if they really feel that the public will not respond to a clean, wholesome play, how do they account for the huge success of *Life With Father?*
>
> There is one word that some guy has coined here of late that gets on my nerves when ever I hear it—"corny," that is the baby. Anything at all that hasn't to do with West 52nd Street night life is absolutely "corny" to the smart alecks in their ready made dinner suits (two pair of pants). These are the birds who call a saloon that will not permit women to stand at the bar a "corny joint." A mother song is "mush," but some rotten, dirty little off-color ditty sung by a well-manicured, highly perfumed, effeminate guy with black velvet hair is a "wow." Yes, they pull some funny words on us these days, and if you don't keep up with their lingo and their utter disregard and contempt for anything that has to do with yesterday you're "corny." Gosh, how I hate that word. Well, I daresay the Greeks

had a word well suited to the kind of guy I'm talking about and I've got a word for him, too, but I wouldn't dare say it right now.

Best to you, old pal, and love and kisses, to all the members of the Catholic Actors' Guild.

Presidentially yours,

George M. Cohan

Cohan missed the old ways, the old players. Among the new players, he found few really interesting actors, and as to who were his peers he had very decided opinions. This was Cohan the Egoist at his most decisive, although these opinions were known to few and almost always never volunteered. His daughter, Mary, remembers a time when as a result of her pleading, he took her to see Alfred Lunt and Lynn Fontanne in Ferenc Molnar's *The Guardsman.* Cohan had never seen the Lunts but he rather suspected they were not his kind of actors. Invariably as a playgoer, he sat in the back row and on this occasion when Molnar's sophisticated parry and thrust began, Cohan seemed to wish that his back seat were out in the lobby. If ever a play cohered perfectly to its interpreters, it was *The Guardsman* to the Lunts, and Mary watched them, enthralled, along with the rest of the audience. At the end of the first act, Cohan asked his daughter if she wanted to leave. She looked at him in disbelief. He subsided but crossed and uncrossed his legs impatiently the rest of the evening. Walking home, Mary, curiosity considerably aroused, asked her dad who in the American theatre he preferred, if he didn't care for the Lunts? Cohan looked at her, thrust his right thumb emphatically at himself, and he was not smiling.

This failure to appreciate two of America's greatest actors, like his treatment of Rodgers and Hart during *I'd Rather Be Right,* reveals Cohan's blind spot, an exasperating lack of objectivity which verged on childishness. There was a part of Cohan which *was* childish, that part of him which never had a chance to grow up in consequence of his early-set life pattern, his Peck's Bad Boy self. Cohan was probably aware of this identity unconsciously; his autobiography ends with the quotation:

> "And so he snuck off, all alone by himself, and nobody didn't see him no more."
>
> PECK'S BAD BOY

It must be remembered that Cohan was totally self-educated, and even that not under the best of conditions. In James Cagney's words about the man he portrayed in the film, *Yankee Doodle Dandy:* "He was a product of his times, when performers had no guarantee against starvation. It was a very rough period. As far as I know, there was no formal schooling and the strong creative drive gave him no rest."

In any case, Cohan's abounding self-esteem was, on the whole, fully justified. There *were* very few people in the theatre his peer. Cohan, indeed, could only think of one. The choice may seem surprising but only, perhaps, initially. It was Noël Coward.

For a grassroots kind of guy, for a hyperpatriotic American who thought there were too many British actors in the Lambs Club, Cohan was not instinctively inclined to think of Coward as the man he respected most in the theatre. But, on reflection, Coward is almost everything Cohan was: an actor since childhood, manager, playwright, composer, writer of revues, personality singer, a director, and a man who very much enjoys and who for the most part only appears in his own plays. Above all, the two men shared a belief in the primacy of entertainment as the theatre's essential function.

As far as is known, Noël Coward is the only person in the theatre ever to receive a fan letter from George M. Cohan.

In a letter to this writer acknowledging his receipt of Cohan's note, Sir Noël says:

> I shall look forward to your book on George M. Cohan, who I greatly admired. In my opinion he was brilliant in everything he undertook and infinitely charming. A kind man too; he gave me a piano like Irving Berlin's famous one. In those days I could only play and compose in E Flat, so all I had to do was press a little button and get any key I fancied.
>
> I cannot find his letter I am sad to say. I have a feeling he wrote it after seeing me and Gertie in *Tonight at 8:30* which we played in New York at the National late '36–early 37'.
>
> I have a strong feeling that the photograph was taken when I went to Boston for the opening there of *I'd Rather Be Right* in 1937.
>
> Yes, the letter was one of praise, I do remember that; I was touched he had taken the trouble and very proud . . .

Cohan across the years had any number of favorite actors, among them Nat Goodwin, Lucien Guitry, Grant Mitchell, Spencer Tracy, and Walter Huston, but his last recorded preference was for Noël Coward—which in no way diminishes his regard for the others. "It does come as a little bit of a surprise that Noël Coward at the last was Cohan's favorite actor in the theatre," says J. D. Salinger, "but maybe that surprise could break down under a little thought. I suppose we like best what we most approve, and it seems to me that Cohan was bound to wholemindedly approve the way Coward under-read a line, with style—because it was the thing Cohan could and did, too. The styles of under-reading may have been worlds apart, but the intelligence and cleverness of each man's style were terribly close together, I think. They both spoke, conversed, on stage without any obvious theatricality, and they did it equally expertly. Do you remember Coward's performance in the old plummy Ben Hecht movie, *The Scoundrel?* Or some of the speeches Coward had to make to his ship's crew in *In Which We Serve?* The peculiar kind of insouciant understatement was so like Cohan's own—as Cohan was, anyway, in *Ah, Wilderness!*"

That Cohan could deeply appreciate Noël Coward and fail to enjoy the Lunts whose acting style is akin to Coward's is a mystery. (Although one can easily see why the old-fashioned Cohan reacted instinctively against the playful sexuality of *The Guardsman.*) This mystery is simply another contradiction in Cohan's makeup. Ward Morehouse quotes an unidentified Boston lady who had known Cohan all his life: "A complex and amazing man, George was, and one of a million contradictions. Vain and violent-tempered, childish at times, sulky and temperamental, but a man with a heart and a soul, one who was easily hurt and one who could be a great friend. There was a wistfulness always about George and there was never another Irishman born in the world who had his unfailing charm."

In the summer of 1941, a grim irony commenced. Cohan began to experience the symptoms of the form of cancer which killed Sam Harris. But he continued to work. He was crafting *The Musical Comedy Man,* a play marked by almost complete self-identification of Cohan with the leading character throughout. This is Joe Callahan, an Irish-American musical comedy star. His Japanese valet is Hiranto; Cohan's valet was a smiling little Jap named Mike Hirano. Callahan is approached by a lady playwright who asks him to forsake musicals temporarily and appear in her drama, *The Actor Man.* The plot she outlines is only a slight reworking of Cohan's *The Song and Dance Man.* Callahan is intrigued despite his reluctance to do anything other than musical comedy, but suddenly he seizes on the idea that their present situation—this very encounter of theirs—is the perfect springboard for something he has needed for some time: a substantial story line for his next musical. The title of that show, he now decides, will be *The Musical Comedy Man,* and it will concentrate on Callahan's decision to choose between the straight play and the musical. This is an obvious echo of Cohan's own dilemma in choosing to work for other producers. There are Pirandellian overtones when the "real" characters of the first act wander into the second act and, irritated at the dislocation, ask Callahan to explain to the audience their plot function as initiators of the action. Callahan is about to do so when the stage manager impatiently points out that the audience doesn't care anything about the play, they came to see Callahan dance. (Cohan-Callahan's blithe justification for his musicals' threadbare plots.) So Callahan dances, to one of the brightest tunes of Cohan's career as a composer, a song (later used in the Broadway musical, *George M!*) in which he describes himself proudly:

> There he goes on his dancing toes
> With that famous American stride–
> Full of musical comedy pride
> Traffic holds up when he hits Main Street.
> Broadway knows
> That it's all a pose,
> It's a perfect publicity plan.
> But they like the pose,
> The dancing toes,
> They even go to see his shows.
> They've famed him,
> They've even named him:
> The Yankee Doodle
> Yankee Doodle musical comedy man.

Intratheatrical to its every fiber, *The Musical Comedy Man* is principally a series of rehearsals for a musical called *The Musical Comedy Man.* It is a joyous affair, despite its tenuous plot, and it allows Cohan to comment on his own theatrical foibles and predilections, even to speak of his ostensible vanity. Callahan, after the lady playwright has left after the offer of her play to him, explodes to Julie, his customary leading lady:

> CALLAHAN: I'm not excited—I'm hurt, I'm sore—sore as a pig. I am, on the square. I have a sense of my own importance. I've always taken great pride in the fact that I'm not one of the common garden variety of theatre minds. I've given it something. I've created. I've worked—a half century of hard work. And I'm darned proud of the position I've made for myself in a profession that I've done as much for as it's done for me.

Callahan continues in this vein for a few moments, emphasizing that the lady playwright with her record of "about three hits and forty flops" has colossal cheek in offering him a job as an actor. Julie rounds on him, telling him his prating about the lady playwright's swelled head is ironic in view of his own conceited outburst. Callahan reflects, then agrees with her:

> CALLAHAN: You're right, kid. I shouldn't have exploded like that. Maybe I am a little swelled up on myself. I don't know. But I guess it's only natural to get like that when you're used to a lot of applause. But I do know that it's easy enough to get that way with a little success in this business if you don't watch yourself and develop a balance wheel.

Cohan-Callahan further explains that an approach from an outside management has unbalanced him a bit, even provoking him to rudeness:

> You see, it's the first time I experienced anything of the kind since I've been under my own management. I felt I was being sort of—well, not exactly patronized, that isn't the word, but—well, it hurt my dignity or

> whatever you call it . . . It took me down a peg in my own estimation for the moment and I suppose that's the reason I had to start telling myself what a great guy I was to get back in good standing with myself.

In effect, belated apologies to Messrs. Rodgers and Hart.

One of the best songs in *The Musical Comedy Man* is a reworking of one of his earliest songs, "Life's a Very Funny Proposition After All." Titled "Life Is Like a Musical Comedy," it can reasonably be taken as Cohan's final—and light-hearted—comment on mortal existence:

> Life is what you make it, it's just the way you take it,
> Life can be a tragedy or life can be a song.
> Scientific teachers, philosophers and preachers
> Have forty different themes on the way to get along.
> But when all is said and done, why do they worry so?
> To me to look on life is just like looking at a show.

CHORUS

> Life is like a musical comedy,
> Life is like a travesty show.
> Nobody seems to know just what it's about,
> Yet ev'rybody's trying to figure it out.
> Life, with all its girls and comedians—
> Life is like a blackout revue.
> Unexpected scenes, all the way through.
> Life is make believe and spectacular.
> Life will hand you just a few laughs.
> A little dialogue, then somebody sings.
> Just like those Gilbert and Sullivan things.
> Life is just the same over distant seas,
> Life's a series of inconsistencies.
> Lights on, lights out—before you know:
> Life's just a great big musical show.

The Musical Comedy Man, like any play, cannot be fully assessed until it is lifted from the printed page and brought to life in the theatre. The plot, despite its heavy intratheatricalities, is something different for him, and the songs are very good if not quite vintage Cohan. Any production of the play would, of course, have a sizable lack: George M. Cohan playing himself.

It was with some thought of playing himself that Hollywood from time to time approached Cohan in the hope that he would sing and dance his way through a biographical film. He had always refused. In 1940, Warner Brothers, convinced that the format of Walter Kerr's *Yankee Doodle Boy* was an entertaining way to tell Cohan's story, sold the idea to him. His previous refusals to authorize a film biography were influenced by a reluctance to reveal his personal life but the *Yankee Doodle Boy* format was quite another thing. Cohan approved it on the condition that his personal life would be covered only briefly and that it would center around his wife Agnes, using her middle name, Mary. Robert H. Buckner who did most of the screenplay of *Yankee Doodle Dandy* talked at length with Cohan and submitted a preliminary shooting script for approval in 1941.

Cohan, despite the heavy drain on his vitality made by intestinal cancer, wrote almost a book-length series of notes on the script, including long scenes in dialogue understandably more in the nature of a play than film scenario. The longest of these episodes is a sentimental account of Cohan's meeting Agnes Mary Nolan. Totally fictional in details (they actually met backstage, not aboard an ocean liner as Cohan has it), it is a deeply touching sequence because it reveals that after thirty-two years and despite occasional love affairs, Cohan was still pulsatingly in love with his wife.

But this episode, along with most of Cohan's dialogue submitted to Warner Brothers, could not be fitted into the film because of the necessary precedence of the musical material. Cohan wholeheartedly approved the choice of James Cagney to play him. "When it was decided that I was to do the job," says Cagney, "I sat down with Lynne Overman, Frank McHugh, Spencer Tracy, and Pat O'Brien to find out what I could about the man himself. They all had known Cohan. I was the only one in our group who hadn't met him or worked with him. I had seen him in *Ah, Wilderness!* and from that I keyed the mannerisms. He was a fine actor and often did much with very little. The dancing I got from Johnny Boyle who had staged dances for Cohan and who had appeared in *The Cohan Revue of 1916*. The Cohan walk Johnny had not forgotten. In any case, George M. was quite a fellow, and in summing up, I have said many times that we took fifty years of a very troubled life and set it to his music. That it turned out well was because of the material we had to work with—and he did it. Happily for all of us, he liked it when he saw it."

Cohan, indeed, liked *Yankee Doodle Dandy* but with some reservations about the dialogue. After an abdominal operation in October 1941 he went up to his country estate at Monroe to rest and there was shown a print of the film. He watched the film in the company of his son, George, and at the end of the showing, his son asked, "How did you like it, Dad?" Cohan shook his head admiringly, and referring to the Cagney performance, said, "My God, what an act to follow."

The greatest praise that can be given *Yankee Doodle Dandy* is that it befits its subject absolutely. It is a beguiling film because it is the Cohan music set to a pace as fast as any Cohan musical, which indeed it is, and if the book is slight and perfunctory, that is in the Cohan tradition, too. The film's greatest virtue is its happy marriage of the dynamic Cagney performance with the crisp and pounding rhythms of Cohan's songs. For his performance, James Cagney won the Oscar as Best Actor of 1942 by the Academy of Motion Picture Arts and Sciences. The story has nary a problem which is just the way Cohan wanted it. Speaking of *Yankee Doodle Dandy,* Georgette Cohan said, "That's the kind of a life Daddy would have liked to have lived."

On January 2, 1942, Cohan had a second operation which revealed that his cancer had spread devastatingly. He was aware that a virtual death sentence had been passed on him, but his bravery was unwavering. He continued to revise *The Musical Comedy Man,* his pencil and yellow pad never far from his bedside. By late summer of 1942 his weakness was pronounced, but one evening he announced to his nurse a determination to take a ride down Broadway. She argued, but he was adamant. They drove down Fifth Avenue, through Times Square and the theatre district, stopping briefly at the southeast corner of Broadway and 43rd Street to look at the movie house which had once been the George M. Cohan Theatre. Then down to 14th Street to the site of Tony Pastor's Music Hall, then to Union Square where the Four Cohans had made their New York debut, finally back uptown to the Hollywood Theatre (now the Mark Hellinger Theatre) where Cohan and his nurse sat in the back row, unnoticed, to watch a few minutes of *Yankee Doodle Dandy.* Cohan smiled as he heard the actor playing President Roosevelt and James Cagney speak two of the very few lines Cohan actually wrote for the film which were retained in the script: "Where else in the world could a plain guy like me sit down and talk things over with the head man?"; "Well now, you know, Mr. Cohan, that's as good a definition of America as I've ever heard." In Cohan's view, it made a pretty good ending to a pretty good picture. As "Over There," the last number in the film, was playing, he walked out of the theatre and was driven back to his apartment. He had given his last regards to Broadway.

On the evening of November 4, it was apparent that he was slipping into a coma. To his bedside in his apartment at 993 Fifth Avenue came Monsignor John J. Casey, representing Archbishop Spellman, and Father Francis X. Shea, to administer the last rites of the Roman Catholic Church. Just before he lost consciousness, Cohan spoke his last words, "Look after Agnes."* She was there, together with Cohan's

* His request was honored. Mrs. George M. Cohan was lovingly attended by her children until her death at eighty-nine on September 9, 1972. Quite hale during most of her bed-ridden years, she was a great television fan and whenever *Yankee Doodle Dandy* was shown, joined in the songs with resonant voice. She remembered their lyrics in detail and sang them with much the gusto she did as an original cast member of *Little Johnny Jones.*

children, Georgette, Mary, Helen, and George M., Jr. As the dawn was breaking on November 5, 1942, Mary Cohan, holding her father's hand, felt it go limp. He had gone easily, without pain.

Along Broadway in the last thirty years, there has been a popular impression that George M. Cohan died embittered. Those who say that did not know their man. Unhappy with the failure of *The Return of the Vagabond*, concerned about his health, Cohan was hardly euphoric in his last two years of life, but to the end he was stoutly optimistic, writing and waiting for his return to Broadway. George M. Cohan was a man who believed in miracles. He no longer pondered why his kind of theatre failed to flourish; he accepted the change even if he didn't relish it. Now he did not look back. He would have to go on to something new. His innate resiliency—a word that cannot be overused about Cohan—convinced him he must and would.

One of the last things he said when the end was near came in response to an impulsive comment by Gene Buck. "By God, George," Buck said, "no man ever did what you did in the theatre. No man. Doesn't that make you proud as hell?" Cohan aroused himself from his sedation and said with a warm grin lighting his still youthful features, "No complaints, kid. No complaints." It was a phrase he coined years before about his life situation, and it obtained to the very end, bespeaking his utter self-content. To the end he was an optimist and a man with a justifiably good self-image. In *The Return of the Vagabond* Cohan wrote a poem which the Vagabond speaks, a poem which encapsulates Cohan, essential humorist, and a man well at ease with himself:

I'm the best pal that I ever had,
  I like to be with me;
I like to sit and tell myself
  Things confidentially.

I often sit and ask me
  If I shouldn't or I should
And I find that my advice to me
  Is always pretty good.

I never got acquainted with
  Myself till here of late;
And I find myself a bully chum,
  I treat me simply great.

I talk with me and walk with me,
  And show me right and wrong;
I never knew how well myself
  And I could get along.

Just get together with yourself
  And trust yourself with you,
And you'll be surprised how well yourself
  Will like you if you do.

"In the days just before my dad died, we talked of many things," says Mary Cohan. "We talked of things we had never talked of before. We admitted to each other our own stubbornness, and the things we would have done differently. I sat beside his bed and held his hand by the hour while we talked—and the one thing I know with certainty is that he was a deeply happy man. The Equity affair was the only thing in his life that ever really upset him. For the rest —it was a glorious life, and no one knew it better than he."

A Solemn Requiem Mass was held for Cohan at St. Patrick's Cathedral at 10 A.M., Saturday, November 7, 1942. The Cathedral was filled with people from all classes and creeds but theatrical people dominated. After the Mass, when the casket was lifted up to be borne down the aisle by the pallbearers, a touch of beautifully crafted drama was added, a touch the master showman for whom it was offered would have loved. For the first time in St. Patrick's long history, a secular song was played on its great organ. Pietro Yon, the Cathedral's organist, had the inspired idea of playing "Over

There" slowly, softly, in funeral march tempo. This totally unexpected tribute triggered a release of tears from many in the Cathedral. The funeral procession, after making its way through the thousands lining Fifth Avenue, drove north to the Bronx. There, in the family mausoleum at Woodlawn Cemetery, Cohan was laid to rest with his mother, his father, and his sister. The Four Cohans had finished their tour.

"He was stubborn," says Jack McGowan. "The Irish *are* stubborn, they hate defeat. That was his principal fault but it was never objectionable, deep down. You had to love him in spite of it. Maybe I liked him too much but I don't think I did. I don't think you could like a man with all that talent too much. The sum total of the man, not the individual pieces, made him the most talented man in the history of the American theatre."

"The last time I talked to him was after a performance of *I'd Rather Be Right*," remembers Peggy Wood. "I went backstage to his dressing room, and they said he was on stage. So I went there, and I found him still in his costume—the cutaway, striped pants, and top hat. Just a few spotlights were on. He was wandering about the stage, dancing a bit here and there with cane in hand, poking at things, working out some things. Now—he'd been playing that show for *months*, yet here he was rehearsing, improving his performance, trying out new bits of business. We had the grandest chat, sitting on one of the benches on the set. He didn't have time to take me back to his dressing room to talk: he was concerned with what he was going to be doing at the evening performance. After we chatted, he said, 'Glad to see you, darling' and he just went back to his work, in total concentration, still looking for perfection.

"Knowing him gave me the sense of what it meant to search for things in the theatre, never to *stop* searching. That was our last visit. I looked back at him—working patiently, alone on that deserted stage. He had never stopped thinking about the theatre."

APPENDIX A

Listing of George M. Cohan Productions in New York

(and his stage appearances)

TITLE	AUTHOR	DATE	FEATURED PLAYERS
The Governor's Son	George M. Cohan	Feb. 25, 1901 (32 perf.) Savoy Theatre	with the Four Cohans Produced by L. C. Behman
Running for Office	George M. Cohan	April 27, 1903 (48 perf.) 14th Street Theatre	with the Four Cohans Produced by Fred Niblo
		Several songs and sketches by Cohan were incorporated into *Mother Goose,* a musical extravaganza by J. Hickory Wood (sic) and Arthur Collins, produced by Klaw and Erlanger, at the New Amsterdam Theatre, Dec 2, 1903. (105 perf.)	
Little Johnny Jones	George M. Cohan	Nov. 7, 1904 (52 perf.) Liberty Theatre. Revived at New York Theatre May 8 to Aug. 26, 1905, and from Nov. 13 to Dec. 9, 1905	with the Four Cohans Produced by Sam Harris
Forty-five Minutes from Broadway	George M. Cohan	Jan. 1, 1906 (90 perf.) New Amsterdam Theatre	with Fay Templeton and Victor Moore Produced by Klaw and Erlanger

George Washington, Jr.	George M. Cohan	Feb. 12, 1906 (81 perf.) Herald Square Theatre	with George, Nellie and Jerry Cohan and Ethel Levey Produced by Sam Harris

Cohan and Harris Productions

Popularity	George M. Cohan	Oct. 1, 1906 (24 perf.) Wallack's Theatre	with Thomas W. Ross
Little Johnny Jones	George M. Cohan	April 22, 1907 (16 perf.) Academy of Music	with George, Nellie and Jerry Cohan
The Honeymooners	George M. Cohan	June 3, 1907 (72 perf.) Aerial Gardens atop the New Amsterdam Theatre	with George, Nellie and Jerry Cohan
The Talk of New York	George M. Cohan	Dec. 3, 1907 (157 perf.) Knickerbocker Theatre	with Victor Moore
Fifty Miles from Boston	George M. Cohan	Feb. 3, 1908 (32 perf.) Garrick Theatre	with Edna Wallace Hopper
The Yankee Prince	George M. Cohan	April 20, 1908 (28 perf.) Knickerbocker Theatre	with the Four Cohans
The Cohan and Harris Minstrels	George ("Honey Boy") Evans and George M. Cohan	Aug. 16, 1909 (16 perf.) New York Theatre	with Julian Eltinge
The Fortune Hunter	Winchell Smith	Sept. 4, 1909 (345 perf.) Gaiety Theatre	with John Barrymore

The Man Who Owns Broadway	George M. Cohan	Oct. 11, 1909 (128 perf.) New York Theatre	with Raymond Hitchcock
Get-Rich-Quick Wallingford	George M. Cohan	Sept. 19, 1910 (424 perf.) Gaiety Theatre, and later the Cohan Theatre	with Hale Hamilton and Edward Ellis
The Aviator	James Montgomery	Dec. 6, 1910 (44 perf.) Astor Theatre	with Wallace Eddinger
The Little Millionaire	George M. Cohan	Sept. 25, 1911 (192 perf.) Cohan Theatre	with George, Nellie and Jerry Cohan
The Only Son	Winchell Smith	Oct. 16, 1911 (32 perf.) Gaiety Theatre	with Wallace Eddinger
The Red Widow	Book: Channing Pollock and Rennold Wolf Music: C. J. Gebest	Nov. 6, 1911 (128 perf.) Astor Theatre	with Raymond Hitchcock
Officer 666	Augustin MacHugh	Jan. 29, 1912 (192 perf.) Gaiety Theatre	with Wallace Eddinger
Forty-five Minutes from Broadway	George M. Cohan	March 14, 1912 (36 perf.) Cohan Theatre	with George M. Cohan
Broadway Jones	George M. Cohan	Sept. 23, 1912 (176 perf.) Cohan Theatre	with George, Nellie and Jerry Cohan
Hawthorne of the U.S.A.	J. B. Fagan	Nov. 4, 1912 (72 perf.) Astor Theatre	with Douglas Fairbanks

Stop Thief	Carlyle Moore	Dec. 25, 1912 (149 perf.) Gaiety Theatre	with Frank Bacon
Nearly Married	Edgar Selwyn	Sept. 5, 1913 (123 perf.) Gaiety Theatre	with Bruce McRae and Ruth Shepley
Seven Keys to Baldpate	George M. Cohan	Sept. 22, 1913 (320 perf.) Astor Theatre	with Wallace Eddinger
The Beauty Shop	Book: Channing Pollock and Rennold Wolf Music: C. J. Gebest	April 13, 1914 (88 perf.) Astor Theatre	with Raymond Hitchcock
It Pays to Advertise	Roi Cooper Megrue and Walter Hackett	Sept. 8, 1914 (399 perf.) Cohan Theatre	with Grant Mitchell
The Miracle Man	George M. Cohan	Sept. 21, 1914 (97 perf.) Astor Theatre	with Frank Bacon and Percy Helton
Hello, Broadway!	George M. Cohan	Dec. 25, 1914 (123 perf.) Astor Theatre	with George M. Cohan and William Collier
Young America	Fred Ballard	Aug. 28, 1915 (105 perf.) Astor Theatre	with Otto Kruger, Peggy Wood and Percy Helton
The House of Glass	Max Marcin and George M. Cohan	Sept. 1, 1915 (245 perf.) Candler Theatre	with Mary Ryan
Hit-the-Trail Holliday	George M. Cohan	Sept. 13, 1915 (336 perf.) Astor Theatre	with Fred Niblo
Cohan Revue of 1916	George M. Cohan	Feb. 9, 1916 (165 perf.) Astor Theatre	with Richard Carle and Charles Winninger

The Intruder	Cyril Harcourt	Sept. 26, 1916 (31 perf.) Cohan and Harris Theatre	with Frank Kemble Cooper
Captain Kidd, Jr.	Rida Johnson Young	Nov. 13, 1916 (128 perf.) Cohan and Harris Theatre	with Otto Kruger
The Willow Tree	J. H. Benrimo and Harrison Rhodes	March 6, 1917 (103 perf.) Cohan and Harris Theatre	with Fay Bainter
A Tailor-Made Man	Harry James Smith	Aug. 27, 1917 (398 perf.) Cohan and Harris Theatre	with Grant Mitchell
The King	G. A. Caillavet, Robert de Flers and Emmanuel Arene	Nov. 20, 1917 (127 perf.) Cohan Theatre	with Leo Ditrichstein
Going Up	Book: Otto Harbach Music: Louis Hirsch	Dec. 25, 1917 (351 perf.) Liberty Theatre	with Frank Craven, Ruth Donnelly and Donald Meek
Cohan Revue of 1918	George M. Cohan	Dec. 31, 1917 (96 perf.) New Amsterdam Theatre	with Nora Bayes and Charles Winninger
The Little Teacher	Harry James Smith	Feb. 4, 1918 (128 perf.) Playhouse Theatre	with Mary Ryan
Once Upon a Time	Rachel Crothers	April 15, 1918 (24 perf.) Fulton Theatre	with Chauncey Olcott
		Cohan played in J. Hartley Manners's *Out There* at the Century Theatre with an all-star cast for benefit of the Red Cross, 8 performances beginning May 17, 1918. Then on three-week tour in leading American cities	

Three Faces East	Anthony Paul Kelly	Aug. 13, 1918 (335 perf.) Cohan and Harris Theatre, then to Longacre Theatre	with Emmett Corrigan and Violet Heming
The Matinee Hero	Leo Ditrichstein and A. E. Thomas	Oct. 7, 1918 (64 perf.) Vanderbilt Theatre	with Leo Ditrichstein
A Prince There Was	George M. Cohan	Dec. 24, 1918 (159 perf.) Cohan Theatre	with George M. Cohan
The Voice of McConnell	George M. Cohan	Dec. 25, 1918 (30 perf.) Manhattan Opera House	with Chauncey Olcott
Mis' Nelly of N'Orleans	Laurence Eyre	Feb. 4, 1919 (127 perf.) Henry Miller's Theatre	with Mrs. Fiske
The Royal Vagabond	George M. Cohan (utilizing book and lyric material by Stephen Ivor-Szinney and William Cary Duncan and music by Anselm Goetzel)	Feb. 17, 1919 (208 perf.) Cohan and Harris Theatre	with Frederick Santley and Tessa Kosta
The Acquittal	Rita Weiman and George M. Cohan	Jan. 5, 1920 (138 perf.) Cohan and Harris Theatre	with William Harrigan and Chrystal Herne

George M. Cohan Productions

Genius and the Crowd	John T. McIntyre and Francis Hill	Sept. 6, 1920 (24 perf.) Cohan Theatre	with George Renavent

The Tavern	George M. Cohan	Sept. 27, 1920 (252 perf.) Cohan Theatre	with Arnold Daly
The Meanest Man in the World	Augustin MacHugh	Oct. 12, 1920 (202 perf.) Hudson Theatre	with Frank M. Thomas (George M. Cohan replacing Thomas during the run)
Mary	Book: Otto Harbach and Frank Mandel Music: Louis Hirsch	Oct. 18, 1920 (219 perf.) Knickerbocker Theatre	with Janet Velie and Jack McGowan
Nemesis	Augustus Thomas	April 4, 1921 (56 perf.) Hudson Theatre	with Emmett Corrigan and Pedro de Cordoba
The Tavern	George M. Cohan	May 23, 1921 (27 perf.) Hudson Theatre	with George M. Cohan heading the Chicago company of the play
The O'Brien Girl	Book: Otto Harbach and Frank Mandel Music: Louis Hirsch	Oct. 3, 1921 (164 perf.) Liberty Theatre	with Elizabeth Hines
Madeleine and the Movies	George M. Cohan	March 6, 1922 (80 perf.) Gaiety Theatre	with James Rennie and Georgette Cohan (George M. Cohan replacing Rennie during the run)
So This Is London	Arthur Goodrich	Aug. 30, 1922 (343 perf.) Hudson Theatre	with Lily Cahill and Edmund Breese
Little Nellie Kelly	George M. Cohan	Nov. 13, 1922 (248 perf.) Liberty Theatre	with Elizabeth Hines and Charles King

Two Fellows and a Girl	Vincent Lawrence	July 19, 1923 (132 perf.) Vanderbilt Theatre	with John Halliday and Alan Dinehart
The Rise of Rosie O'Reilly	George M. Cohan	Dec. 25, 1923 (87 perf.) Liberty Theatre	with Virginia O'Brien and Jack McGowan
The Song and Dance Man	George M. Cohan	Dec. 31, 1923 (96 perf.) Hudson Theatre	with George M. Cohan
American Born	George M. Cohan	Oct. 5, 1925 (88 perf.) Hudson Theatre	with George M. Cohan
The Home Towners	George M. Cohan	Aug. 23, 1926 (64 perf.) Hudson Theatre	with Robert McWade
Yellow	Margaret Vernon	Sept. 21, 1926 (135 perf.) National Theatre	with Chester Morris and Spencer Tracy
The Baby Cyclone	George M. Cohan	Sept. 12, 1927 (184 perf.) Henry Miller's Theatre	with Grant Mitchell and Spencer Tracy
The Merry Malones	George M. Cohan	Sept. 26, 1927 (208 perf.) Erlanger's Theatre	with George M. Cohan
Los Angeles	Max Marcin and Donald Ogden Stewart	Dec. 19, 1927 (16 perf.) Hudson Theatre	with Frances Dale and Alison Skipworth
Whispering Friends	George M. Cohan	Feb. 20, 1928 (112 perf.) Hudson Theatre	with Chester Morris and William Harrigan
Elmer the Great	Ring Lardner	Sept. 24, 1928 (40 perf.) Lyceum Theatre	with Walter Huston

By Request	J. C. and Elliott Nugent	Sept. 27, 1928 (28 perf.) Hudson Theatre	with J. C. and Elliott Nugent
Billie	George M. Cohan	Oct. 1, 1928 (112 perf.) Erlanger's Theatre	with Polly Walker and Joseph Wagstaff
Vermont	A. E. Thomas	Jan. 7, 1929 (15 perf.) Erlanger's Theatre	with John T. Doyle and Allyn Joslyn
Gambling	George M. Cohan	Aug. 26, 1929 (152 perf.) Fulton Theatre	with George M. Cohan
The Tavern	George M. Cohan	May 19, 1930 (32 perf.) Fulton Theatre	with George M. Cohan
The Song and Dance Man	George M. Cohan	June 16, 1930 (16 perf.) Fulton Theatre	with George M. Cohan
The Rhapsody	Louis K. Anspacher	Sept. 15, 1930 (16 perf.) Cort Theatre	with Louis Calhern and Natalie Schafer
Friendship	George M. Cohan	Aug. 31, 1931 (24 perf.) Fulton Theatre	with George M. Cohan
Pigeons and People	George M. Cohan	Jan. 16, 1933 (70 perf.) Sam H. Harris Theatre	with George M. Cohan
		Cohan appeared in Eugene O'Neill's *Ah, Wilderness!* in a Theatre Guild production for 289 performances in New York, beginning Oct. 2, 1933, at the Guild Theatre	
Seven Keys to Baldpate	George M. Cohan	May 27, 1935 (8 perf.) National Theatre	with George M. Cohan (for the Players Club)

Dear Old Darling	George M. Cohan	March 2, 1936 (16 perf.) Alvin Theatre	with George M. Cohan

Cohan and Harris Productions

Fulton of Oak Falls	George M. Cohan	Feb. 10, 1937 (37 perf.) Morosco Theatre	with George M. Cohan

Cohan appeared in Kaufman and Hart's *I'd Rather Be Right* in a Sam Harris production for 290 performances in New York, beginning Nov. 2, 1937, at the Alvin Theatre

George M. Cohan Productions

The Return of the Vagabond	George M. Cohan	May 17, 1940 (7 perf.) National Theatre	with George M. Cohan

NOTE: The length of Broadway run usually had little to do with the financial success of Cohan's productions. Road company tours, sale of stock company rights and profits from sheet music—printed by his own publishing company—made most of his productions highly profitable.

APPENDIX B

Plays Written by George M. Cohan

(Asterisk indicates one-act play or sketch.
All plays listed under year of composition.
If co-author, so stated. Cohan never allowed his name to be used as co-author unless he was responsible for well over half the play. In the case of *The Meanest Man in the World, The Acquittal* and *So This Is London,* he did not bill himself as co-author although he was, in fact, responsible for most of these plays' dialogue by the time they had reached Broadway.)

1895 *On the Road**
*Money to Burn**

1896 *The Professor's Wife**

1897 *A Tip on the Derby**
*Running for Office** (Later expanded to full-length)
*His Wife's Hero**
*A Hot Old Time** (Later expanded to full-length)

1898 *A Game of Golf**
*The Dangerous Mrs. Delaney**
*The Charitable Mrs. Jones**
*The Governor's Son** (Later expanded to full-length)

1899 *The National Game**
*To Boston On Business**
*The Town Clown**
*Hogan of the Hansom**
*A Wise Guy** (Later expanded to full-length)

1900 *A Wise Guy* (Full-length)†
The Governor's Son (Full-length)

† *A Wise Guy* is technically Cohan's first full-length play but he always referred to it as his first full-length "musical show." It is little more than a number of vaudeville sketches centering around a blustering piano mover who hates work. It totally lacks the cohesion of *The Governor's Son* which Cohan called his first full-length "play."

1901 _A Hot Old Time_ (Full-length; written with Edgar Selden)

1903 _Running for Office_ (Full-length)

1904 _Little Johnny Jones_

1905 _George Washington, Jr._
Forty-five Minutes from Broadway

1906 _Popularity_

1907 _The Young Napoleon_*
Fifty Miles from Boston
The Honeymooners
The Talk of New York

1908 _The Little Blonde Lady_*
The Yankee Prince

1909 _The Belle of the Barbers' Ball_* (Incorporated in _Cohan and Harris Minstrels_)
Cohan and Harris Minstrels (Written with George "Honey Boy" Evans)
The Man Who Owns Broadway

1910 _The Firemen's Picnic_* (For Friars' Frolic that year)
Get-Rich-Quick Wallingford

1911 _Hogan's Millions_*
_The Pullman Porters' Ball_* (For Friars' Frolic that year)
The Little Millionaire

1912 _All Members of Our Club_* (For Friars' Frolic that year)
Broadway Jones

1913 _Seven Keys to Baldpate_

1914 _Hello, Broadway!_
The Miracle Man

1915 _Hit-the-Trail Holliday_
The House of Glass (Written with Max Marcin)

1916 _The Moving Picture Studio_* (For Friars' Frolic that year)
Honest John O'Brien
Cohan Revue of 1916

1917 _Cohan Revue of 1918_

1918 *A Prince There Was*
The Voice of McConnell

1919 *The Royal Vagabond*

1920 *The Farrell Case**
The Tavern
The Acquittal (Written with Rita Weiman)
The Meanest Man in the World (Written with Augustin MacHugh)

1922 *Madeleine and the Movies*
Little Nellie Kelly
So This Is London (Written with Arthur Goodrich)

1923 *The Song and Dance Man*
The Rise of Rosie O'Reilly
Two Fellows and a Girl (Written with Vincent Lawrence)

1925 *American Born*

1926 *The Home Towners*

1927 *The Baby Cyclone*
The Merry Malones

1928 *Billie*
Whispering Friends

1929 *Gambling*

1930 *All in the Game*
A Well-Known Woman

1931 *Friendship*

1932 *Confidential Service*
Pigeons and People

1935 *Dear Old Darling*

1937 *Fulton of Oak Falls*

1940 *The Return of the Vagabond*

1941 *The Musical Comedy Man*

NOTE: Mary Cohan has a distinct memory of her father writing a play called *Step Into My Parlor,* based on the notorious Everleigh Sisters of Chicago, but neither script nor record of try-out performance seem to have survived.

ACKNOWLEDGMENTS

For the fullest information on George M. Cohan, I am principally indebted to the dedicatee. All of Mr. Cohan's family were helpful, particularly Mrs. George M. Cohan, Georgette Cohan, and George M. "Mike" Cohan, Jr.

One old actor assured me: "You'll only find the real Georgie on the stage—and in his plays." Whether or not that is true, I have had at least all of the latter to examine closely, thanks to the George M. Cohan Collection of the Museum of the City of New York. For helpful access to it, I am most grateful to the late Sam Pearce, ever-patient Curator of the Theatre Collection and his staff.

In a comparatively full and unsheltered life, I have never met people who combined professional expertise and personal kindness more functionally than librarians. Among theatre librarians, I am most indebted to Paul Myers, the unendingly helpful Curator of the Theatre Collection, Library and Museum of the Performing Arts, Lincoln Center, and his staff; and to Louis A. Rachow, Librarian of the Walter Hampden Memorial Library at the Players, a model for his profession.

Most of the photographs in the book come from the Cohan material held by the Hoblitzelle Theatre Arts Library, University of Texas at Austin. I am grateful to its Curator,

Frederick J. Hunter, to W. H. Crain of the Library, and to my friend, Professor James Moll of the Drama Department at Austin, who helped select many of the photographs.

My deep gratitude also goes to:

Brooks Atkinson for several comments on Cohan. His *Broadway* was also invaluable for source material.

David Black and Konrad Matthaei, producers of *George M!* for tape recordings of many Cohan songs which they made in preparation for their production.

James Cagney for his impressions of the man he portrayed so magnificently in the Warner Brothers film, *Yankee Doodle Dandy.*

Ida Cohen of the firm of O'Brien, Driscoll and Raftery, attorneys for the Cohan estate, for help in determining the names and copyright dates of many Cohan plays.

Marian Shockley Collyer for an account of Cohan during the run of *Dear Old Darling.*

Sir Noël Coward for his memories of Cohan.

Ruth Donnelly for stories of George M. Cohan's world.

Parker Fennelly for a copy of his play, *Yesterday's Lilacs,* which was Cohanized into *Fulton of Oak Falls.*

Abel Green, editor of *Variety,* for several insights into Cohan legend and fact, and for many kindnesses through the years.

Kathryn Givney for her memories of Cohan during the run of *Fulton of Oak Falls.*

Katharine Hepburn for precious time taken from her stint in *Coco* to tell me some of Spencer Tracy's affectionate memories of his old mentor.

The late Percy Helton for memories of his days as a child actor in Cohan shows.

Celeste Holm for her memories of Cohan during the run of *The Return of the Vagabond.*

Walter Kerr for details of his experiences with Cohan during and after the Catholic University production of *Yankee Doodle Boy.*

Larry Kasha for help at a time when it was especially needed.

Dan Langan for allowing me to tape all of his precious original Cohan recordings.

Nedda Harrigan Logan (Mrs. Joshua Logan) for information about her father, Edward Harrigan, and her brother, William Harrigan.

Herbert A. Marks for information about Cohan the composer. I am grateful to Mr. Marks and the company he headed before his retirement, the Edward B. Marks Music Corporation, for permission to quote from various Cohan songs, all of which are now owned by the Marks Music Corporation.

The late (and how I hate to use those words about that vital, delightful man) Chester Morris for a number of anecdotes about the Cohan of the mid-twenties.

Jack McGowan for one of the most pleasant afternoons of my life in telling me stories about the man he worked for so felicitously in *Mary* and *The Rise of Rosie O'Reilly*.

Elliott Nugent for his memories of Cohan.

Pat O'Brien for anecdotes of Cohan and for being such damned fun.

Dr. Francis J. O'Neill for particulars of the life of Cora Dick Gantt. Also helpful in this respect were Dr. Arthur Zitrin and Dr. Norman S. Wikler.

Arvid Paulson, now a leading Strindberg scholar, for memories of his acting days with Cohan in *Pigeons and People* and other plays.

William Post, Jr. for stories of Cohan the actor.

Selena Royle Renavent, whose dimples will live happily in cinematic history, for memories of her old boss.

J. D. Salinger for some words and for that most practical form of support—moral.

Larry Swindell for Cohan anecdotes both from his own fund and from his book, *Spencer Tracy*.

Margaret Webster for insight into Cohan with her account of the weeks she spent as his director in *Madam, Will You Walk?*

Peggy Wood for her memories of Cohan and Willie Collier.

I am also grateful for the help of Art Bannon; David Blair; Herb Borre; Brown University Library Archives; Mrs. Rosalie J. Coyle of the Theatre Collection, Free Library of Philadelphia; Vaughan Deering; Harvey Friedman; Wynn Gibson; Charlie Haubert; Lake Superior State College Library; Dr. William A. Lynch; Maisry MacCracken and Geraldine Hughes of the original Mackinac College Library; William Maury of the U. S. Capitol Historical Society; Vija and Linny McCabe; Frank McHugh; W. T. Rabe, E. J. Sundstrom, and Florence Wallach.

The Cohan-Keith interchange in Chapter Four is from *American Vaudeville: Its Life and Times* by Douglas Gilbert, Dover Publications, Inc., N.Y., 1963. Reprinted through permission of the publisher.

The Cohan-Harris interchange in Chapter Five is © 1941 by The New York Times Company. Reprinted by permission.

The George M. Cohan letter to George W. Buck in Chapter Fifteen appeared in the June 1941 issue of *The Call Board*, publication of the Catholic Actors' Guild of America, and I am grateful to the Guild for permission to reprint it.

I am grateful to Leo Feist, Inc., for permission to reprint the lyrics of "Over There."

A number of details of Cohan's life were taken from Ward Morehouse's *George M. Cohan, Prince of the American Theater*, J. B. Lippincott, Philadelphia, 1943. It should be referred to for biographical details which my work in its particular orientation does not cover. Cohan's autobiography, *Twenty Years on Broadway* (1924, Harper & Brothers, N.Y.) provided information on his early life. Other source books I used with profit were Lehman Engel's *The American Musical Theatre*, David Ewen's *The Story of America's Musical*

Theater, Stanley Green's *The World of Musical Comedy*, and Robert Baral's *Revue*.

The quotation from "George M. Cohan in Hollywood" by Teet Carle appearing in Chapter 14 is taken from the March 1969 issue of *Screen Actor*, and is reprinted through the courtesy of Mr. Carle and Screen Actors Guild.

Thanks to Harper and Row, Inc., for permission to publish George M. Cohan's preface to the Row and Patterson edition of *Remember the Day* by Philo Highley and Philip Dunning.

Last, my special thanks to a Cohan intimate, Danny Healy, superb entertainer—the Night Mayor of Broadway Jimmy Walker properly dubbed him—who first encouraged me in this work and who, alas, did not live to see its completion. Those nights in the Lambs bar when you charmed us all with your sprightly stories will always warm the soul, old friend.

J. McC.
Mackinac Island, Michigan
1972

INDEX